Fendall House with its hip roof and the back of the boyhood home of Robert E. Lee (607 Oronoco Street). The building in the right foreground was owned by Al-exandria merchant John Dundas. It was sometimes called "Dundas Castle" or "Castle Thunder," and was later abandoned and considered to be haunted.

William Francis Smith

*F*irst Commonwealth Savings Bank and The Lyceum of Alexandria, Virginia are proud to present this limited edition copy of Alexandria: A Pictorial History. Special recognition must be extended to the authors T. Michael Miller and William Francis Smith for the many hours they willingly relinquished to bring the community this documentation of Alexandria's beginnings.

Both The Lyceum and First Commonwealth have a great interest in preserving the history of Alexandria. This publication will make an outstanding contribution toward maintaining the heritage of the city.

We know that the community will treasure this collector's volume for many generations. The Lyceum and First Commonwealth Savings Bank are proud to take part in the continuing history of Alexandria, Virginia.

THE
DONNING COMPANY
PUBLISHERS
NORFOLK/VIRGINIA BEACH

A SEAPORT SAGA

Portrait of Old Alexandria, Virginia

by William Francis Smith
and T. Michael Miller

DEDICATED TO:

A Patient and Long-Suffering Wife—Nancy Smith

and

My Parents—Madeline and Nathan Miller, Sr.

Edited by Elizabeth B. Bobbitt
Richard A. Horwege, Senior Editor

Library of Congress Cataloging-in-Publication Data:

Smith, William Francis, 1924-
  A seaport saga : portrait of Old Alexandria, Virginia/by
William Francis Smith and T. Michael Miller.
    p.   cm.
  Includes bibliographical references.
  ISBN 0-89865-781-4 (lim. ed.)
  1. Alexandria (Va.)—History—Pictorial works.
2. Alexandria (Va.)—Description—Views. I. Miller, T. Michael.
II. Title.
F234.A3S57   1989
975.5'296—dc20   89-16989
                             CIP

Printed in the United States of America

*View of Creighton's Emporium, a
hardware and dry goods store on the
southeast corner of King and South Pitt
streets, before 1888.*

CONTENTS

PREFACE

by William Francis Smith

My interest in old photographs has been a part of me since my earliest days. I have always been fascinated by the thought that, except for the existence of a camera-produced image of a building, scene, or person taken seventy-five or a hundred years ago, no written description could ever adequately describe the appearance of that building, scene or person once it was gone. I can recall pictures of the Sphinx covered up to its neck in sand (taken in the late 1850s), of the Washington Monument in its unfinished state (1870s), of San Francisco before the earthquake (before 1906), of the Arch-Duke Franz-Ferdinand and his wife climbing into a carriage at Sarajevo moments before they were dispatched by an assassin in June 1914, among many others. Because of the presence of a photographer at the time we are able today to experience an accurate visual rendition of a scene or event which might never be reproduced again.

Growing up in a town which was founded in 1749, I often wondered what Alexandria really looked like back in its earlier days. Except for a few yellowed copies of elderly photographs framed and hanging on the walls of private residences, I had no idea where to look or whom to approach to learn if there might be an answer to my quest. I knew that wartime pictures had been taken in Alexandria because many were included in Miller's *Photographic History of the Civil War,* issued in 1911, but the publisher had expired during the Depression so there was no hope for information from that quarter. One day, about 1950, Mrs. Arthur King, a long time Alexandrian who worked in the photographic depart-ment of the National Archives, mentioned the Brady Collection (consisting of thousands of original glass plate negatives all taken during the War Between the States) and that it included some local views. This was the opening that I had hoped for although it was no easy task since the Archives was not open on weekends, it closed daily at 5:00 P.M., the positive prints were not catalogued and many scenes were either incorrectly identified or not identified at all. I was able to spend an occasional two-hour session after leaving work early and this took the better part of a year to complete. One major triumph occurred when a view showing many ships lined up at docks in a river town (someone had written "Savannah?") convinced me that it might be Alexandria. Rather than chancing the purchase of an unwanted scene (after all an eight-by-ten-inch glossy cost fifty cents and it took at least a week to receive the copy), I memorized the order in which buildings were placed, then went home to check a copy of the 1863 Charles Magnus *Birdseye View of Alexandria.* Every building in the photograph was matched by an identical structure in the print, thus successfully con-cluding a first attempt at detective work. Another good collection in the Archives consisted of pictures taken all over town by the Bureau of Public Roads in 1929 in anticipation of the building of the Mount Vernon Boulevard, which would pass directly through the middle of town.

At this time, the Library of Congress had very little to offer that satisfied my interest (although this has changed drastically in recent years) but other sources began to surface. A Mr. William Palmer Gray walked the streets of Alexandria in 1923-1924 and took about sixty excellent snapshots which he gave to the Valentine Museum in Richmond. Mrs. William A. Moore, widow of a prominent insurance agent, gave me about fifteen glass negatives which were all that were left from the several hundred that he had taken prior to their marriage about 1901. After his death, she, thinking no one would be interested, systematically broke and disposed of the negatives. A cousin, Col. James D. McLean, lived through a number of violent hurricanes in the 1920s during his Marine Corps years in Central America and in the process lost a collection of photographs taken by his father including one showing the present City Hall steeple under construction about 1873.

Many single pictures were lent me for copying by elderly ladies who had, or whose husbands had had, roots set deeply in Alexandria's past. Mrs. Virgil Davis gave both the Alexandria Library and me a large group of views taken in the 1940s by her late husband who had given slide lectures on the doorways of Alexandria. Miss Katie Uhler gave an earlier set of doorway scenes. Probably the greatest coup of my collecting career occurred when I was lent a large scrapbook of snapshots which had been compiled by Mrs. Virginia Evans O'Brien, aunt of Miss Laura Hulfish, the lender. The scenes in this book ranged from the 1880s to about 1900 and from this collection I was able to obtain a hundred rare views. Oddly enough, about twenty-five years later an almost identical book formerly owned by Miss Esther Green was given to the Alexandria Library.

My wife, Nancy, sometimes used to complain that I was giving away my collection in bits and pieces and while I had always hoped that some sort

of publication might result from my hobby, I tried to be cooperative when pictorial information was needed on particular buildings. The city was given copies of every print in my possession concerning the City Hall and Market Square when remodelling was being planned. The Fauber architectural firm was given similar assistance when it was working on the rehabilitation of both Carlyle House and Gadsby's Tavern and many individuals received like treatment when they showed interest in particular structures. One scene of the 300 block of Cameron Street, of which I had the original glass negative dating to about 1866, appeared on the dust cover of a book with the credit line "Courtesy of Wilson Design," whatever that is. Unfortunately, this problem can backfire because there are a few of my early pictures whose donors have been lost. It has always been my intention to give proper credit for gifts or loans but time and forgetfulness have wreaked their vengeance.

What a fantastic book this would be if we could resurrect all the photographs which we know were taken but have been lost. Even without them I hope that those who know Alexandria from the "old days" will derive pleasant nostalgia from these pages while those who have come to know the old town in more recent times will be able to appreciate the contributions of the past toward the making of what is today a truly unique community in the Washington metropolitan area as well as a vital link in the history of the Commonwealth of Virginia.

William Francis Smith

ACKNOWLEDGMENTS

hanks must be extended to numerous persons and institutions but the major indebtedness we both feel is to Mrs. Jeanne Plitt, Director of the Alexandria Library and to the Alexandria Library, Lloyd House, for its generosity in time and use of its equipment. This book would have been several years longer in preparation had it not been for the kindness, understanding and backing of the entire Library staff. The Valentine Museum, Richmond, Virginia, the Lee Society, Mrs. Eleanor Lee Templeman, the Alexandria Lyceum, Mr. Benjamin F. Baggett, Jr., Mrs. Lewis Gordon Porter, through her daughter Elizabeth Porter Sibold, U.S. Army Military History Institute, Carlisle Barracks, Pennsylvania, Episcopal High School, the Alexandria-Washington Lodge, No. 22, A.F. & A.M., the Alexandria Archaeology Center, and Northern Virginia Park Authority must all be recognized for their cooperation and generosity.

The Historic Alexandria Foundation kindly allowed unlimited use of its many contemporary photographs used in Ethelyn Cox's *Historic Alexandria Virginia—Street by Street* and the invaluable information contained in her book. The Alexandria Association generously permitted copies to be made of photographs utilized in their publication *Our Town—1749-1865.* Mr. John Stobart cheerfully gave permission for the use of his painting *Alexandria* as the cover illustration, even supplying the color slide from his Maritime Heritage Prints, Boston, Massachusetts.

INTRODUCTION

lexandria, Virginia, with its charming ambience is truly a historic city where almost every cobblestone has a story to tell. During the past eleven years, it has been my pleasure to study the town's architecture, historic houses, and socio-political heritage. Nearly 250 years old, Alexandria is rich in tradition including its association with the Republic's early founding fathers. Washington, Mason, Jefferson, Madison, and Monroe were frequent visitors here and walked its narrow alleys and thoroughfares. Established first as a tobacco inspection station in the 1730s, thousands of hogsheads were later transshipped from Alexandria's wharves to the ports of Glasgow and Whitehaven while its merchant princes and salty sea captains established trade links with the West Indies, Iberian Peninsula, Africa, and Europe. Honeycombed with hundreds of bricklined wells and privies, Alexandria contains the physical remnants of that generation whose artifacts remain largely buried beneath the substrata of the town's streetscape. In 1977-1978, I worked for the Alexandria Archaeology center investigating many of these deposits. Every day a new discovery would come to light as thousands of shards of earthenware pottery, ceramics, bone, and metal were unearthed from these sites and served as interpretive tools in unraveling the threads of Alexandria's eighteenth and nineteenth-century legacy.

By the summer of 1978, I had traded in my archaeological trowel and subsequently became curator of the Lee-Fendall House. One of Alexandria's major museums, it was home to thirty-seven members of the Lee family from 1785 to 1904. Constructed by Philip R. Fendall, a Lee, this historic house was resided in briefly by Light Horse Harry Lee, governor of Virginia, Edmund J. Lee, prominent lawyer and mayor of Alexandria, and the grandchildren of Richard Bland Lee, Northern Virginia's first Congressman. From childhood I have always had a fascination with this premier Virginia family and the many contributions they have made to the nation. During their residence in Alexandria, the Lees owned extensive tracts of real estate and played a seminal role in the town's development.

After leaving the Lee-Fendall House, I was employed by the Lloyd House, the historical and genealogical adjunct of the Alexandria Library. For several years I have served as Research Historian at this fine institution. With more than seventeen thousand volumes in its collection, Lloyd House also houses photographic archives, vertical files, cartographic resources and original manuscript materials on Virginia and the South. Frequently these items, whether they be old letters, diaries, or account ledgers, provide an interesting window on the past. The large photographic archives at Lloyd House has been particularly useful in the production of *Seaport Saga* and in conclusion I would like to thank the Alexandria Library for the use of their excellent facilities and assistance in promoting this volume.

T. Michael Miller

John Summers (1688-1790), the son of an English Protestant family, was an early pioneer who constructed a cabin on the Potomac River where the town of Alexandria now stands. "He was a man of very robust constitution, broad in chest, powerful in limb" and spent his time hunting and fishing. In 1716, Summers was a tenant of John West and is credited with constructing the first tobacco warehouse on Hunting Creek. He also attended many surveys and was frequently consulted on all questions of title and boundaries. Upon his death in 1790, he was buried at what is now the corner of Beauregard and Barnum streets off Route 236. His tombstone may still be seen there, along with those of his son, Francis, a Revolutionary War hero who died in 1800, and Francis' wife, Jane, who "met her Maker" in 1814.

TOBACCO TRADERS
AND REVOLUTIONARY PATRIOTS
1742 TO 1780

lexandria, Virginia, is a community of delightful charm with its brick-lined streets, ivy-covered walls, and stately Federalist and Georgian mansions. It has been home to U.S. presidents, governors, congressmen, as well as salty sea captains and merchant princes. Its streets and alleyways are pregnant with the sights and sounds of the past. George Washington owned property, voted, and frequented the taverns of the old seaport town. He literally was the "first and most beloved of its citizens" and Alexandrians took every opportunity to pay him homage. George Mason, author of the Virginia Declaration of Rights, the Fairfax Resolves, and a leading eighteenth century intellectual, was a town trustee and practiced law here. In 1810, eleven years after Washington's death, a carriage rumbled into Alexandria and deposited the Henry Lee family at 611 Cameron Street. "Light Horse" Harry Lee, a renowned Revolutionary War hero and former governor of Virginia removed his family from Stratford Hall Plantation as a result of financial reverses. In 1811, he leased the impressive Fitzhugh mansion at 607 Oronoco Street. It was in this house that his young son, Robert E. Lee, lived his formative years, hunted and fished in the woods to the west of town, and spent countless hours playing along the docks and waterfront of Alexandria. After serving in the U.S. military for thirty-five years, he resigned his commission in 1861 to become commander of Virginia forces. One year later, he headed the Confederate Army of Northern Virginia and led the Southern people through four years of fratricidal Civil War. His military exploits are emblazoned upon the pages of history as he

marched his army across the fields and valleys of Virginia. Faced by a well supplied and numerically superior Union Army, Lee and his tattered troops were forced to surrender at Appomattox Courthouse in April 1865. After the conflict, he urged a policy of national reconciliation and spent the remainder of his life as a prominent educator at Washington College, later Washington and Lee University. General Lee never forgot his love for his hometown, however. In May 1869, while visiting friends in Alexandria, a large reception was held for him at which time he remarked: "There is no community to which my affections more strongly cling than that of Alexandria, composed of my earliest and oldest friends, my kind school fellows and faithful neighbors." Since Washington and Lee were but two of Alexandria's illustrious citizens, let us focus our attention on the city's early history.

The site of Alexandria was initially a seven-hundred-acre patent issued to Mistress Margaret Brent by Virginia Royal Governor Richard Bennett on September 6, 1654. Brent, an early feminist and advocate of women's right to vote, had played a seminal role in the Maryland colony as a kinswoman of Cecil Calvert, Lord Baltimore, the proprietor, and of his brother Leonard Calvert, the first governor. Brent, subsequently moved some fifty miles upriver from St. Mary's, Maryland, to a home called Peace constructed by her brother Giles near Aquia in Stafford County, Virginia. Although she had re-patented her seven hundred acres "in the Freshes of Potomac River beginning at the Mouth of Hunting Creek" in 1662, Governor Berkeley had also issued an overlapping patent of six thousand acres to

Robert Howson in October 1669. Howson, a mariner, had received his grant for transporting 120 persons to Virginia. He quickly sold his real estate to John Alexander, a Stafford County planter, on November 13, 1669, for 6,000 pounds of crop tobacco. Alexander, who did not realize that Brent's seven hundred acres were encompassed in his grant, had to pay for the parcel twice. He paid the heirs of Margaret Brent 10,500 pounds of tobacco in 1674 for a clear title to the same. Upon John Alexander's death, his holdings were devised to his two sons, Robert and Philip, and a portion became the site of Hugh West's Hunting Creek Warehouse—thence Alexandria.

Many of the early settlers who emigrated to old Prince William County in the early 1700s were primarily interested in cultivating tobacco. The Virginia legislature passed a tobacco inspection act in 1730 which called for the construction of tobacco warehouses along the major tributaries in order that the weed might be inspected, packed, and shipped to Great Britain. Initially the warehouses at Alexandria were supposed to be constructed upon Charles Broadwater's land on Great Hunting Creek. This location, however, proved unsatisfactory, and instead they were built on Simon Pearson's property. Pearson had once owned a one-hundred-acre plantation just north of old Alexandria prior to 1730 and had maintained a rolling house there for the transshipment of tobacco. The region near the foot of Oronoco Street soon became known as Hugh West's Hunting Creek Warehouse and by the early 1740s other English and Scottish merchants including John Pagan, John Carlyle, and William Ramsay had settled here. Since the warehouse site was "the last and best Virginia anchorage for ocean vessels before the Potomac Falls," Lawrence Washington and Lord Thomas Fairfax joined the ranks of the early traders and petitioned the Virginia General Assembly for the right to establish a town in October 1748. (Thomas Preisser, *18th Century Alexandria Before the Revolution, 1749-1776*) (James Munson, "A New Look at the Founding of Alexandria, Va." in *Fairfax Chronicles,* May-June 1985) Officially called Alexandria, the early hamlet was later known as Belhaven in honor of John Hamilton (1654-1708), the second baron of Belhaven, who had been a patriotic figure in Scotland.

George Washington as a young surveyor made an unofficial plat of the region in 1748. It showed a fine improvable marsh with two springs and a road leading to the tip of Point West. On the point there were several buildings identified as Mr. West's house and warehouses. (1748 plat map by George Washington, *The George Washington Atlas,* plate 19)

The petition to establish the town was debated in April 1749 at a session of the Virginia House of Burgesses in Williamsburg and finally passed on May 11th of that year. The legislation stated that within four months after the passage of the act, sixty acres of land, parcels of Philip and John Alexander and Hugh West, should be vested in eleven trustees (Thomas Fairfax, William Fairfax, George Fairfax, Richard Osborne, Lawrence Washington, William Ramsay, John Carlyle, John Pagan, Gerrard Alexander, Hugh West, and Philip Alexander). These trustees were appointed to oversee the sale and construction of the town which would be called Alexandria in honor of the Alexander family.

In the spring of 1749 the trustees hired John West, Jr, assistant surveyor for Fairfax County, to lay out the town. There were originally sixty acres which were divided into eighty-four one-half-acre lots. The date for the sale of the first lots was scheduled for July 13th and 14th, 1749, at Hunting Creek Warehouse. During the first day the trustees met at the tobacco warehouse near Oronoco Street and walked down the riverfront to the northwest corner of Cameron and Lee streets. There a Mr. West, the town crier, struck off the first lot to John Dalton, a tobacco merchant.

Alexandria soon became the major town in Fairfax County which had been formed in 1742. The county courthouse had originally been situated at a location called Springfield near current Tyson's Corner but was moved to Alexandria in May 1752. Thus, the town became the central locus of political, economic, and ecclesiastical power in Northern Virginia and continued to flourish during much of the 18th century. The mainstay of this economic growth was the production of tobacco. Large quantities were shipped to Great Britain and then to the European continent. By 1775, the wheat and grain trade had begun to replace tobacco. As productive farmland was leached, the cultivation of tobacco moved south and west. Wheat was easier to transport and could be shipped throughout the world since it was outside the British Navigation Acts. A system of roads leading from Alexandria to the hinterland of the Shenandoah Valley permitted grain merchants and farmers to move their produce to the wharves of Alexandria and thence to the Caribbean and Europe. There were twenty major mercantile firms in Alexandria in 1775 and twelve of these were involved in the transshipment of wheat. (Thomas Preisser, *op. cit.*)

War also had a major impact on the early economy of Alexandria. In 1755 Gen. Edward Braddock

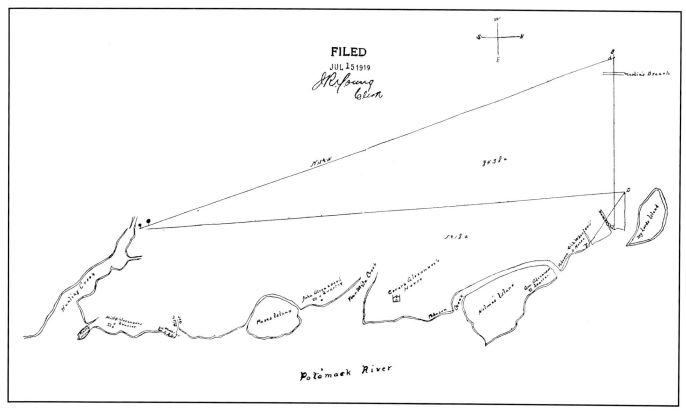

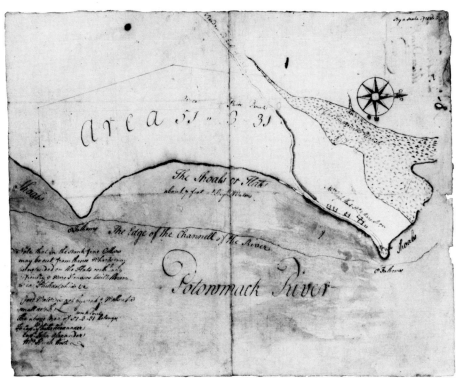

The Daniel Jennings Survey, 1746 of Robert Howson's six-thousand-acre patent (1669) was prepared by Theodore Bland, surveyor of Stafford County in February 1693. After a territorial suit was filed by Gerrard Alexander against John Awbrey, Daniel Jennings resurveyed the Howson patent in 1746. National Airport is now located in the vicinity of Holmes Island while Pases Island is presently known as Daingerfield. The structures south of Ralph's Gut, Hugh West's Hunting Creek Warehouses, were the genesis of the town of Alexandria and were situated near the present terminus of Oronoco Street. Piper's Island corresponds to current Jones Point.
Cox Collection, Maps

This very early plat of "the land whereon stands the town of Alexandria," was drawn by George Washington in 1748. It clearly depicts the old rolling road as it enters town and continues to Hugh West's Hunting Creek Warehouse (lower right). The huge improved marshland was not totally filled in until the late nineteenth century and precluded development of the northern sector of town. Washington penned the following remark on the plat: "Note that on the bank fine cellars may be cut. From thence wharves may be extended on the flats without any difficulty and more houses built thereon as in Philadelphia. Good water may be got by sinking wells to small depth. The above area of 51 acres, 3 rods, 31 perch belongs to: Capt. Philip Alexander, Capt. John Alexander, Mr. Hugh West. The shoals or flats about 7 feet at high water."

Print from Harpers New Monthly Magazine, February 1880

15

and several thousand British regulars bivouacked in and around town and later mounted an unsuccessful expedition to force the French out of the Ohio Valley. Alexandria became a major supply center for the Braddock expedition.

During the 1760s the British imposition of a tea and stamp tax were topics of fierce debate in Alexandria. Thus, when the English closed Boston Harbor in 1774, disgruntled Alexandria citizens passed a resolution calling on all the colonies to terminate trade with the mother country. Accordingly, various committees of correspondence were established throughout the country to trumpet the news of the perilous situation and to register public outrage.

In Alexandria, several inhabitants (James Hendricks, John Carlyle, William Ramsay, John Dalton, Dr. William Rumney, Robert Adam, James Kirk, Robert Harrison, George Gilpin, Capt. John Harper) formed such a committee. On May 29, 1774, Dalton and Carlyle, writing on behalf of the organization, informed the Bostonians that they were "deeply interested in the fate of Boston now suffering the scourge of oppression . . . and make no doubt that the spirit which has distinguished Virginia as the intrepid Guardian of American Liberty, will again shine forth in all its former Lustre." (*Virginia Calendar of State Papers,* volume 8, page 5). On July 18, 1774, several townspeople including George Washington and George Mason met at the courthouse to approve the Fairfax Resolves. Penned by George Mason, these resolutions were a firm statement of the Colonists' position regarding their constitutional rights under British law.

When hostilities commenced at Lexington on April 19, 1775, Alexandrians were not long in volunteering for service. Many enlisted and took part in the seige of Boston in 1775-1776 and the Battles of Trenton, Princeton, Brandywine, and Monmouth. Among those who displayed exceptional military prowess were Col. James Hendricks, Lieut. Col. Charles Simms, and Col. John Fitzgerald. After the conflict, all three of these soldiers were later chosen to serve as mayor of Alexandria. (Joseph Mitchell, "The Price of Independence," in *A Composite History of Alexandria, Va.,* page 65)

During the war General Washington selected Dr. William Brown to be surgeon general of the Hospital Middle Department and in addition, Dr. James Craik, Washington's personal confidant and physician, became chief physician and surgeon to the Continental Army. (Mitchell, *op. cit.,* pages 64, 65) Alexandria was also the center for the Southern department inoculation hospitals. Dr. William Rickman, surgeon in charge of these facilities from September 22 to November 30, 1777, reported that 775 men had been received into his hospitals; of whom 695 were discharged to duty; 28 died, and 58 remained. The condition of the infirmaries left much to be desired as is evidenced by an affidavit signed by Hardee Murfree. He wrote:

. . . the men being almost naked, Dr. Parker said it was not worth while to give them physic when the men were so naked and lying on the cold floor . . . One of the sick men had no clothing but an old shirt and half an old blanket . . . that night one of the men died and some few the others died and I believe it was for want of clothes to keep them warm. (Louis C. Duncan, *Medical Men in the American Revolution, 1775-1783*)

During the colonial and Revolutionary eras, Alexandria was populated by a diverse group of artisans and craftsmen. Among the many trades and occupations represented were; blacksmiths, butchers, hatters, house carpenters, music teachers, cabinet makers, coopers, ropemakers, silversmiths, tanners, tobacconists, weavers, and wheelrights. These tradesmen supplied the local population and the back country with many goods and services. Foreign trade was also a major factor in the life of the town as sea captains in their ships and brigs plied the sea lanes of the world transporting cargoes of wheat, corn, tobacco, and hides. In turn, shipments of rum, molasses, and manufactured goods were offloaded at Alexandria's wharves.

In 1779, Alexandria underwent a significant political metamorphosis. With the passage of the October 4, 1779, Act of Incorporation, the town's oligarchical trusteeship government was replaced with a mayor-council system. This legislation provided for the selection of twelve elected officials who formed a Board of Aldermen and Common Council. From 1780 to 1843 the Mayor of Alexandria was chosen by the Common Council until a February 1843 amendment to the city charter that year provided for his direct election by freeholders. Thus, with the election of a popular government by freeholders in 1780, Alexandria entered into a new age of prosperity and enlightenment.

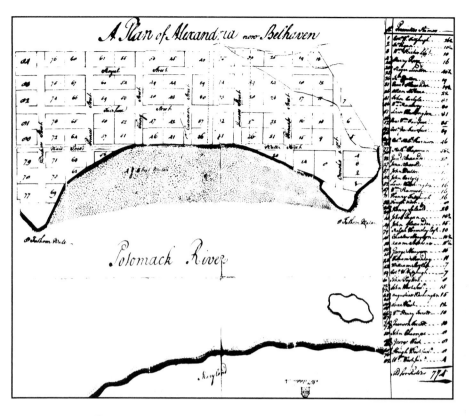

A Plan of Alexandria now Belhaven

Potomack River

Drawn by young George Washington, this map depicts the hamlet of Alexandria in 1749 with seven streets running north and south and three east and west. As planned, Alexandria, or Belhaven as it was known locally, was laid out on sixty acres of ground which were subdivided into eighty-four one-half-acre lots. Typical of many tidewater towns, the plan for Alexandria was the traditional grid pattern which allowed for orderly expansion and ease of record keeping as new territory was acquisitioned.

During the first two days of lot sales, July 13th and 14th, 1749, forty-two parcels were struck off to various planters and merchants. By 1753 all of the original block of eighty-four lots had been sold. It is conjectured that George Washington may have drawn this map for his half-brother Lawrence who later purchased lots No. 51 and No. 52 containing one acre at the southwest corner of King and Water (Lee) streets in September 1749.

On May 11, 1749, Virginia Gov. William Gooch approved a bill passed by the House of Burgesses which established the town of Alexandria at Hunting Creek Warehouse. Provisions of this statute directed that the eleven town trustees "shall lay out sixty acres into lots and streets not exceeding half an acre of ground in each lot: & also set apart such portions of said land for a market place . . ." shown here. Lots No. 42 and No. 43 comprising one acre bounded by Royal Street on the west, Cameron on the north and Fairfax on the east were set aside for this purpose. Ninety-two men petitioned the Virginia House of

Market Square— stock and pillory

Burgesses to move the Fairfax County Courthouse from Spring Field (near Tyson's Corner) to Alexandria. On April 25, 1752, the Governor's Council "ordered that the Court House and prison be removed . . . to the Town of Alexandria." On May 3, 1752, the first session of the new court convened at its new location on the north side of the square, facing Fairfax Street and nearly opposite the Carlyle House. It was in September 1752 that John Carlyle was paid fifteen hundred pounds to construct a pillory and stocks on the ground and by 1753 the Fairfax County jail also occupied the site. It was not until February 21, 1753, that the Alexandria town trustees ordered that "deeds be executed to the Justices of Fairfax County . . . for the lots No. 43 & 44, otherwise called the Market Place." Market Square quickly be-

came the locus of town activity as militiamen drilled, farmers sold their produce, and local crowds gathered to buy meat, poultry, fruit, and vegetables.

In 1774 the Friendship Engine House was placed at its west end, and in 1775 the Sun Engine House was put alongside the courthouse on its east side. In 1784 Alexandrians petitioned for a new Market House. The new building which measured seventy-eight by twenty-four feet was situated on the southeast corner of Cameron and Royal streets. The first floor was occupied as a market place; the second was utilized by the local Hustings Court from 1785 to 1802 and by the Fairfax County Court from 1790 to 1800.
(Penny Morrill, Alexandria Virginia's Market Square)

This circa 1900 view of the Ramsay House at the northeast corner of King and Fairfax streets shows how the structure was left "high and dry" when the

two streets were graded to allow for a gentler slope to the river front.

William Ramsay (1716-1785), an early town trustee and tobacco factor from Kirkcudbright, Scotland, had this home removed from another location in the late 1740s. Reputed to be the "oldest house" in Alexandria, architectural historian Milton Grigg surmised from the house's original gambrel roof that it may have been constructed in the early decade of the eighteenth century. The structure was home to the Ramsay family for over a hundred years. William Ramsay was a leading citizen of his day. In 1751, he was on a committee to superintend the construction of the courthouse; 1754, adjuster of seals and weights at Hunting Creek Warehouse; 1756-1760, overseer of the Alexandria Academy. A business partner of both John Carlyle and John Dixon, Ramsay took an active role in the

town's commercial affairs. He later served as Alexandria's postmaster in 1772 and as Fairfax County justice of the peace. Ramsay was so generally respected that he was made the town's first and only honorary lord mayor in 1761. He married Sarah McCarty by whom he sired eight children. (Papers of George Mason, volume 1, page 90)

Through the years numerous businesses have occupied the old Ramsay House including a cigar shop and tavern. After a destructive 1943 fire a group of historically minded Alexandrians formed the Ramsay House Restoration Committee and prevented the building from being razed. The Alexandria City Council purchased it for nine thousand dollars about 1949 and it was later restored and currently houses the Alexandria Visitor and Tourist Bureau.

O'Brien/Hulfish Collection

The John Dalton House at 207 North Fairfax Street is perhaps one of the most historically important buildings in Alexandria for it was the residence of one of the town's first trustees (by 1750) who in partnership with John Carlyle acted as agent for George Washington in the sale of his tobacco and wheat. He was joined with George Mason of Gunston Hall in constructing armed ships as well as supplying food and arms for Continental

troops during the early days of the Revolutionary War. Mason, writing to Washington, later described Dalton as "a steady, diligent man." He became wealthy as a result of his successful mercantile and entrepreneurial projects and died in 1777. The house, originally all frame, was smaller in its original state. During restoration work in the early 1980s, an exterior painted frame wall was found in use as a room divider just to the left of the

center doorway. A brick facade was added in the nineteenth century and true mutilation occurred when the left end of the structure was torn away and a strange brick excrescence was raised, thus eliminating the left dormer window. There are still traces of very early interior woodwork.

Milton Grigg Collection

In its very early days the town crier was an important institution in old Alexandria, now superceded by printer's ink. He was employed for many purposes such as auction sales, town meetings, and announcing the time. In the 1830s, a very tall and a very old black man named Peter Logan, not only was the crier but also a piper. On great holidays, accompanied by a drummer, he aroused the town from its slumber.

Carlyle House, Alexandria's first mansion, was built by John Carlyle in 1752 to 1753 on the east side of the 100 block of North Fairfax Street. The backside originally overlooked the river, scene of much commercial activity in which Carlyle had considerable financial interests. He was a founding trustee and first overseer of the town (1749), customs collector for the South Potomac District (1758), member of the Fairfax Committee of Safety (1774-1775) and a justice of the peace for Fairfax County. Upon the arrival of Gen. Edward Braddock and his troops at Alexandria in 1755, this house was taken over as headquarters and on April 14, 1755, the Council of Governors met here with Braddock and his staff to plan the initial campaign in what would become known as the French and Indian War. On Carlyle's death in 1780, it was inherited by his minor grandson, John Carlyle Herbert, whose parents, Sarah Carlyle and William Herbert, moved their family into the house and occupied it at least till the death of Mrs. Herbert in 1827, resulting in local references to the Herbert House. It was purchased in 1848 by James Green, a prominent furniture manufacturer, who incorporated it into his Mansion House hotel complex. Over the years, the vicissitudes of time and neglect left the structure in very poor condition and only after 1969 was its preservation assured when its purchase

by the Northern Virginia Regional Park Authority resulted in its restoration and maintenance as a museum.
Print from Harpers New Monthly Magazine February 1880
Portrait of John Carlyle courtesy of Northern Virginia Park Authority

John Carlyle wrote to his brother George in Scotland on August 15, 1755, informing him that "There was the Grandest Congress held at my house ever known on the continent." On April 13 to 16, 1755, five Royal Governors (hence the name Royal Governor's Conference) and Gen. Edward Braddock assembled at the Carlyle House to discuss strategy for the campaign against the French. They included: William Shirley of Massachusetts, Robert Dinwiddie of Virginia, James Delacey of New York, Robert Morris of Pennsylvania, and Horatio Sharpe of Maryland. The conferees discussed the establishment of a common defense fund for the colonies and the execution of military campaigns against Crown Point on Lake Champlain and Fort Niagara on Lake Erie. In addition, a Colonel Johnson was sent to form an alliance with the Iroquis Confederation, the Six Nations. On the 16th of April, the assembly adjourned and the participants departed Alexandria "on their way to

Governor Shirley

their respective Governments." Ross Netherton, "The Carlyle House Conference: . . . " in Northern Va. Studies Conference, 1983. Alexandria: Empire to Commonwealth.

Governor Dinwiddie

General Braddock

Arriving in Alexandria in March 1755, Gen. Edward Braddock commanded the largest military force to set foot on the American continent. His troops bivouacked northwest of town while the general took up residence in a home owned by Scottish merchant John Carlyle, a brother-in-law of Col. William Fairfax, a member of noted Northern Neck of Virginia gentry. After remaining in Alexandria for a few days, Braddock and his army departed in April and marched over rugged Virginia and Maryland terrain to

Fort Cumberland. On July 9, 1755, his troops were ambushed by French, Canadian, and Indian forces eight miles from Fort Duquesne—the present site of Pittsburgh, Pennsylvania. Braddock was mortally wounded and his troops sustained severe casualties. Thus, the British attempt to oust the French from the Ohio Valley failed miserably.

Burial of General Braddock by his men courtesy of the Library of Congress Print Division

With George Washington as his aid de camp, Maj. Gen. Edward Braddock left Alexandria in April 1755 with a little army of regulars and provincials on this ill-fated expedition against the French and Indian allies. He left behind a number of cannon that were later planted with muzzles pointing skyward at the entrances to several of the principal alleys of the city of Alexandria. "A few years ago these cannon were turned over to the Colonial Dames, who intended to use them to mark what is known as the "Braddock trail." For this purpose one has been erected at Winchester, Virginia, and another at the juncture of Russell Road and Mushpot (or Braddock Road) on Braddock Heights in the northwestern section of Alexandria. A third cannon was made the central part of a public drinking fountain, which was presented to the city of Alexandria by the Colonial Dames and stood at the intersection of Cameron and Royal streets for several years. The fountain was knocked from its foundation by an army truck four years ago and is now said to be stored in the market building while city council deliberates on a new location for it. The remaining cannon are lying in Christ Church yard. It is understood that the Colonial Dames will present them to the George Washington Masonic National Memorial Association to be mounted on the grounds of Shuter's Hill, Alexandria, as a memorial to Washington." (Alexandria Gazette, March 31, 1922). The fountain was restored but the location of the rest of the cannon is unknown.

With a population of twelve hundred inhabitants in 1762, Alexandria felt a need to expand its physical perimeter. This map drawn by George West on March 10, 1763, was prepared for the trustees' sale of lots on May 9th of that year. An advertisement from the Maryland Gazette of February 24, 1763, noted the sale of fifty-eight additional parcels as follows: "To be Sold at Public Vendue on Monday the 9th day of May next, pursuant to an act of the General Assembly of Virginia, for enlarging the Town of Alexandria. Fifty eight lots, or half acres of land. This town is beautifully situated near the Falls of Potomac, one of the finest Rivers in north America; it affords good Navigation for the largest Ships in Europe, up to the Town, where there is an excellent Harbour. The Country back is very extensive, and the soil capable of producing Tobacco, Corn, Wheat, Flax, Hemp in great perfection."
Cox Collection

There are few shrines in Virginia which evoke such a deep sense of history as does Christ Church. Founded in the early 1750s, the congregation played a seminal role in the religious life of Alexandria. An early Anglican "Chapel of Ease" stood at Pitt and Princess streets. It was not long, however, before the parish wanted to construct a more substantial building and in January 1767, James Parsons agreed to build a new church, designed by James Wren, for six hundred pounds. Parsons was unable to finish his charge and John Carlyle was requested to complete the job in 1772. By 1773, the edifice now known as Christ Church was a reality but its location, at some distance from the built-up part of town, caused it to be referred to as the "Church in the woods." Many members of Alexandria's ruling elders including George Washington and the Lee family were members of this celebrated church. Robert E. Lee was confirmed here by Bishop Johns in 1853. A bell tower was added in 1799 but it was replaced by the present steeple in 1818 and other buildings including an old parish hall and firehouse dotted the church grounds. In the early years the cemetery served as the town's main burying ground until burials were prohibited by an 1809 statute. A split in the congregation in 1809 led to the founding of St. Paul's Church in that year. During the War Between the States, the building was seized by the Union Army but church services continued throughout the war under their auspices.

Christ Church has undergone several alterations and in 1891 Glen Brown, Alexandria's first professionally trained architect, restored the interior to be what he considered a close approximation of its colonial appearance. During this century many American presidents, including Taft, Coolidge, Hoover, Roosevelt, Truman, and Eisenhower have worshiped in this important Virginia shrine. Ballou's Pictorial Drawing Room Companion, 1854

This clapboard house at 517 Prince Street was built about 1775 by Patrick Murray who in 1774 had acquired the one-half-acre lot on which it sits from John Alexander, the purchase of which included the payment of an annual ground rent of £13.5s forever. Upon its disposal by Murray, it had a succession of owners, including Dr. Elisha Cullen Dick from 1794 to 1796, finally being purchased for three thousand dollars by John Douglas Brown in 1816, whose descendants (Hooff, Fawcett, and Cheeseman families) have continued to own and occupy it to the present day. Probably the least altered of all early Alexandria houses, it is a fascinating microcosm of the complete single family dwelling, containing in addition to the usual living, dining, and bedrooms a kitchen, a necessary, rooms for slaves or servants and storage rooms, all under one roof. Carne Collection, before 1900

This is Old Presbyterian Meeting House. Richard Arell conveyed the property in the west 300 block of South Fairfax Street to the minister William Thom in July 1773. On May 11, 1775, John Carlyle and William Ramsay placed the following notice in the Maryland Gazette: "To be let to the lowest undertaker, the building of a brick church . . . sixty feet by fifty foot and 28 foot pitch." (Ethelyn Cox, Alexandria, Street by Street) The meeting house is rich in its colonial associations. It has been immortalized, however, as the place where George Washington's funeral service was conducted on December 29, 1799. Thereafter, the Washington Society, which was formed to perpetuate his memory, marched to the church on the General's birthday to hear orations by such renowned individuals as John Marshall and Francis Scott Key. Lightning struck the meeting house in 1835 and it was severely damaged by fire. The edifice was quickly rebuilt and a vestibule was added to its front while the bell tower was added in 1843. Many of Washington's comrades in arms sleep within the walled cemetery. This print from Harpers New Monthly Magazine, February 1880, is considered to be a fairly accurate depiction of the church before the great fire.

George Mason (1725-1792), Fairfax County planter and leading eighteenth-century American Revolutionary statesman, served as an Alexandria town trustee (1754-1779) and was also a gentleman justice of the Fairfax County Court. Mason resided at his beautiful home, Gunston Hall, south of town overlooking the Potomac, and took an active interest in the affairs of Truro Parish. When the vexing Stamp and Townshend acts crippled Anglo-American trade, Mason proposed resolutions which resulted in the formation of a non-importation association. After the port of Boston was closed in 1774, he penned the Fairfax Resolves which stated the colonies' constitutional position, vis-a-vis Great Britain. In 1776, as a member of the Virginia Committee of Safety, he authored the Virginia Declaration of Rights which became the basis for the first ten amendments to the U.S. Constitution. After the war, Mason served as a member of the Potomac and Ohio Companies whose purpose was to open up trade with the West. An opponent of slavery, he opposed the ratification of the U.S. Constitution because it didn't guarantee personal freedoms. "More than perhaps any other American statesman of the period, he represented the rationalist spirit, the Enlightenment in its American manifestation."
Dictionary of American Biography
Print courtesy of the Alexandria Association

A Pay Roll of Captd Dennis Ramsay's Company of
Militia under Colo Wm Rumney from Fairfax county Virga
for 70 days from 5th Sept 1777 to the 12th day of Nov both days inclsd

Name	Rank	Time (mos/days)	Pay month (Doll)	Virga Curr
Dennis Ramsay	Captain	2 10	40	28 — —
Nathaniel Sibbett	1st Lieut.	2 10	27	13 18 —
Robert Muir	2d ditto	2 10	27	18 18 —
George Minor	Ensign	2 10	20	14 — —
John Adam	Serj Major	2 10	9	6 6
Walter Bayne	S. Major	2 10	9	6 6
Gideon Moss	1st Serjt	2 10	8	5 12
Richard Govard	2 ditto	2 10	8	5 12
John Gisler	3 ditto	2 10	do	5 12 2
Charles Govard	4th ditto	2 10	do	5 12
Charl Bell	Fifer	21	7/3	1 12 2
London	Drummer	2 10	do	5 2 2
Jackson Hunter	Private	2 10	6/8	4 13 4
Thomas Fleming		2 10	do	4 13 4
William Munday		2 10	do	4 13 4
Jas. Chapman		2 10	do	4 13 4
John Hoor		2 10	do	4 13 4
John Bowling		2 10	do	4 13 4
John Page		2 10	do	4 13 4
Saml Symmonds		2 10	do	4 13 4
Henry Roberts		2 10	do	4 13 4
Ralph London		2 10	do	4 13 4
Christopher Shell		2 10	do	4 13 4
John Keech		2 10	do	4 13 4
Thomas Hedrick		2 10	do	4 13 4
Robert Hedrick		2 10	do	4 13 4
Richard Sanford		2 10	do	4 13 4
Jonathan Hatchison		2 10	do	4 13 4
John Goble		2 10	do	4 13 4
Cumberland Ferguson		2 10	do	4 13 4
James Hawkins		2 10	do	4 13 4
Charles Bryan		2 10	do	4 13 4
Ludwick Zimmerman		2 10	do	4 13 4
Christopher Hartman		2 10	do	4 13 4
Joseph Ballinger		2 10	do	4 13 4
Philip Fry		2 10	do	4 13 4
James Crump		2 10	do	4 13 4
Hezekiah Williams		2 10	do	4 13 4
James Petit		2 10	do	4 13 4
Howard Cash		2 10	do	4 13 4
			Carried Over	252 4 2

This unique page from a contemporary ledger lists the payroll due members of Capt. Dennis Ramsay's company of militia, under Col. William Rumney, for the period of September 5, 1777, to November 12, 1777. The men listed were from Alexandria and Fairfax County. Since the local militia was not part of the Continental Army and since its main aim was to protect militarily the immediate area from which it was formed, it is difficult to determine just where these troops might have been located at the time of the preparation of this document. Dennis Ramsay was the son of William Ramsay, one of Alexandria's true founders. *Ramsay Papers, Smithsonian Institution*

This house at 708 Wolfe Street, of eighteenth-century vintage, was owned in 1802 by Jonathan Butcher and tax records for that year indicated the house and quarter block on which it sat to be valued at one thousand dollars. A 1930 visitor described this as a "small house, its walls . . . of solid brick covered with weather boarding, its garden . . . full of crippled old shrubs" (Cox, *Street by Street*) In the 1920s to 1940s the door was painted a shocking vibrant color, and it entered into its commercial life becoming what was probably the town's first true antique shop (as opposed to many used furniture and junk stores which abounded in the city) known as the Blue Door. It was operated by one of Alexandria's sharp-tongued but lovable characters, Miss Nannie Jones.

George Washington's associations with Alexandria were many and varied throughout his life. Following his birth in 1732 in Westmoreland County in the Northern Neck of Virginia, his family moved several times. After his father's death in 1743, he lived with relatives in various locations, finally spending most

The Alexandria Gazette for July 29, 1873, contained this interesting commentary: "Within the memory of even young men a very great change has come over the appearance of the town, and its principal streets. Heads without a silver hair in them can well remember when one story frame houses were common on King Street and when log cabins filled the space now occupied by Sarepta Hall (400 block) and by Washington Hall (600 block). Now there are only eight frames, all two stories or more, below Washington street and not more than thirty frames, less than ten percent of the whole number of buildings . . . The general change which has occurred in very nearly the same proportion in all other parts of the town . . . has swept away nearly all the houses more than a century old." "A recollection of the buildings in the whole of that portion of the town from the market house to the fish wharf, which may be called 'Old Town of Alexandria' will show that from thence the town took its rise." The two structures shown here, both Alexandria houses undoubtedly built during the first several decades following the official founding of the town but at unidentified locations, were the types of buildings being referred to in the preceding article. The fascinating small, gambrel-roofed house must have been fairly typical of the very early structure which the ordinary, hard working, non-office holding citizen might call "home." O'Brien/Hulfish Collection

of his time with his elder half-brother, Lawrence, who owned Mount Vernon. Lawrence's wife, Ann Fairfax of Belvoir, was a kinswoman of Lord Fairfax who, through an early land grant, was the owner of thousands of square miles of land in the northern part of Virginia. Through this connection, young George had the opportunity to accompany surveying parties tramping over this vast acreage. His training was sufficient for him (age seventeen) to be appointed in 1749 as county surveyor for Culpeper. It was about this time that the town of Alexandria was being laid out and despite tradition, there is no proof whatsoever that George assisted John West in his platting of the new town. Half-brother Lawrence, however, was very interested and was one of the initial purchasers of lots as they were offered in July 1749. It is a fact that two different plats of the town were drawn by young George, and we may assume that they were drawn for Lawrence's use, by one who was trained in the art. Shortly after Lawrence's death in July 1752, Mount Vernon became the property of George.

About this time George was appointed by Governor Dinwiddie to several military posts in the Virginia militia which caused him to lead several forays into the western lands, including serving as aide on the staff of the disastrous Braddock expedition, but all this gave him valuable training in military tactics and a great knowledge of the sparsely settled lands to the west of Tidewater. In addition his ability to command was enhanced by the time spent in military musters and drills of the Virginia militia, much of this taking place in Alexandria. In the fall of 1755, Dinwiddie appointed him colonel and commander in chief of all Virginia forces which gave him the dubious honor of defending three hundred miles of mountainous frontier with about three hundred men. He performed admirably and added to that store of knowledge which would become so important to him and the new nation only a few years in the future. He resigned his command shortly before marrying Martha Dandridge Custis, widow of Daniel Parke Custis, on January 6, 1759. He then settled down to the life of a gentleman farmer at Mount Vernon and for the next fifteen years led a rather uneventful but happy life in upgrading his beloved Mount Vernon farming operation, serving as a burgess from Fairfax, of which Alexandria was the county seat, serving in the Virginia legislature at Williamsburg, and making neighborly visits to nearby towns. He frequently visited Alexandria where he owned property, including a small townhouse on Cameron Street in which he could spend the night when it was inconvenient to ride back home. He shopped, visited friends, and attended church services in the town with some regularity and served as a justice of Fairfax from 1760 to 1774, holding court in Alexandria.

After 1770 the question of British taxes in the American colonies assumed increasing importance in the colonies. Washington had experienced the arrogance of British military officers toward their provincial counterparts as well as the growing conflict between Parliament and the American colonies over its handling of trade restrictions and related taxes as a member of the House of Burgesses. While he did not approve of the Boston Tea Party, he was in total sympathy with the refusal of Massachusetts to submit to British restrictions. He was one of the burgesses who met in Raleigh Tavern on May 27, 1774, after the Assembly had been dissolved by the governor, and signed the proceedings of that unauthorized but important meeting. On July 18 he acted as chairman of a meeting in Alexandria, at which the important Fairfax Resolves, the work of George Mason, were adopted. He was elected to both the First and Second Continental Congresses but between the two, he was chosen to command the independent militia companies of Fairfax and four other counties. The buff and blue uniform chosen by the Fairfax Company was the uniform worn by Washington throughout the Revolution and so has become fixed in the public mind as the Continental Army uniform.

His election as a delegate to the Second Continental Congress and his subsequent appointment to command the Continental Armies on June 15, 1775, ensured his inability to relax in his beloved Northern Virginia and Alexandria, for at least the next six years.

An interesting feature of this view is the very old frame house in the center background located on the east side of the 100 block of South St. Asaph Street. When first built, it might have been considered somewhat substantial, but it fell upon poorer times during the entire nineteenth century, when it changed ownership at least five times and was occupied by a series of people, mostly renters, who worked essentially in blue collar jobs. Interestingly enough, as early as 1836 there lived here a series of black families, some free, some slave, and some a combination of the two. There were cases where, in some black households, some members might be free, while their kinsmen were owned as slaves. In 1849, tax records indicate that the head of household was one Harriet Williams, identified as a slave, and whose owner, Samuel Lindsay, lived three doors away. It is thought that the old house was demolished around the turn of the twentieth century. This view, taken about 1870, shows the Relief Fire Company ladder truck in front of the Columbia Steam Fire Engine Company (which later moved into a new firehouse across the street) and the house on the left which the writer recalls in the 1930s and 1940s to be known as the Jac Lane Apartments which were lived in by members of the Columbia Company because of its proximity to their workplace.
Gift of Mike McKenney

THE GOLDEN EPOCH
1781 TO 1800

s the Revolutionary War drew to a close, Alexandria prospered as a vibrant seaport town and mercantile center. Having supplied the Continental Armies with wheat and grain, its merchant princes basked in the sunshine of economic prosperity.

Robert Townsend Hooe, Alexandria's first mayor, was certainly representative of this class. Born in King George County, Virginia, in 1743, Hooe migrated to Alexandria sometime before 1780. He organized and was an active participant in several Alexandria business enterprises including Hooe, Stone and Company and Jennifer and Hooe. Primarily a wheat and flour merchant, Colonel Hooe operated an extensive wharf and warehouse complex on Union Street south of Duke. In addition to his commercial endeavors, he also owned extensive tracts of real estate including a beautiful three story Georgian house at the southwest corner of Prince and Water (Lee) streets. Here, he entertained many members of the local gentry including George Washington. On the political scene Hooe was mayor of Alexandria when Gen. George Washington designated it as a collection place for the state's quota of war supplies. Washington wrote Gov. Thomas Jefferson: "Alexandria is to be the depository of 40,000 gallons of rum, 80 tons of hay and 40,000 bushels of corn."

On April 21, 1781, General Lafayette and his Continental troops marched through Alexandria in pursuit of General Cornwallis who was entrenched at Yorktown. Annoyed by the actions of penurious merchants, Lafayette complained bitterly to Governor Jefferson that after two days notice "not a single wagon could be procured in Alexandria."

After the war, British privateers continued to harass the town's shipping. Combined with the fact that European demand for grain had also diminished, Alexandria experienced a recession from 1781 to 1782. Fortunately the economy recovered and its merchant class survived the economic malaise. Meanwhile, while many other seaport communities continued to rely upon tobacco exports, Alexandria was wise in diversifying its market. Thus, it prospered while Dumfries and Colchester languished.

Johann Schoepf, a German traveler who visited Alexandria in 1783, left an interesting impression of the community. He wrote:

... the streets are straight and there are 200 not unpleasing houses, the number of inhabitants may be about 2,000. This was next to Norfolk, even before the war, one of the wealthiest and most respectable towns in Virginia; its trade was flourishing and apparently is reviving again. Ships of all sizes are vigorously building there ... many new buildings, wharves and warehouses have gone up within a brief space, ... (*The German of Johann D. Schoepf*, Bergman publishers, 1968)

In December 1785, Italian Count Luigi Castiglioni described Alexandria as having three hundred houses and a population of three thousand. The public buildings included two churches, (a Presbyterian and Anglican), a Quaker Assembly and the municipal building. Alexandria then had various factories for the manufacture of bricks, which as the surrounding land was of soft, strong clay, could be made very cheaply. ("Count Luigi Castiglioni—An Early Italian

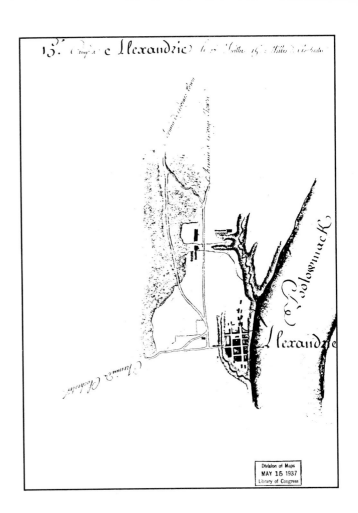

After the siege of Yorktown in October 1781 and the subsequent American and French victory over Lord Cornwallis, commander of French forces, Count Rochambeau and his army bivouacked near Williamsburg that winter. In the spring the French Army marched north to depart for France. On July 19, 1782, the army encamped on a large plain near Alexandria. The map shown here was drawn by French officers and depicts Alexandria and its surrounding environs. Two roads led to Georgetown while an east-west artery probably traversed what is now Duke Street into the Virginia hinterland.
First published in 1782 in Amerique Compagne 1782; Plans des Differents camps occupes par L'Armee aux Ordees de Mr. le Comte de Rochambeau. *Rochambeau Map Collection in the Library of Congress.*

Traveler to Virginia . . . " *Virginia Magazine of History and Biography* volume 58, page 473)

During this era one of the town's chief cultural attributes was the Alexandria Academy. Constructed in 1785, it was the first free school in the state of Virginia. George Washington who was one of its first trustees contributed one thousand pounds for the education of twenty orphans.

With the construction of so many new buildings, Alexandria was a virtual beehive of activity from 1785 to 1786 as the sounds of the hammer and trowel could be heard throughout the town. The first issue of the *Virginia Journal and Alexandria Advertiser*, a forerunner of the *Alexandria Gazette*, came off the press on February 5, 1784. By the next year, over fifty Alexandria merchants had placed advertisements in this journal. These represented a virtual cornucopia of goods and services which included: adzes, backgammon boxes, buckles, crockery, chimney pieces, artificial flowers, gloves, guitars, horsewhips, ironmongery, microscopes, muskets, ostrich feathers, writing cases, etc.

Flour milling remained the town's chief industry during this era. The product was, however, inferior to the superfine flour manufactured at Philadelphia, New York, and Baltimore. Therefore, after the price of flour declined, concerned Alexandria merchants petitioned the Virginia House of Delegates in 1782 requesting that exports be more strictly inspected. Another disadvantage under which Alexandrians labored was state imposed tariffs on marketable commodities. This was partially a result of the fact that Virginia's political arena was dominated by planters who were opposed to business and commercial interests. (Stoessel, *op. cit.*, page 61)

Alexandria merchants were also at the forefront of the movement to establish a strong national government. In March 1785, George Mason and Alexander Henderson of Virginia met in Alexandria with Maj. Daniel Jenifer, Thomas Stone, and Samuel Chase of Maryland to discuss navigational and boundary disputes on the Potomac River and Chesapeake Bay. The meeting adjourned to Mount Vernon on March 28th where a compact was signed by the two states which guaranteed free navigation of the Potomac. This conference precipitated the Annapolis Convention of 1786 which in turn led to the Constitutional Convention at Philadelphia in 1787. It was no surprise that Alexandrians were Federal to a man and supported the ratification of the Constitution. Crippled by trade restrictions, Alexandria merchants and traders sent a memorial to the Virginia General Assembly in November 1785 requesting that "Congress should be vested with certain rights and

A Gallery of Notable Eighteenth Century Alexandrians
from the Pen of Saint-Memin

JOHN CARLYLE HERBERT
Merchant

WILLIAM FITZHUGH
Planter

MRS. JOHN THOMAS RICKETTS

ADAM LYNN
Silversmith

WILLIAM YEATON
Builder

Taken from: Saint-Memin in Virginia: Portraits and Biographies *by Fillmore Norfleet (Richmond, Virginia: The Dietz Press publishers, 1942)*

This interesting structure on the south-east corner of North Fairfax and Queen streets was, at the time of its demolition in 1915, considered to be one of Alexandria's very early buildings. The Alexandria Gazette (March 26, 1915) stated that it "was one of the first brick and stone structures" erected in town and that it "was previous to the Revolutionary War, the store and place of business in Virginia, of the wealthy and extensive House of Glasford & Co., of Glasgow, Scotland." It was later purchased and remodeled by Isaac Milton Kell into a residence and he, followed by his son, occupied it for about a hundred years. A stable was erected in its place, and subsequent uses for the site included a used furniture store, gift shop (Iberian Imports), and office building.
Esther Green Scrapbook, Alexandria Library

authorities to be properly defined . . . over foreign trade and commerce of the several states." When the Constitution was finally ratified in 1788, Alexandrians celebrated with fireworks and illuminations. Washington wrote to Tobias Lear that: "this flood of good news . . . gave abundant cause for rejoicing . . . the inhabitants of which Alexandria are all federal. The cannon roared and the town was illuminated yesterday." (*Writings of Washington*, volume 30, page 569)

It was also in May 1785 that the gentry of Virginia and Maryland met in Alexandria at Lomax's Tavern on Princess Street to organize the much heralded company to improve the navigation of the Potomac. Known as the Potomac Company, it was spearheaded by Gen. George Washington who served as its first president. The enterprise was formed to construct a lateral canal around the Great Falls of the Potomac at Matildaville and to improve navigation along this commercial artery as far north as Cumberland, Maryland. Opened by 1801, the canal linked the western frontier to the eastern ports of Georgetown and Alexandria, thus ensuring that trade would flow east instead of down the Mississippi River. Beset by many problems including labor riots and foul weather, the canal was not a viable financial venture and the company passed into oblivion on August 15, 1828, when it was purchased by the Chesapeake and Ohio Canal Company.

In 1789, Maryland and Virginia donated land on the Potomac River for a new federal city. With the creation of a federal government, there was a strong impetus to move the capital to a more central location than the city of Philadelphia, Pennsylvania.

In turn, a committee of ten men from Alexandria and Georgetown including John Fitzgerald, Robert T. Hooe, and George Gilpin published a broadside which listed the commercial advantages of the Potomac region. Congress later passed legislation on July 10, 1790, which created the new Columbian District. Alexandria, however, was not included within the original confines of the federal district until the Residency Act was amended in February 1791. Unfortunately, the provisions of this bill precluded the construction of public buildings on the south side of the Potomac River—a measure which was highly detrimental to the economic well-being of Alexandria and which was a major factor in the town's retrocession to Virginia in 1847.

On April 2, 1791, in a very impressive ceremony, Mayor Philip Marsteller, the commonalty, leading citizens, and Masonic officials marched to Jones Point to dedicate the laying of the first cornerstone of the District of Columbia. During the next ten years, Alexandria would witness unparalleled growth and development. Its population nearly doubled from 2,746 inhabitants in 1790 to 4,971 residents in 1800. This was the golden epoch when wealthy merchants constructed many of the exquisite brick Federal houses which now dot the streetscape. Much of this wealth was generated by the Napoleonic Wars in Europe and the increased demand for wheat and grain.

Alexandria's economic fortunes continued to improve when the Virginia General Assembly chartered the Bank of Alexandria in 1792, the first bank in the state. Thomas Twinning, a visitor, was impressed in 1795 by the vast number of houses under construction: "The number of people employed as

While this circa 1866 scene shows mostly early to mid nineteenth century structures, the two-and-one-half-story building (with dormers, right of center) was being operated as Duvall's Tavern in 1783 when the gentlemen of Alexandria entertained General Washington. It was later occupied by Daniel Roberdeau (1787) and Charles Lee, collector of the port (1788-1791) Afterwards it was the banking house for the first bank in Virginia, the Bank of Alexandria, which used the location from 1792 to 1807, when it moved across the street to its new building on the southeast corner of Cameron and North Fairfax Street. The building looming in the right background is Wise's Tavern under construction in 1777 when its builder, John Dalton, died.
Reese Collection

The original cornerstone of the District of Columbia was laid in April 1791 at Jones Point. It appears dimly in this 1929 photograph within a stone enclosure built in 1912. The laying ceremony was a colorful one, starting at Mr. Wise's (tavern) with a glass (or two) of wine and the statement: "May the stone we are about to place in the ground remain an immovable monument of the wisdom and unanimity of North America." A large procession moved on to the Point and the stone was placed with proper Masonic rites, overseen by the master of Lodge No. 22 (the name of Washington had not yet been added) and followed by remarks by the Reverend Muir, minister of the Presbyterian Church. The Virginia Gazette and Alexandria Advertiser (April 21, 1791) stated: "May this stone long commemorate the goodness of God in those uncommon events which have given America a name among the Nations—

Under this Stone, may Jealousy and Selfishness be forever buried . . . " Additional stone markers were subsequently laid at one-mile intervals around the entire ten-mile square of the District of Columbia.
National Archives

Built around 1780 on the southwest corner of South Lee and Prince streets, this was the handsome residence and business site of Colonel Robert Townshend Hooe, Alexandria's first mayor (1780-1781). He was a successful merchant with varied business interests and owned a wharf at the end of Duke Street as well as parcels of property throughout the town. He was an ardent Federalist, being a strong backer of Washington, who "dined at Colonel Hooe's" on several occasions. At least a part of the first floor of this house and its attached wing along Lee Street were used for commercial purposes. The wood paneling and unique (for Alexandria) stairway were outstanding; most of the stair still exists in the house but a goodly portion of paneling from the second story drawing room was sold to the St. Louis Art Museum where it was reassembled and has been on display for many years. Two years after Hooe's death in 1809, the property was bought by the Farmer's Bank of Alexandria and it remained a banking house for ninety-nine years. The Farmers Bank merged in 1848 into the Exchange Bank of Alexandria

which was closed by Federal authorities in 1861. In December 1864, the assets and organizers of the Exchange Bank represented by Lewis McKenzie became the foundation for the newly approved First National Bank which occupied this building until 1910 when it moved to the 500 block of King Street. Through various mergers, it subsequently became the First and Citizens National Bank, United Virginia Bank, and finally is known today as the Crestar Bank.

This view shows paneling in the Robert Townshend Hooe House after its removal and sale to the St. Louis Art Museum in the late 1920s. The main block of the original house did not have entrances from the street but rather had a doorway in the west front which faced a garden plot. The two-and-one-half-story Lee Street wing which is contemporary with the main house had a street ingress which presumably entered the commercial area of the establishment. Colonel Hooe was born in King George County, Virginia, in 1743, lived in Charles County, Maryland, for a time during which he served as lieutenant colonel in the twelfth Maryland Battalion and on the Committee of Safety (during the early Revolutionary period) before coming to Alexandria. He and his wife died without issue, but other Hooe kinsmen were prominent members of the community for several generations to come.

This fine group, sometimes referred to as "Gentry Row," was built by Captain John Harper over several years, approximately 1786 to 1793. Two of the physicians who attended Washington in his final hours, Dr. James Craik and Dr. Elisha Cullen Dick, lived here on the north side of the 200 block of Prince Street. (The five brick houses are numbered, from right to left: 207, 209, 211, 213, 215.) The traditional residence of Dr. Dick has long been 209 and, while he may have spent some time there, most recent evidence indicates that he was living in 211 at least as early as 1802 and possibly remained there until 1820 when he moved out of town into the country. Dr. Craik resided at 209 in 1789 and may have been there till 1796 when he moved to 210 Duke Street. The end of the row (215 Prince) was apparently a two story brick house in 1796. Aaron Hewes had purchased the lot in 1783 from Captain Harper but by 1829, it had been raised to its present height.
William A. Moore, circa 1900

carpenters and masons . . . the hammer and trowel was at work everywhere." Another commentator noted that the streets were as muddy as Baltimore, "but there was more luxury in Alexandria, if a miserable luxury; you see servants in silk stockings and their masters in boots . . . They have set up superb wharves and vast warehouses."

All did not augur well for the future of town however. The passage of the Jay Treaty in 1794 gave preferential treatment to Great Britain and alienated the United States from its former ally, France. In retaliation France initiated an "undeclared naval war" upon American shipping and it is estimated that at least twenty Alexandria vessels were captured during this period. As a hedge against hostilities, a fort was constructed at Jones Point in 1795 and the Alexandria City Council voted to arm the military and purchase gunpowder. The war furor later subsided and the century ended on a gloomy note with the death of Gen. George Washington on December 14, 1799. His funeral was virtually an Alexandria affair as townspeople streamed to Mount Vernon to pay homage not only to a national hero but to their beloved friend and neighbor. Washington's death marked the end of an era. The Fairfax County Courthouse was moved to Providence, Virginia, in March 1800 and Alexandria became an integral part of the District of Columbia in February 1801.

Built by Captain Harper, the same row, suffered considerable damage in a high windstorm about 1913, the most apparent damage having been inflicted on the home of the family of R. E. Knight at 207 Prince Street. The quarter block on which this house sits was purchased in July 1749 by Colonel William Fairfax of Belvoir at the first sale of lots in the newly designated town site. His son, George William Fairfax, sold it in 1771 when he left permanently for England, and it was later sold to William Hodgson in 1790 by Captain John Harper. It is very likely that the house was built during Harper's ownership. The corner of the building on the right edge is the Bank of the Old Dominion, built 1851-1852, later occupied for about forty years by the Citizens National Bank, still later by the Free Methodist Church, and finally and currently under the name Athenaeum, by the Northern Virginia Fine Arts Association.

The Stabler-Leadbeater Apothecary Shop, a business established in 1792 which finally died in the Great Depression in 1933, occupied one of these buildings (107 South Fairfax Street to the left) as early as 1796. It was erected by coopersmith Philip Dawe sometime between 1774 and 1785 and he had tenants, Porter and Ingraham, from 1787 to 1795. Edward Stabler advertised himself as an "Apothecary and Druggist" in 1796 at this location. He purchased the structure in 1805, and as business expanded, bought the building next door at 105 South Fairfax in 1829. Eventually the corner building on King and Fairfax was purchased, which rounded out the holdings of the company in the immediate area. When a Leadbeater son married a Stabler daughter, the transition to the extensive wholesale and retail drug business of E. S. Leadbeater and Sons began.

Numbers of well-known people dealt with this venerable business and the best remembered item is the note sent from Mount Vernon on April 11, 1802, which stated that: "Mr. Stabler, Alexandria— Mrs. Washington desires Mr. Stabler will send by the bearer, a quart bottle of his best Castor Oil, and the bill for it." Upon its demise in 1933, the Landmarks Society of Alexandria composed of a dedicated group of ladies, was formed to preserve the shop, which it did and continues to do. Mr. L. Manuel Hendler of Baltimore bought all the pharmaceutical equipment at the auction in 1933 but allowed it to stay in what became a museum, and finally and generously donated it to the Society in 1945. This view, one of the earliest in this volume, may predate 1852, since in that year, the firm's name was changed from Stabler to Leadbeater. Perkins Library, Duke University

Few of the remaining structures on the south side of the 300 block of King Street were of eighteenth century vintage. A devastating fire visited the block in 1827 and destroyed many of the street front buildings as well as the rear ells and outbuildings. A happy exception, however, was the silversmith shop of Benjamin Barton at 324 King Street. Barton came from England to Alexandria in 1801 and engaged in the clock and watch making business until his death in 1816. The establishment was carried on by his son Thomas and a grandson, Benjamin, who added the jewelry and silversmith trade in 1834. Alexandria was home to over seventy silversmiths during the late eighteenth and nineteenth centuries including W. W. Adam, John Duffy, William A. Williams, Adam Lynn, and Mordecai Miller.
Gift of William Adam, circa 1850

Dr. James Craik, *courtesy of the Alexandria Association*

Popularly known as the Craik House, this imposing structure was built between 1783 when John Short purchased the lot and 1789 when he offered for sale the lot and a "three-story brick house." The purchaser was John B. Murray who resold the house in October 1795 to Dr. James Craik who made this his primary residence until 1809, when he offered it for rent. He moved into the countryside of Fairfax County, where he died at the age of eighty-four years in 1814. He had been a friend of George Washington's from early days, having accompanied him on his mission to the French in 1754, served together under General Braddock in 1755, surveyed lands together in the Ohio and Kanawha valleys in 1770, and he served under Washington during the Revolution as surgeon-general in the Continental Army. He moved to Alexan-

dria from Port Tobacco, Maryland, in 1785 and one of his first places of residence before settling in this house was in the 200 block of Prince Street. He was one of three physicians attending Washington at the time of his death in 1799. The clapboard flounder to the left was long thought to have been the home of George Coryell, an artisan builder from New Jersey, who is reputed to have been persuaded by Washington to move to Alexandria because of the need for his skill in a fast growing and developing community. Coryell's lot was actually two lots east of the Craik house and this flounder was owned by a sailmaker, Joseph Robinson, in 1783. After near total dilapidation, it was covered with a brick veneer and was incorporated as an extension of the Craik House.

Loeb Collection circa 1920

The Bank of Alexandria had its beginnings in 1792 by act of the Virginia Assembly and it spent its first fourteen years at 305 Cameron Street in what had been Duvall's Tavern. The corner building seen here in this circa 1940 view (North Fairfax and Cameron) may be the second oldest structure in the United States erected specifically as a bank building. The bank moved into the building in 1807 and occupied it until 1834 when it failed. The building was considered, and rejected, by Robert Mills when a new courthouse for Alexandria, D. C., was being planned in the mid-1830s. It was purchased by James Green in 1848 and subsequently incorporated as a part of his new hostelry, "Green's Mansion House Hotel." The writer's mother, a native of Gloucester County, Virginia, remembered as a child an elderly aunt, who sometimes stayed at the Mansion House when visiting cousins in Alexandria. This entire complex became one of Alexandria's many hospitals for Union soldiers during the war. In the mid-1970s the hotel portion (to the right) was torn down in order to remove the obstruction standing between the Carlyle House and Fairfax Street, but the original bank building was preserved and restored.

Loeb Collection, Alexandria Library

Timothy Mountford

Lawrence Hooff

George Deneale

Elisha Cullen Dick

The Alexandria-Washington Lodge No. 22 has long played a seminal role in the life of Alexandria. First organized in 1782 by Michael Ryan, William Hunter, Sr., Dr. Elisha Cullen Dick, Peter Dow, and Robert Adam, the Lodge No. 39 as it was

then called was chartered from a warrant obtained from the Grand Lodge of Pennsylvania in 1783. Its first place of meeting was at the second floor of Lamb's Tavern, situated on the west side of Union Street between Prince and Duke. The

lodge was later housed at John Wise's Tavern, northeast corner of Cameron and North Fairfax streets in 1785, at William Page's Tavern in 1788 and at the Common Council chambers in 1790. In 1797, the Lodge occupied a long room situated in William McNight's tavern located on the northwest corner of King and Royal streets and it was here that Washington was frequently entertained. By 1802, the Alexandria-Washington Lodge had constructed permanent quarters over the market building at Cameron and Royal streets. The hall occupied a space fifty by twenty-two feet and cost $1,988.83. Many distinguished guests including General Lafayette were entertained in this hall until the Market House burned on May 19, 1871. Fortunately the many relics housed in the museum were saved and a new elegant hall forty-six by twenty-eight feet, anteroom, and banquet hall were later constructed within the new City Hall, built in 1873. The Alexandria-Washington Lodge continued to meet here until the George Washington Masonic Memorial was constructed atop Shuter's Hill in 1932.

Pictured here are many prominent members of Alexandria Lodge No. 22 who gave unsparingly of their time and shaped the destiny of their community.

Silhouettes courtesy of the Alexandria-Washington Lodge No. 22

Probably the least altered (both interior and exterior) of Alexandria's finer residences, the Dulany House at 601 Duke Street was built shortly after the purchase of its lots from David Arell in September 1783 by Benjamin Dulany, a wealthy and

arrogant Marylander who had moved across the river a short time before. He married Elizabeth French, an heiress, ward of George Washington and daughter of Daniel French of Rose Hill in Fairfax County, and was soon consorting with

the most affluent members of Alexandria society. General Washington noted, on February 15, 1785, that he "Went to Alexandria with Mrs. Washington. Dined at Mr. Dulany's." In 1799 Dulany purchased and moved to Ludwell Lee's mansion on Shuter's Hill (at the west end of King Street) and subsequently rented this house till its purchase by Robert J. Taylor, a prominent attorney and civic leader in 1810. Tradition has it that general Lafayette, when being greeted by throngs of town citizens in 1824, was unable to respond effectively from the low level of the front step of the Lawrason house across the street, so he moved to the high front steps of this house where he addressed those assembled in his honor. This view, circa 1900, gives an idea of its appearance before the advent of bumper-to-bumper automobiles. Perhaps things might still be a bit quieter if the cobblestones had not been removed in favor of smooth blacktop surfacing. To the left of the house may been seen one of the original stables still existing in town.
O'Brien/Hulfish Collection

Portrait by William Williams, 1794; courtesy of the Alexandria - Washington Lodge, No. 22

With the signing of the Treaty of Versailles on September 3, 1783, the Revolutionary War formally came to an end. After eight and one-half years of conflict the American colonies had secured their freedom from Great Britain. Gen. George Washington had emerged as the preeminent hero of the Revolutionary struggle and his prestige could not have been any higher than the day he rode into Alexandria on December 31, 1783, having recently resigned his commission at Annapolis, Maryland, on the 23rd of the month. His arrival in Alexandria was announced by the discharge of thirteen cannon after which a reception was tendered by the town's leading citizens at DuVall's Tavern at 305 Cameron Street. Attending the festivities, Mayor Richard Conway delivered an emotional speech! "We experience a singular satisfaction in reflecting that your residence in our neighborhood will have a happy Influence as will the Growth and Prosperity of this infant Town . . ." And General Washington replied thusly: "While your friendly concern for my welfare demands my best acknowledgement, I beg you will be persuaded, Gentlemen there is a certain heart-felt Gratification in receiving the approbation and good wishes of those with whom we have been long acquainted, and whose friendship we value . . ." After an elegant dinner at the tavern and sev-

eral effusive toasts, Washington retired for a time to Mount Vernon to pursue his favorite occupation—farming.

For many years until his election as first president, Washington was a frequent visitor to his hometown. He patronized its stores and shops, worshipped at old Christ Church and enjoyed the camaraderie of many of his former officers who had settled in Alexandria after the war. Washington owned real estate in town, conducted business here, and cast his ballot at the courthouse for election

of representatives to the Virginia General Assembly. On April 16, 1789, Alexandrians were the first to fete the newly elected president on his way to New York to be inaugurated. After his retirement from this high office, General and Mrs. Washington attended a birthnight ball at Gadsby's Tavern in 1798 in honor of the president's birthday. Upon Washington's death on December 14, 1799, a veil of gloom settled over Alexandria, as its townsmen bade farewell to their "First and most beloved of Citizens."

Mason's Ordinary or the Little Fountain Tavern was located on the west side of the 100 block of North Royal Street just south of the City Hotel. A hospice had been operated on this site by Charles and Ann Mason from 1754 to 1761. Innkeeper William Hawkins obtained a license to keep an ordinary in this building on May 21, 1771, and upon his death his wife took over the establishment. George Washington noted in his diary for January 17, 1774, that he "Supp'd at Mrs. Hawkins' and came home afterward." Edward Owens, a merchant, bought the little tavern in 1778 and conveyed it to John Wise in 1782. J. Everette Fauber, Jr., an architectural historian, suggests in his analysis, Restoration Gadsby's Tavern, that since the dimensions of the building that John Carlyle advertised Mason as having constructed do not fit the current dimensions of the Fountain Tavern, Wise either remodeled the earlier structure or built an entirely new one. Wise also constructed the large 1792 addition to the north and built the rear stable and outbuildings. Wise, Alexandria's tavern king, also owned and operated the Indian Queen at the northwest corner of King and St. Asaph, Lomax Tavern on the south side of Princess Street, between Water (Lee) and Union, and Wise's Tavern, described later.

In 1796 Wise leased the Royal Street facility to John Gadsby. Mr. Gadsby soon gained an unrivaled reputation for his viands and liquors. "His canvas back suppers were a common theme, for the like of them was never known before or after . . . "
National Archives 1929

OLD TOWN TAVERNS

Alexandria was a town of many taverns. There were some fifty here by 1800 and these included: the Lomax, Indian Queen, McKnight's, Washington's Tavern, Ship's Tavern, the Red Lion, Rainbow Inn, Reeder's Tavern, and Union Tavern. Generally, these establishments were of two types: those which served gentlemen and aristocrats; and others catering to drovers, sailors, and the common citizenry. "For the townspeople, the tavern served as a meeting place for civic groups, private businesses, and social hobnobbing." In addition, it was the scene of "Masonic Balls," "music and dancing lessons" as well as "tutoring in French," "auctions held in the courtyard," "fire company elections," "political dinners" and the "organization of horse races for the Jockey Club." (Dona M. Ware, "Tavern Life") Private subscriptions for the use of coffeehouses were available. "Here members could come to exchange the news of the day, read newspapers from other communities, enjoy a meal among friends, and even deposit their mail in the letter bag left by the local post master for the next ship due to set sail." (Dorothy Kabler, The Story of Gadsby's Tavern, Alexandria, Virginia, 1952)

A

B

City Hotel or Gadsby's Tavern is certainly the best known of all Alexandria's hostelries. During the winter of 1792, John Wise relocated his tavern from North Fairfax Street to Royal where he constructed a handsome three-story brick inn. The Fountain Tavern, also owned by Wise, abutted the new structure on the south and by 1796 a Mutual Fire Insurance Map of the one-half acre at the southwest corner of Royal and Cameron streets showed seven structures. Leased to John Gadsby from 1796 to 1808, it reached its pinnacle of fame as a superior hostelry in both foods and accommodations.

Commonly known as the City Hotel during most of the nineteenth century, Gadsby's Tavern has had a succession of owners including William Caton, 1808; Thomas Brooke, 1809; Thomas Triplett, 1812 and Horatio Clagett, 1820s. During the first part of the twentieth century the building was occupied by Thomas Lucas, an auctioneer and junk dealer. View A shows both buildings before 1870, with a

C

D

corner of the old George Tavern appearing on the right, and the small gable roof which covered the street opening of the brick-lined icehouse built under the sidewalk on Cameron Street.
(Rebecca Ramsay Reese Collection)
B. This beautifully proportioned ballroom was the scene of assemblies, Washington birthnight balls, and testimonial dinners, at which distinguished guests included Washington, Jefferson, Madison, Monroe, both Adamses, and Lafayette. Traveling players and musicians performed here regularly and meetings of the Alexandria Library Company, St. Andrews Society, and the local golf club were attended by the eligible townspeople. This view of the Gadsby's ballroom shows it reinstalled in the Metropolitan Museum, New York City.
(Courtesy of the Metropolitan Museum, New York City)
C. A rare view of Gadsby's Tavern vividly depicts the gallery and one of the outbuildings which once dotted the courtyard. There was a kitchen, necessary,

wooden stable, and wash house, which were destroyed by fire in 1839. During the tavern's heyday, carriages would arrive in the courtyard and deposit passengers and luggage. Colonel Arthur Herbert, a prominent Alexandria citizen and banker, penned a fascinating account of riding the stage from Alexandria to Winchester, he wrote: "Some time then in the early fifties, a coach drawn by four horses passed from the courtyard of this old hotel under the arched gateway and into the streets of the ancient city of Alexandria in search first of the U. S. Mail and then for the passengers who were picked up at parts designated on the 'Waybill', they having paid their fare and been 'booked' for Leesburg, Winchester or intermediate points the evening before. We passed out of the old gateway, my seat being the deck just back of the driver, the time being early dawn, my eyelids and my senses not entirely awake. The court yard referred to is now entirely metamorphosed and its ancient archway, in ruins, was just as you see them in old English Inns to-

day where the vandal touch of improvement has not destroyed them and this was the only typical one I have ever seen in this country." ("A Wild Stage Coach Ride," edited by T. Michael Miller in Northern Virginia's Heritage, February 1982)
(Photograph from the O'Brien/Hulfish Collection)
D. In 1929 the American Legion, along with other civic organizations, raised money and purchased Gadsby's Tavern for its headquarters. It was subsequently deeded to the city of Alexandria in 1972 and today the site houses a restaurant and an excellent eighteenth century interpretive tavern museum.

A portrait of John Gadsby, painted in the early nineteenth century by John Gadsby Chapman, is displayed today in Gadsby's Tavern Museum, along with a portrait of his wife.
(Gadsby's Tavern Museum, Alexandria Library)
John Gadsby, courtesy of the Smithsonian Institution

Wise's Tavern (also known at various times as Globe Tavern, Bunch of Grapes, and Abert's Tavern) is one of Alexandria's oldest structures. Situated at the northeast corner of Cameron and North Fairfax streets, it was the scene of many resplendent events. Construction of the building was commenced by John Dalton and upon his death in 1777, it was finished by his son-in-law, Thomas Herbert. In the mid-1780s Herbert leased it to tavern keeper Henry Lyles who entertained General Washington here on September 26, 1785. A succession of innkeepers operated this facility before it was converted into a dwelling house during the early part of the nineteenth century. Among these were: George H. Leigh, 1787-1788; John Wise, 1788-1792; John Abert, 1794-1799; Peter Kemp, 1799-1800. (Cox, Street by Street)

It was in this building that George Washington, after being elected to the presidency in 1789, was feted by the citizens of Alexandria prior to his departure for New York City where he was to be inaugurated. For the occasion, Colonel Light Horse Harry Lee penned an address which was delivered by Mayor Dennis Ramsay. A description of the gathering has been left to us by the Reverend William McWhir who attended the ceremony: ". . . I was at the public meeting of the citizens of Alexandria called to receive General Washington and to take farewell of him, when he was called to the Presidential chair. The large hotel was crowded to overflowing, and as great a multitude surrounded the doors and windows . . . the reply of General Washington was longer than the address. The style of oratory was grave and commanding, nor was it possible, when he spoke, to deny the most fixed and earnest attention. His sentiments fell upon the people like oracles. During the delivery of Colonel Lee's address, and especially during the reply of Washington, a breathless silence pervaded the multitude and in common language, 'you might have heard a pin drop.' He closed his reply with these words—'My kind friends and good neighbors, I bid you an affectionate fare-well.' There was not a dry eye in the assembly." (Alexandria Gazette, January 3, 1853.

In September 1798, a dinner was held here in honor of John Marshall, the future chief justice of the Supreme Court, and local groups such as the Potomac Company and the Alexandria Jockey Club were entertained on numerous occasions. The building was modified circa 1916 and the high steps and double doorway visible in this photograph were removed and replaced by a Colonial Revival porch. From that time to 1974 it served as the Anne Lee Memorial Home for elderly ladies.
Library of Congress, circa 1905

Officers of the First District Volunteers pose for A. J. Russell, photographer, around the doorway of the City Hotel on the southwest corner of North Royal and Cameron streets in 1863. This structure, erected in 1792 by innkeeper John Wise, was leased to John Gadsby from 1796 to 1808 during which period it and the adjoining building were known as Gadsby's Hotel or Gadsby's Tavern and gained favorable notoriety far and wide for luxurious fittings and a fine table. The interesting building appearing dimly across Cameron Street is the very old George Tavern which William Ramsay advertised in the Maryland Gazette on March 6, 1760, to be for rent. "There are three fire places below stairs, a very good bar, and six rooms above; a kitchen adjoining, with two good rooms below and above, a dining room 24 feet by 18, a room of the same dimension above it, in which is a very good London Billiard table: There are also, a garden, stable, smokehouse, etc. . . ." It was demolished in February 1870. One wonders if the two small Sunday-clad citizens belong to one of the officers, or were escapees from the arms of their Southern sympathizing parents.
Library of Congress

Arell's Tavern, originally situated on the corner of Sharpshin Alley and Market Alley (southeast of the south entrance of present City Hall), was operated by Richard Arell from 1768 to 1773. Diaries of George Washington indicate that the general dined there some sixteen times between 1771 and 1774. It was at Arell's Tavern on July 18, 1774, that a committee of Fairfax citizens, chaired by George Washington, was appointed to draw up resolutions disapproving actions taken by the British Parliament against the city of Boston in retaliation for its Tea Party. Written by George Mason, these became the famous Fairfax Resolves which later developed into the Virginia Declaration of Rights and still later into the Bill of Rights of the U. S. Constitution. Arell later leased his tavern to one John Rich. Upon the former's death, Arell's heirs reentered against Rich for nonpayment and a subsequent description of the property in 1811 states that there was "no dwelling house thereon." Thus the original Arell's Tavern ceased to exist sometime around 1810 to 1811. The construction date of the structure in the photograph is not known but it served as Zimmerman's Oyster House until it was razed during the 1960s urban renewal process. Eleanor Van Swearingen, "Richard Arell, His Times, Tavern & Neighbors," Arlington County Historical Society, volume 2, number 4; volume 3, number 1.

Washington Tavern was constructed circa 1797 on the southeast corner of King and Pitt streets and was adorned with a sign showing George Washington on horseback on one side, and a dun backing on the other. About the year 1826, a new keeper of the tavern changed its appellation to the Franklin House. Then upon the death of Chief Justice John Marshall in 1835, the hostelry was renamed the Marshall House in his honor. This hotel was made memorable by the death of Colonel Elmer E. Ellsworth who was shot by James Jackson at the commencement of the War Between the States for tearing down the Confederate flag which flew over it and for the blood Jackson shed while defending his property. On February 25, 1873, the building was nearly destroyed by fire. "The whole of the back building and entire interior of the third story of the main building, together with the roof were destroyed and the first and second stories were badly damaged. Alexandria Gazette, February 25, 1873. Subsequently rebuilt, the old Marshall House was demolished in the 1950s and a Virginia State liquor store was erected on the site.
National Archives, Brady Collection, circa 1864

Yeates' (also Yates') Garden The region surrounding 414 Franklin Street was leased by Peter Billy who operated a greenhouse and botanical garden where he sold an assortment of plants and shrubs. William Yeates, a Quaker, leased the real estate from James H. Hooe in 1813 and bought it outright for $750 in 1818. In 1826 the description of the vacant lot changed to a "House and Garden, Royal to Pitt on Franklin Street" valued at $4,000. Upon Yeates' death in 1826, his son William Yeates, Jr., inherited the structure and grounds and subsequently advertised it as Yeates' Botanical Garden in 1841: "William Yeates and Son respectfully call the attention of the public to their collection of Trees, Evergreens and Greenhouse plants; all of which they are determined to dispose of on moderate terms. Much attention has lately been bestowed upon the grounds and many improvements added affording a delightful resort for citizens and strangers. At the solicitation of a number of citizens they have concluded to furnish ICE CREAM and other refreshments, including the finest fruits of the season, refreshments will be served on and after the 5th of July . . . Tickets of admission can be had at the Garden. Price 12½ cents. . . . Visitors will be allowed the deduction of Ticket money, in refreshments, cut flowers or plants."
Alexandria Gazette, July 2, 1841

Walter Gahan, an Alexandria resident, reminisced that in the 1860s, Yeates Garden was a pleasure ground with swings and other amusements. During the War Between the States, Federal soldiers enjoyed horse racing on a track which was situated west of the gardens and subsequently the black population used the surrounding grounds for recreational purposes. In the 1890s Yeates Garden "was the favorite walk of the belles and beaux, in the southern part of the city, to drink of the cool and sparkling water from the

pump, that always hung conveniently by its rusty chain; after that a stroll in the well kept garden. What was said I leave to the imagination of the reader; but it must have been very sweet and sentimental, for it was called the 'lovers' walk' . . ."
(Alexandria Gazette, April 24, 1890)

The Virginia House Hotel opened as a hotel as early as 1823, situated at the southwest corner of King and Peyton streets. In November 1853, Lucien Peyton advertised that he would lease the hotel which had recently been thoroughly repaired, having had a large addition—another story—constructed thereon. The facility contained about thirty bedrooms, many of them double ... a large dining room, barroom, sitting room, and parlor. "Besides the tavern house, there is on the premises a new stable, capable of accommodating 50 horses, a feed house, store house and shedding for carriages. The lot attached contains near 2 acres with a pump of the best water in the city ..." (Alexandria Gazette, November 2, 1853) W. B. Scarce, proprietor there in 1857, advised the public that board at the Virginia House would be one dollar per day. On July 4, 1889, a chimney fire erupted at the hotel and it suffered such severe water damage that one of the walls of the building collapsed three weeks later. During the latter nineteenth century, the Virginia House catered mostly to a working class clientele. Nearly destroyed by a tornado in 1927, the hotel was subsequently razed.
O'Brien/Hulfish Collection

Catts' Tavern, situated near the intersection of Duke and Diagonal Road, was established in 1815 and was known as a drover's tavern where cattle sales of the District of Columbia on the Virginia side of the Potomac took place for over a century. Elections and political meetings for the eastern part of Fairfax County also occurred here. On New Year's Day from 1815 until the outbreak of the War Between the State, many employers from Alexandria and outlying counties congregated at Catts' Tavern in the West End where they would contract for the services of servants and field hands. Here the small farmer could look for three or four able-bodied fellows to help cultivate

his fields; the citizen of town hunt his porter or house servants, and the childless widow look for a "girl." After the tavern was destroyed by fire on September 24, 1896, the Pennsylvania Railroad

purchased the property in 1903. (Alexandria Gazette, September 25, 1896 and June 10, 1903)
Milton Grigg Collection

The Lee-Fendall House was built at 429 North Washington Street in 1785 by Philip Richard Fendall on a half-acre lot purchased the previous year from Light Horse Harry Lee, his stepson-in-law. Fendall's first wife was a cousin, Lettice Lee of Maryland; his second wife was Elizabeth Steptoe Lee, who had inherited the famous Stratford Hall Plantation and whose daughter Matilda had been Light Horse Harry Lee's first wife. Fendall's third wife was Mary, Light Horse Harry Lee's sister! In addition to liking Lee wives, Fendall was a director of the Potomac Company and one of the founders of the Bank of Alexandria and its first president in 1793.

The Lee-Fendall House was lived in by thirty-five members of the Lee family from 1785 to 1903 and is now a shrine

to Light Horse Harry Lee. From 1836 to 1843, Edmund Jennings Lee resided here and from 1850 to 1856, Harriott Stuart Cazenove, great-granddaughter of Richard Henry Lee occupied the structure. During the War Between the States, the home was utilized as a Union military hospital and from 1870 to 1904, five grandchildren of Richard Bland Lee, Northern Virginia's first congressman, lived here. The Lee-Fendall House is now a public museum and is open for tours for an admission fee. Another notable who domiciled here was Philip R. Fendall, Jr., member of the Washington Monument Commission, district attorney for the city of Washington, D. C., and editor of the papers of President James Madison, under the auspices of the Library of Congress in the early 1860s.

THE LEE FAMILY

From 1784 to 1815 a remarkable concentration of the Lee family settled in Alexandria and its vicinity. They were mostly of the fifth generation of that family in Virginia and numbered about thirty individuals. Over the years, the Lees acquired and occupied dozens of properties in and around Alexandria. While some of the Lees in Alexandria traced their ancestry through Thomas Lee of Stratford Hall, it was the Lees of Leesylvania who played a more important role in the socio-economic fabric of the community.

Leesylvania was a plantation located about twenty miles south of Alexandria between the towns of Dumfries and Colchester, Virginia. Henry Lee II, a nephew of Thomas, was the progenitor of this clan. He had five sons and three daughters and four of these sons were intimately connected with the history of Alexandria.

The oldest son, Henry Lee III, commonly known as Light Horse Harry, was Robert E. Lee's father and George Washington's favorite cavalry officer. He arrived on the scene in Alexandria as early as 1783 and purchased as many as thirty lots there. In fact, the Lee-Fendall House was built on property bought by Lee from Baldwin Dade in November, 1784. It was also this Henry Lee who was a brilliant orator and personal political advisor to George Washington. According to family tradition, he penned the "Farewell Address' from the citizens of Alexandria to George Washington in the dining room of the Lee-Fendall House in March 1789 and was later chosen by the Sixth Congress of the United States to deliver the funeral oration for the first president. This oration contains those immortal words about Washington as being "First in War, First in Peace and First in the Hearts of his Countrymen."

His brother, Charles Lee, was the first Lee to settle in Alexandria. He had the foresight to buy land outside the 1762 limits of the town—one half acre on Wilkes and Fairfax street, two acres between Oronoco and Pendleton and Pitt streets and, with Philip and Mary Fendall, ten acres west of town between Patrick and Fayette, Queen and Oronoco streets. Charles Lee was practicing law in Alexandria in the early 1780s. He later served as George Washington's personal attorney, secretary of state pro tem and was twice attorney general under the Washington and Adams administrations. During the administration of the latter, he was offered the position of chief justice of the Supreme Court but declined. He was counsel for the plaintiffs, Robert T. Hooe and Dennis Ramsay of Alexandria and William Marbury of Maryland, in the landmark court decision resulting from *Marbury vs. Madison*. Charles was a shrewd real estate investor and bequeathed two hundred thousand dollars, a considerable sum for that time, to his children upon his death in 1815.

The third brother of the clan was Richard Bland Lee who lived much of his life at Sully Plantation in Fairfax County. In 1811 he moved to Alexandria and resided at 404 Duke Street. He was Northern Virginia's first congressman and was primarily responsible for having the capital of the United States moved from Philadelphia to the banks of the Potomac.

Edmund J. Lee is the last of the Leesylvania brothers to be mentioned. Not as nationally prominent as his other brothers, he was far more intimately involved in the day to day affairs of Alexandria. He was twice mayor of town, from 1814 to 1818, and had Cameron Street extended and a new town jail built as well. As clerk of the U.S. District Court for Alexandria, he served as a commissioner and executor for the court in buying and selling scores of properties at public auction and handling bankruptcies and settling personal estates. Edmund was also president of the Alexandria Canal Company, vestryman at Christ Church, and upon Light Horse Harry Lee's death in 1818, he became Robert E. Lee's unofficial guardian.

Lee Corner (Oronoco and North Washington streets) was the focal point of the clan's interaction and it is for this reason that an investigation of the Lees and their real estate holdings should begin here. The oldest of the Lee homes on the corner is the Lee-Fendall House.

Edmund Jennings Lee bought this property at 428 North Washington Street from his brother Charles Lee in 1801 and resided here until 1836. His son Cassius later lived in this lovely house from 1839 until the War Between the States when he was forced to emigrate to Canada. Edmund J. Lee was born at Leesylvania, Prince William County, on the 20th of May, 1772, and died at the Lee-Fendall House in May 1843. He married Sarah, the youngest daughter of Richard Henry Lee, a signer of the Declaration of Independence. Edmund was actively involved in the affairs of the Episcopal Church in Virginia and was one of the founders of the Episcopal Seminary. He was also responsible for preventing the confiscation of the glebe land of Christ Church. After selling these lands, Christ Church utilized the funds to erect a new church steeple, placed a substantial fence around the churchyard and purchased the house at 407 North Washington Street as a permanent rectory (former Charles Lee Home). An exceptionally pious man, Edmund was a gadfly to evildoers and vigorously prosecuted those in town who gambled. Bishop Meade wrote of him: ". . . he was a man of great decision and perseverance in what he deemed right—obstinate, some of us thought . . . There was no compromise at all in him with anything which he thought wrong. He was fearless as Julius Caesar."

Matilda Lee Love, Edmund's great niece, attended a party at this home in 1807. She writes: "I spent the next winter in Alexandria (1807), and we had a fine time, as my uncle, F. L. Lee (Francis Lightfoot Lee II) was married that winter to Miss Fitzgerald. It was the cause of great gaiety, as they both had large connections. At the party given at Mr. E. J. Lee's who married my aunt, I danced a cotillion with W. Meade, the present bishop of Virginia . . ."
Photograph by W. P. Gray, 1924, Valentine Museum

This photograph depicts two historic Lee homes at 607 and 609 Oronoco Street. John Potts, secretary of the Potomac Company, originally constructed the beautiful Federalist house, No. 607 on the right, in 1795. In 1796, William Fitzhugh of Chatham, the largest landowner in Fairfax County, Virginia, purchased this property for his city townhouse. Mary, his daughter, age sixteen, married George Washington Parke Curtis here and later became mistress of Arlington House. General Light Horse Harry Lee moved his family here from 611 Cameron Street in 1811. By 1813 Lee had journeyed to Barbados to convalesce from an attack made upon him by a Baltimore mob. His family continued to reside at No. 607 until 1816 when they moved to 407 North Washington Street (Charles Lee's home). In 1820, Ann Hill Lee and her family again occupied No. 607. It was here that young Robert E. Lee grew to manhood and spent many of his happiest years hunting, fishing, and playing in the woods surrounding Alexandria. During Lafayette's triumphant visit to Alexandria in 1824, he made two courtesy calls on Mrs. Lee at this residence. It was from this house that Robert E. Lee applied for admission and was accepted to West Point in February of 1824. After his departure in June 1825, his mother moved to Georgetown, D.C., to reside with her oldest son Carter, a prominent lawyer. Portia Lee Hodgson who was a daughter of William Lee of Greenspring, one of the famous Stratford Lees, also lived at No. 607 from 1825 until her death in 1840.
(National Archives, 1929)

Edmund Jennings Lee (1772 to 1843) was intimately engaged in the day-to-day affairs of Alexandria as a member and president of the Common Council, 1809-1810; mayor of Alexandria, 1814-1818; Clerk of the U.S. Circuit Court, 1818-1837; and president of the Alexandria Canal Company, 1830. During his residency here, he lived at: 407 North Washington Street, 1798-1800; 515 King Street, 1800; 428 North Washington Street, 1801-1836; the Lee-Fendall House, 429 North Washington Street, 1836-1843. His wife, Sarah (1775-1837) was the youngest daughter of Richard Henry Lee and she died at the Lee-Fendall House on May 8, 1837.
Courtesy the Lee Society and the Lee-Fendall House

Another view of 607 Oronoco Street was taken in the 1870s or 1880s before dormer windows had been added. William Yeaton, noted Alexandria attorney, was the occupant then, and the two ladies standing on the front steps are probably his daughters. During the 1940s, 607 Oronoco Street was also home to Archibald MacLeish, librarian of Congress. In the early 1960s this lovely home was purchased by the Lee-Jackson Foundation and converted into one of Alexandria's major museums. Thousands of visitors frequent it annually, now known as the boyhood home of Robert E. Lee. (Gift of Sayers family; Lloyd House)

The first known portrait of Robert E. Lee was painted by William E. West at Baltimore, Maryland, in 1838. A young thirty-one-year-old lieutenant of engineers in the U.S. Army, Lee has been described by the eminent biographer, Douglas Southall Freeman, as being "five feet, ten and a half inches in height . . . with bright eyes that sometimes seemed black. His hair was ebon and abundant, with a wave that a woman might have envied. There was dignity in his open bearing, and his manners were considerate and ingratiating. He had candor, tact, and good humor. The self control he had learned from his mother was his in large measure . . . It was easy for him to win and hold the friendship of other people."
Courtesy of the Lee Society

House view courtesy of Viola Barrett Greenland Pope

The Lee Hopkins House was at 609 Oronoco Street built in 1795 by William Wilson as a twin house to the one at No. 607. Cornelia Lee, also a daughter of William Lee of Greenspring, was the first Lee to occupy this dwelling. William was one of that famous band of Lee brothers born at Stratford Hall along with Richard Henry, Arthur, and Francis Lightfoot. Following her father's death, Cornelia and her sister Portia became wards of Richard Bland Lee of Sully. Cornelia married John Hopkins, a Richmond

banker, on the 16th of October 1806 and died at No. 609 twelve years later in 1818. John Lloyd, who married Edmund J. Lee's daughter, Ann Harriotte, was the tenant at No. 609 from 1821 to 1823. In the autumn of 1824, Benjamin Hallowell, the famous Quaker schoolmaster and Robert E. Lee's teacher, opened his academy at the same location. Cornelia Lee's widowed step-daughter, Lucy Lyons Hopkins, was living here in the 1850s. When Cassius F. Lee's wife, Hannah Philippa, died in childbirth in January

1844, it was Aunt Turner, "as she was affectionately called by the family, who cared for and raised Cassius Lee, Jr. After Aunt Turner's death in 1871 the house was purchased by Mrs. Pierson Barton Reading, the widow of Major Reading who was General Fremont's paymaster of the California battalion. Other notable inhabitants included: Thomson F. Mason, a grandson of George Mason of Gunston Hall and Judge William Cranch, supreme court jurist, and judge of the Circuit Court of D.C.

45

This is the Charles Lee House at 407 North Washington Street. Most of this three-story brick house was refashioned in the Victorian mode except for the rear wing. Built around 1790, it was the home of Charles Lee who was born in 1758 and died in 1815. Charles Lee was the first member of the Lee family to settle in Alexandria and was practicing law here in 1785. A brilliant scholar, he attended the College of New Jersey (Princeton University) like his brothers, Edmund and Henry. A 1774 newspaper account of the prizes he had won concluded: "This youth, it seems is but seventeen years of age, and it is thought . . . that he will shortly be one of the greatest ornaments of the country." His later personal accomplishments seemed to bear out the truth of this early prediction. Upon visiting Charles Lee in 1800, John Adams wrote his wife, "I am particularly pleased with Alexandria. Mr. Lee lives very elegantly, neatly and agreeably there among his sisters and friends and among his fine lots of clover and timothy and I scarcely know a more eligible situation." Charles married Anne, one of the daughters of Richard Henry Lee in 1789. After her death in 1804, he married Margaret Scott in 1809 and later moved to "Leeton Forest" near Warrenton in 1814. Lucinda Lee, Charles' daughter, inherited the house in 1821 and her husband, General Walter Jones, a prominent Alexandria attorney, sold it to Christ Church for its rectory.

Matilda Lee Love visited Uncle Charles' residence in 1806. She stated: "At sixteen (1806) I came out in Alexandria as a young lady. My first entrance into that desirable state was on the 22nd of February, Washington's Birthday. No act of my life had I ever considered of such consequence. My sister and myself spent that winter with an uncle-in-law. (Charles). His wife being dead, his house was presided over by a daughter about my own age, and you may be sure we had nice times; frequently we sat up until two in the morning playing cards when my uncle thought we were in bed. We had a delightful society in Alexandria then." (Recollections of Matilda Lee Love in Lee Chronicle by Cazenove Gardner Lee, Jr., (New York: New York University Press, 1957), page 286, 287.

During his youth, Robert E. Lee resided here from 1816 to 1820.
Historic Alexandria Foundation

This is a portrait of Charles Lee (1758-1815) by an unknown artist. A man of exceptional talent, Mr. Lee served as: Naval officer for the South Potomac, 1777 to 1789; secretary of the Potomac Company 1785; clerk of the Common Council of Alexandria, 1785; trustee of the Alexandria Academy, 1788; collector of the Port of Alexandria, 1789 to 1793; personal attorney for George Washington, 1785 to 1795; director of the Bank of Alexandria, 1792; member of the General Assembly of Virginia, 1793 to 1795; attorney general of the United States, 1795 to 1801; secretary of state pro tem, May through June 1800; mayor of the City of Alexandria, 1804, (resigned); director of the Bank of Potomac, 1804; and Supreme Court jurist.

Charles Lee married a cousin, Anne Lee (1771-1804) at Chantilly, Westmoreland County, Virginia, on February 11, 1789. A daughter of the renowned Richard Henry Lee, Virginia's first senator, Anne died on September 9, 1804, and was interred at Shuter's Hill, the residence of her brother, Ludwell Lee.
Courtesy of the Lee Society

Constructed circa 1797 by John Wise, this house at 220 North Washington Street was occupied by Charles Lee in 1800 and later by James Marshall, brother of Chief Justice John Marshall and assistant judge of the Circuit Court of the District of Columbia. At one time both brothers were business partners with Light Horse Harry Lee and speculated in Virginia lands. James Marshall was also an uncle of Judge William Louis Marshall of Baltimore who married Robert E. Lee's sister, Ann Kinlock, in 1825. Benjamin Hallowell, Robert E. Lee's tutor who prepared him for West Point, moved his school here in 1825. In 1832, John Lloyd who married Anne Harriotte, Edmund Lee's daughter, purchased the structure and his family resided here until the early twentieth century. During the War Between the States, Dr. Joseph Packard of the Episcopal Seminary was ensconced at Lloyd House. Upon President Lincoln's assassination, Federal soldiers demanded that black crepe be placed upon the front door and later that evening, some miscreant in protest tossed a large stone through the first floor window of the dwelling.
Library of Congress

This beautiful home at 207 Prince Street was acquired in 1790 by William Hodgson, an English merchant, who married Portia Lee in 1799. Hodgson brought his bride to this house that year and they resided here until 1801 when they moved to Bellevue an estate about one mile north of Alexandria. Portia Lee (1777-1840) was born while her parents were living in Europe, and it was in London that William Hodgson became a friend of the family. Her parents were William Lee (of Greenspring) (1739-1795), tenth child of Thomas Lee of Stratford and Hannah Phillipa Ludwell of Greenspring. After the death of her father, she and her sister Cornelia lived with Richard Bland Lee at Sully Plantation until they married. Cornelia Lee married John Hopkins and resided at 207 Prince Street from 1810 to 1813. Both Hodgson and Hopkins were well known in Alexandria business circles. This view shows the house as it appeared in 1929 after certain repairs had been made following a devastating windstorm about 1913, resulting in the removal of dormer windows and one chimney top. The structure has long since been restored, by Mrs. Charles Beatty Moore, a pioneer in Alexandria restoration.
Courtesy of the Lee Society, the Lee-Fendall House and the National Archives, 1929

Portia Hodgson

This photograph of Bellevue Plantation shows the old plantation house, outbuildings, and greenhouses. Portia Hodgson who resided at 207 Prince Street until 1801 soon pined for the quietude of the country and convinced her husband to move to Bellevue in Alexandria County. Situated about one mile north of the Alexandria Courthouse at the intersection of Abingdon Drive and Slater's Lane, the estate occupied twelve acres and bordered the Potomac River. The main dwelling house was fifty feet long and twenty-eight feet wide and the outbuildings included a wooden kitchen, smokehouse, and dairy. Valued at four thousand dollars in 1795 the estate offered a panoramic view of the Potomac River and the surrounding Maryland and Virginia landscape. The Lee sisters, Portia and Cornelia, were wealthy and Bellevue was the scene of many splendid parties and receptions, including the marriage in 1806 of Cornelia to John Hopkins, a Richmond banker.

Around 1840, John Slater purchased the old Bellevue property and transformed it into a paradise of vegetation and beauty. Along the banks of the Potomac he grew acres of cabbages, magnificent rhubarb and other produce. Slater was renowned for his luscious strawberries which he sold to Alexandria and Washington restaurants. The estate was also dotted with greenhouses for the propagation of beautiful flowers.

Portrait courtesy of the Lee Society; House courtesy of the Rebecca Ramsay Reese Collection

These are portraits of Gen. Light Horse Harry Lee (1756-1818) and his wife, Ann Hill Carter (1773-1829). Bold, dashing, and intrepid, Henry Lee was a confidant of George Washington and was one of his finest cavalry officers during the Revolution. Lee was also a member of the Confederation Congress, 1785 to 1789; governor of Virginia, 1791 to 1794; a major-general in the U.S. Army, 1798 to 1800 and a U.S. congressman, 1799 to 1801. While in Alexandria he resided first at 611 Cameron Street, (1810-1811) and then moved to 607 Oronoco (1811-1813). Married to Ann Hill Carter on June 18, 1793, the couple produced six children including the famous Robert E. Lee and his brother, Sydney Smith Lee, a U.S. Naval officer for forty years and later served as chief of orders and details of the Confederate Navy.

Richard Bland Lee

Richard Bland Lee was a brother of Charles, Light Horse Harry, and Edmund J. Lee. Born at Leesylvania Plantation on the 20th of January 1761, he was Northern Virginia's first congressman (1789-1795) and also served in the Virginia Assembly. After Sully (Lee's Fairfax County home) was sold, he came to Alexandria with his wife and resided briefly in this lovely house at 404 Duke Street built by Elisha Janney in 1808. They remained here one year before they moved to the

400 block of Prince Street into a house owned by George Taylor. Later in 1813, Richard B. Lee went to live at Strawberry Vale in Fairfax County (near Tyson's Corner). His wife Elizabeth was a close personal friend of Dolley Madison and was one of her bridesmaids. Richard B. Lee II, his son, graduated from West Point and was personally decorated by President Andrew Jackson for bravery during the Seminole Indian Wars. During his thirty years of military service, Lee

was one of the first white men to explore the Rocky Mountains during wintertime. He resigned from the U.S. military in 1861 and joined his cousins in fighting for Southern independence. After having two horses shot from beneath him at the Battle of Shiloh, Lee survived the war and returned to Alexandria in 1865 where he later died in 1875. *Courtesy of the Lee Society*

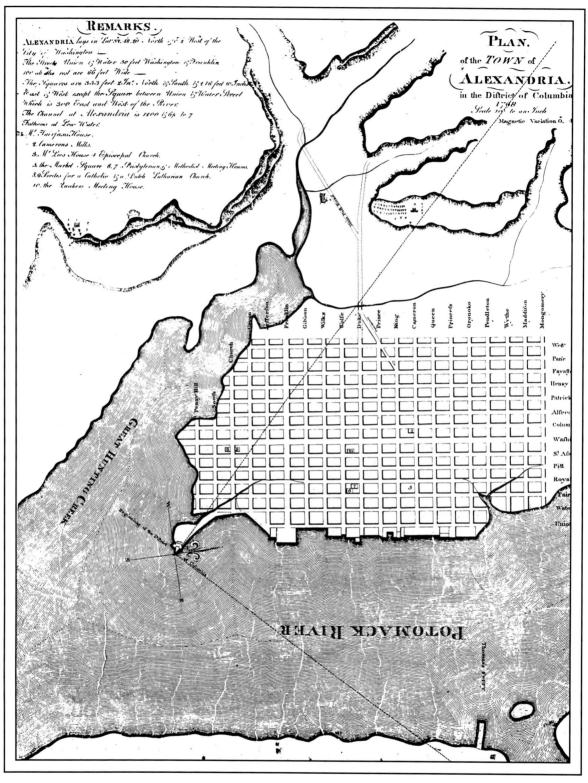

The first published map of Alexandria was drawn in 1797 by George Gilpin, the town surveyor, and published the following year by I. V. Thomas. Comparing it to earlier maps, it clearly shows that much of the waterfront from Water Street east to Union had been filled in by this time.

Gilpin was descended from the Washington's of "Hall Head," Westmoreland, England, and enjoyed a close relationship with George Washington and the Mount Vernon family. Upon Washington's death in 1799, Gilpin was an honorary pall bearer at the funeral. He died December 23, 1813, aged seventy-three, and was interred at Christ Church cemetery. (Mary Powell, George Washington's Last Guard of Honor)

ALEXANDRIA, DISTRICT OF COLUMBIA 1801 TO 1847

ven though the District of Columbia had been established in 1791, Alexandria did not officially become a part of it until the U.S. Congress formally accepted it on February 27, 1801. For the next forty-six years the town would be orphaned from its mother state, Virginia. It would be an era of momentous change punctuated by two major fires, an embargo, two financial panics, and a military invasion by the British.

Trouble commenced almost immediately when Alexandria was visited by yellow fever in 1803. The venerable Dr. Elisha C. Dick estimated that nearly three thousand inhabitants left town and of those who remained many became permanent residents of Penny Hill Cemetery. As a seaport community, Alexandria was continually exposed to plagues, epidemics, and other serious diseases. Therefore, a quarantine station was established at Jones Point to inspect incoming vessels and the Board of Health vigorously enforced local health ordinances. Still, a fever swept the city in 1821 and again in 1839 when a scourge invaded the Potomac Street region—a low lying area running into Wolfe Street along the south waterfront.

Alexandria's commerce had scarcely recovered from the 1803 epidemic when President Thomas Jefferson implemented a naval embargo of American ports in 1807. Since trade was the lifeblood of the town, the president's course of action nearly destroyed Alexandria's economy. Between the years 1801 and 1815, Alexandria's annual exports averaged about $1,114,000 per year or eight times that of its neighbor, Georgetown. During this epoch, the town shipped to foreign countries: 1,154,778 barrels of flour; 323,920 bushels of wheat, and 592,954 bushels of corn. Due to the embargo there were no exports of these commodities in 1808. The best customer for Alexandria's corn was Portugal which took 57 percent of its total from 1801 to 1815 and 27 percent of its flour. Spain also imported 27 percent of its wheat and corn while the West Indies was the best flour market. Flour inspections at Alexandria for the year June 1816 to June 1817 reached a high figure of 209,000 barrels—a level never attained again. The town also carried on an extensive coastwise trade with New England and shipped bread, butter, corn, peas, beeswax, bacon, shingles, and lard to these states. (Arthur Petersen, "The Alexandria Market Prior to the Civil War." *William & Mary Quarterly,* series 2, volume 12, pages 104-114)

In 1808, Capt. Henry Massie visited Alexandria and described it:

as a very handsome town ... Flour appears to be the principal article of exportation in return they receive groceries of various kinds such as sugar, salt, rum. The streets of Alexandria intersect each other at right angles, they are well paved, of an extensive width and kept perfectly clean ... There is here open every morning, an abundantly supplied market with all kinds of meat and every species of vegetables. The buildings are chiefly of brick some of them very stately and elegant... (*Tyler's Quarterly Magazine,* volume 9, no. 2, October 1920, pages 78-81)

The first decade of the nineteenth century ended with a spectacular fire that ravaged the waterfront. It commenced in a cooper's shop near the wharves adjoining Union Street on September 24,

Early nineteenth-century Alexandria, D.C., was a town populated by many business enterprises. The Alexandria Gazette is replete with dozens of advertisements for umbrella makers, coopers, carpenters, gunsmiths, silversmiths, cobblers, and hatters. An occupational census of the area for 1810 identifies: 7 attorneys, 20 bakers, 18 blacksmiths, 11 bricklayers, 5 cabinetmakers, 22 coopers, 4 gardeners, 4 hatters, 1 lamp lighter, 95 merchants, 10 physicians, 2 pump makers, 9 saddlers, 76 seamstresses, 4 cigar makers, 15 tavern keepers, 33 washer women, and 8 wheelwrights. These artisans and professionals offered the public a wide spectrum of goods and services.

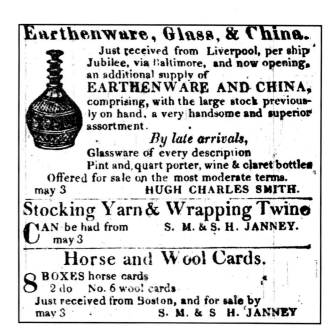

1810, and consumed nearly every building from Prince to Duke Street.

On the heels of this disaster the town was occupied without resistance by the British fleet during the War of 1812. The Common Council after securing loans from the Bank of Alexandria and the Bank of Potomac lent the federal government thirty-five thousand dollars to improve fortifications and defenses south of the Potomac. Little was accomplished however and on August 20 and 21, 1814, the town was left defenseless as its militia was ordered to cross the Potomac River and take up positions between Fort Washington and the Piscataway. (Donald G. Shomette, *Maritime Alexandria*, Alexandria Archaeology, page 120.) On August 29 a British squadron under the command of Capt. James Gordon sailed up the Potomac River and captured Alexandria. For the next five days the enemy occupied the town with no opposition from its seven thousand inhabitants. The British looted stores and warehouses of valuable flour, tobacco, and cotton. Although the grain trade recovered briefly, this occupation together with the severe economic panic of 1816 sounded the death knell for Alexandria as a major seaport. It was an era when local banks failed and numbers of merchants declared bankruptcy.

A highlight of the early 1820s was General Lafayette's visit. No stranger to Alexandria, the French hero of the American Revolution had frequented it on at least five other occasions. On Saturday October 16, 1824, Alexandria took on a gala appearance as thousands of citizens gathered to watch the welcoming ceremonies. Greeted with music from two fine bands and a salute of artillery, Lafayette entered town in a splendid barouche drawn by four fine greys. During the procession the windows of houses were filled with ladies who waved handkerchiefs and dozens of children who displayed flags. Lionized by

Alexandria society, Lafayette enjoyed the special hospitality of the old seaport community for nearly a month.

In 1826, Ann Royall, an itinerant writer, published a wonderful pen portrait of Alexandria. Among other things she stated:

... it was a very handsome town ... There are no squares in Alexandria, except the market square, enclosed and or surrounded with buildings ... Besides these market houses, the other public buildings are two churches for Episcopalians, two for Presbyterians, one for Methodist ... ten in all—a court house, a museum, a town hall, a library, an insurance office, a theater, six banks, a collection office and a post office ... Besides the manufacty of tin and leather a great quantity of sugar is refined ... Great attention seems to be paid to education: There are academies and several schools ...

The people of Alexandria are mild and unassuming ... Alexandria has a gradual ascent from the river back to the western limits, the streets are spacious and paved with stones and the sidewalks with brick. The houses in Alexandria are built of brick mostly 3 stories high. They are comfortable and convenient but not very splendid ... Instead of bells, the watch is preceded by a number of loud trumpets, which blow a tremendous peal at the hour of ten at night, when the watch goes out. (Ann Royall, *Sketches of History, Life & Manners in the U.S.*)

This tranquil scene was rudely interrupted in January 1827 when a massive fire nearly destroyed the city. Originating in the workshop of Mr. James Green, cabinetmaker, on Royal Street, the fire ravaged dozens of businesses and private residences on Fairfax Street, and on Prince between Water (Lee) and Union Street before it was subdued. Fifty-three

Levi Hurdle

Chair Manufacturer and Ornamental Painter,

THANKFUL for the patronage he has already received from his friends and the public, respectfully informs them that he will continue to make, and keep constantly for sale at fair prices, at his Manufactory, south-west corner of King and Columbus streets, opposite J. & J. Douglass store, a general assortment of

Grecian, Fancy and Windsor CHAIRS.

The public are invited to call and examine his present assortment. He feels assured that they will be found not to be inferior either in the durability of their materials or the neatness of their execution, to those of any other manufacturer in the District. He will execute

Sign and Ornamental Painting and Gilding, in all their various branches, on the most accommodating terms.

Old chairs will be taken in part payment for new ones, or will be repaired and repainted at the shortest notice.

☞ Chairs purchased at this manufactory will be sent, free of expense, to any part of the District.

oct 17—3mo

HATS!!

Morse & Josselyn,

Corner of King and Royal sts. Alexandria,

HAVE on hand, and continue to manufacture, HATS of the various qualities and fashions now worn, for sale, wholesale or retail.

They have received, by the latest arrivals from New York and Philadelphia, a complete assortment of

Gentlemen's,

Ladies' and Children's Beavers and Caps

OF EVERY DESCRIPTION:

Together with a full assortment of Hatters' Furs, Trimmings, Dye Stuffs, &c. &c.

Country merchants are invited to call and examine their assortment, as they will sell on as good terms as can be had elsewhere.

Dec 16

Umbrella and Trunk Manufactory,

King-street, two doors below Washington-st.

DANIEL PIERCE has just received per schooner Hilan, from Philadelphia, a number of umbrellas and parasols, which, added to his former stock, comprise a large and general assortment.

Likewise on hand as usual, a complete assortment of trunks of all sizes.

N. B. Old frames new covered in the neatest manner, and all descriptions of repairs promptly executed.

April 28   wstf

Shoes, Hats and Bonnets.

JUST received, and now opening, for sale by   WILLIAM TRUE,

At his store, King-street,

A large assortment of ladies' & gentlemen' shoes of every description.

Gentlemen's fashionable beaver hats

Do.   do.   low priced do.

Boys' fur and felt do.

ALSO,

8 cases ladies' straw and Leghorn bonnets, (some extra fine.)

All the above together with his former stock will be sold at very low prices,

This 1803 map of Alexandria within the District of Columbia is by an unknown surveyor. It is particularly noteworthy in showing the names of several wharves along the Alexandria waterfront as well as other landmarks including an interesting diagram of the fort at Jones Point constructed by Jean Vermonnet, a French engineer, in 1794. Soon after the turn of the century, the fort lay dormant and fell into decay. In 1808, Jon Williams, colonel commandant of engineers, and a Colonel Burbank, proceeded to Alexandria to conduct a field investigation of the site. "They walked to a point about a mile below that city, where they saw the vestige of an old Fort which presented a circular battery in the front, and 2 small bastions in the rear; the whole ditched round in the usual way. The fort did not occupy the whole ground; but appeared to the subscriber to be tolerably well designed . . ." Courtesy of Alexandria Library, Lloyd House.(Alexandria Deedbook G, Circuit Court of the District of Columbia for the County of Alexandria, page 465)

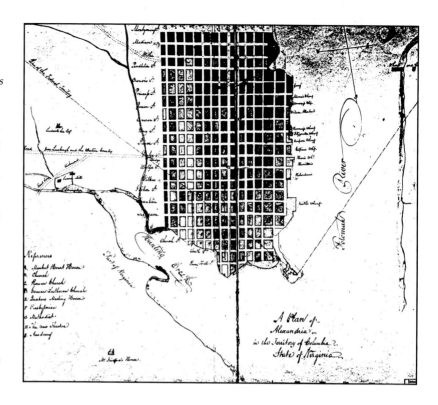

Alexandria houses were burned in the conflagration, involving a loss of more than $150,000.

In 1827, Alexandria subscribed $250,000 to the Chesapeake and Ohio Canal on condition that a lateral canal would later be constructed to town. A charter was granted to the Alexandria Canal Company in 1830 and initial construction commenced in 1831. Completed by 1843, the canal stretched about seven miles from the Aqueduct Bridge across the Potomac at Georgetown to a large outlet basin near the current Ramada Inn at Montgomery and North Union Streets. Thousands of tons of coal from Western Maryland were shipped to wharves at Alexandria, whereupon it was transported to Panama and San Francisco for the use of steamship lines operating in the China and Japanese trade. Plagued by freshets and constant repair problems, the Alexandria canal never quite lived up to expectations. After tremendous capital outlays on the canal, the city defaulted on its loan and was saddled with enormous debts after the War Between the States. During the conflict, the canal was seized by Federal officials, its ditches drained and its boats scattered. It was renewed after the war but finally succumbed after a break in the Aqueduct Bridge forced its closing in 1886.

Commercially, Alexandria languished during the late 1820s and 1830s. No longer a prime exporter of grain and flour, the export of shad and herring became a major industry. Each year an artificial village called Fishtown would rise phoenix-like on Union between Oronoco and Princess streets. Here, dozens of black women and men with sharp knives cleaned tons of fish which they packed in barrels and salted.

Alexandria's other major industry during this era had a far more unsavory quality. It centered around the slave trade and the transshipment of thousands of blacks to the deep South cotton states of Alabama, Mississippi, and Louisiana. Headquartered at 1315 Duke Street in the old mansion constructed by Gen. Robt. Young, the firm of Franklin and Armfield, slave dealers, commenced operation in 1828. After making a fortune, the firm sold the slave pen to George Kephardt in 1846. Moncure Conway wrote in 1856 that Kephardt and Company "was the chief slave-dealing firm in (Virginia) and perhaps anywhere along the border between the free and slave states." (Conway, 1865, page 21) Advertisements appeared constantly in the local newspaper which stipulated that "cash and highest market prices would be paid for any numbers of likely young negroes of both sexes." Many elements of Alexandria society abhorred this trade in human flesh. In 1823, a branch of the American Colonization Society was founded in Alexandria whose express purpose was to collect money so that freed negroes could be resettled in Liberia. Among its members were Edmund J. Lee, Robert E. Lee's uncle, his brother, Charles Carter Lee, and his first cousin, Philip R. Fendall, Jr. The Colonization Society strongly felt that slavery was not a "good, either moral, political or economical."

After the economic panic of 1837, Alexandria's fortunes plummeted. One visitor in 1840 commented:

As her star was descending others were ascending to take the place of the fallen brightness. Georgetown and Washington prospered at her expense . . . with the benefit of trade once con-

Construction of Colross or Belle Aire, as it was then called, was begun by builder John Potts, secretary of the Potomac Company, around the year 1799 and completed circa 1802. This colonial masterpiece may have been designed by the famous American architect Benjamin Thornton since it is very similar to Woodlawn, one of his plantation homes just south of town. Potts, who experienced financial difficulties, advertised the sale of Colross in 1802:

The subscriber, contemplating a removal from the District of Columbia . . . offers for sale a large handsome brick house, fifty by forty feet with a Brick Stable, Smoke

House, and well of excellent water . . . (Alexandria Advertiser and Commercial Intelligencer, November 11, 1802)

On November 3, 1803, Potts sold the estate to Jonathan Swift, prominent Alexandria merchant, for nine thousand dollars. Swift, well known in the diplomatic corps, was appointed consul to Holland in 1815 and in March 1819, consul to the United Kingdom of Portugal, Brazil, and Argaves. Swift died at Colross in August 1824 and was buried there with Masonic honors. The mansion then came into the possession of Thomson F. Mason, George Mason's grandson and a respected Alexandria attorney and judge of the Circuit Court. Personal tragedy beset the Mason family during their occupancy of Colross. A son named William was crushed to death when a violent gale struck and overturned a dilapidated chicken coop on him and soon afterwards another child, Ann, drowned while taking a bath.

During the War Between the States, Colross was seized by Federal authorities and it was reported that several Union

deserters and a bounty hunter were executed against the brick wall. From 1885 to 1917, William A. Smoot, successful Alexandria lumber merchant and later mayor of town, resided there with his family. His wife, Betty, wrote in her book: Days in an Old Town that the: "grounds at Colross included a whole square and were enclosed with an ancient brick wall 10 feet in height . . . Much of the interior woodwork at Colross was of mahogany . . . At the entrance of the house there was a handsome pillared porch, and semicircular walks, paved with granite . . . At the back there was a large portico, also with pillars . . . No brighter or more cheery place could be found than Colross."

Ravaged by a tornado in 1927, Colross fell into a state of disrepair and neglect when John Munn of Princeton, New Jersey rescued it from oblivion by having the entire structure moved brick by brick over the railroad to Princeton. After his death in 1956, it became the centerpiece of the Princeton Day School where it remains in use today.

Loeb Collection

ALEXANDRIA THEATRE.

THE lower part of the house which has heretofore been considered inconvenient, has been most particularly attended to: it is now partitioned off into eight boxes, and will hereafter be under the same rules as in all regular Theatres, viz.: The Box Office will be open every day, where will remain a plan of the Boxes, which may be taken by a whole box, bench or individual sitting, provided the Tickets are taken at the same time. The public will please to observe that an individual sitting cannot be taken on the *front* benches, nor can those seats held, except with the number of tickets making the complement for the whole bench.

The Pit for the future will be under the same regulations as the Boxes; and the Gallery, which has for several years been closed, will now be opened for the reception of people of color *exclusively.*

It is the wish of the Managers to establish the Theatre on a solid basis; to effect which, Rules and Regulations are essentially necessary; in their choice of

them they have only the public feeling at heart, and they have confidence that in presenting to the citizens of Alexandria a *regular* and well governed Theatre will be crowned with that liberality and support which has been bestowed on anterior exertions.

It is most particularly requested that gentlemen will not smoke in the house, the practice within the walls of a Theatre, is not only offensive, but dangerous.

It having been the practice of a number of ill disposed boys who nightly infest the doors of the Theatre, not only to exercise unlawful means of admission, but, failing in their object, to make a riotous and outrageous noise, much to the discomfiture of the audience and interruption of the performance—The Managers give this timely notice to inform them, that officers will be stationed in future to observe them, who will by their orders, take into custody, the first who shall be found committing either of the above misdemeanors, and that they shall be dealt with according to law.

On Saturday Evening, Dec. 13, 1817.

named lord called

While traveling troupes of actors and entertainers moved from town to town in the late eighteenth century to offer their performances to the local populace, few had anything more than the ballroom or long room of the tavern or ordinary where they were housed, in which to present their thespian endeavors. Williamsburg had possibly the earliest theatre building in English America by 1716 and Charleston had one in 1736 (puritanical and simon-pure New England frowned upon such activity as aiding and abetting the devil) and little, old Alexandria claimed its own, the Alexandria Theatre, in 1799. Thomas Wade West, one of the most successful theatrical entrepreneurs of his day, had come from England to Philadelphia in 1790 with his wife Margaret Sully (aunt of the painter

Thomas Sully) and children. Within a few years, through the sale of shares as well as subscriptions, he had built five theatres (one in Richmond which was lost by fire) in as many towns which gave his troupe guaranteed quarters designed specifically for their kind of entertainment. The Alexandria Theatre was built on a lot on the north side of the 400 block of Cameron Street (across from the side of Gadsby's Tavern) and was a large, three-story brick structure with shops on the second floor and dressing and storage rooms on the third. It was described as a "lofty edifice, decorated with handsome pediments and deep cornices, the window frames, tresses and rustic work of stone." It opened in the spring of 1799, and, tragically, Thomas West died in July of that same year of a fall from the upper

story to the stage of his nearly completed building. He was buried in Christ Church yard. His widow continued the operation for a number of years afterward. In later years the building became known as Liberty Hall and, following some modification, two separate meeting rooms were housed within the same walls: Liberty Hall and American Hall. By 1872 much of the building was occupied by city offices, including the mayor's office and city council chambers, when it was destroyed by fire on June 24. By this time much of the local theatrical entertainment had moved to the newly built Sarepta Hall located in the 400 block of King Street. The pictured portion of an 1817 broadside indicates that nasty small boys were on the scene then as now.

fined to the better known Alexandria. So fickle is fortune . . . But no city in the Union perhaps has exhibited so sad a contrast . . . Alexandria's commerce has dwindled to less than the tithe of what it was, and the trade of a great producing country has gone with it. Many of the streets, for lack of the destroyer man to walk upon them have given a quiet resting place for the rank weed. Blades of grass have come more frequently than the passing stranger and the sight has been a melancholy one—especially to those who have seen Alexandria in her beauty and her decay . . . (*Alexandria Gazette*, January 29, 1840)

In 1846 Alexandria heralded the call of President James Polk to annex Texas and to settle the west. Company B of the First Virginia Regiment, composed of Alexandrians, was escorted to the wharf by the Mount Vernon Guards and Ringgold Cavalry as they boarded the steamer *Phoenix* for Aquia Creek. After arriving in Richmond by train, the troops proceeded to Norfolk where they were put on the bark *Victory* and sailed for Mexico. It would be almost two years before the local boys came marching home to a gala banquet held at Liberty Hall in October 1848. Alexandrians had performed their duty and their townsmen were duly proud of their military prowess.

Initially Alexandria had welcomed the town's inclusion into the ten-mile-square which comprised the District of Columbia. The citizenry expected to share in the economic, financial, and industrial benefits which would accrue as a result of the establishment of the capital on the banks of the Potomac River. Events proved otherwise, however, and Alexandrians soon became disillusioned with their status. Several factors prompted this disenchantment. Provisions of the 1791 act creating the district precluded the construction of any public buildings south of the Potomac. Thus, even though Alexandria had better port facilities, the Navy yard was constructed on the Eastern Branch in Washington. In addition, the 1801 District Act disenfranchised the local populace. They could not vote in presidential elections and had no representation in Congress. On the economic scene, the local economy was exacerbated by President Andrew Jackson's failure to recharter the Bank of the United States in 1836 and President Tyler's subsequent veto of a second National Bank in 1841. Coupled with the panic of 1837 and the failure of the Congress to recharter the Bank of Alexandria in 1834, the town suffered severe economic privation. Inspection of flour had dropped from a high of two hundred thousand barrels to about twenty thousand barrels. While no railroad lines serviced Alexandria, Baltimore had been allowed to siphon off the lucrative trade of the Shenandoah Valley by constructing the Baltimore & Ohio Railroads through Virginia to Winchester. Therefore, a strong impetus developed to retrocede Alexandria to Virginia.

After receiving several local petitions, Congress passed "An Act" to retrocede the town and county of Alexandria to Virginia on July 9, 1846. A referendum on the issue was held in Alexandria on September 1 and 2 and by a vote of 763 to 222 the measure passed. Virginia formally accepted the territory on March 13, 1847, and Alexandrians celebrated the occasion with a huge parade on September 19:

National salutes were fired at sunrise, at noon & at sunset. The flags of the shipping in port were displayed . . . At 10 o'clock a procession formed under the command of Dr. Wm. L. Powell, Chief Marshall . . . and marched through the principal streets. The military made a beautiful display. The Ringgold Cavalry and the Mt. Vernon Guards attracted much attention . . . The Mayor and Common Council and a long line of citizens also united on the occasion. About noon the procession arrived at the Public Square and an address was delivered by George Washington Parke Custis (Martha Washington's grandson) and Francis L. Smith . . . Business was suspended through the day . . . and the streets were crowded . . . Everything passed off in the happiest manner . . . (*Alexandria Gazette*, March 23, 1847)

A new era was at hand.

takes great pleasure in entertaining all the workings of the institutions to visitors." Alexandria Gazette, May 28, 1883)
The original purpose of the property was discontinued in 1927 when the city of Alexandria joined with several other jurisdictions in the erection of a district home at Manassas, Virginia. This building operated as a tourist home for awhile in the 1930s and was finally demolished when a new bridge crossing the railroad tracks at Potomac Yards was built in the 1940s. Milton Grigg Collection

Stagecoach travel in the eighteenth and nineteenth centuries was long, difficult, and tedious. Frequently it would take one day to journey to Fredericksburg from Alexandria and still another day's journey to Richmond. Many of the roads were mere pig paths and were virtually impassable especially during the spring and winter seasons when they became virtual quagmires. A typical American stagecoach was described by a Mr. Jansen, a visitor to America from 1793 to 1806, as being "calculated to hold 12 persons, who sat on benches placed across with their faces toward the horses. The first seat holds three, one of whom is the driver . . . (The Stranger in America in Stage Coach & Tavern Days, by Alice M. Earle)

Stage lines generally ran from Philadelphia via Baltimore to Georgetown, Alexandria, Fredericksburg, Richmond, Williamsburg, and points south. On October 10, 1787, Mr. G. P. Vanhorne announced that: "The Northern Stages will in future arrive and take their departure from Mr. Leigh's Bunch of Grapes Tavern in Alexandria (201 N. Fairfax St.) Passengers will please to take their seats and enter their baggage at the office at Mr. Leigh's the evening previous to their starting in order to render the hour of departure certain, which will take place precisely at 4 o'clock in the morning."

In 1827 the stage line from Alexandria

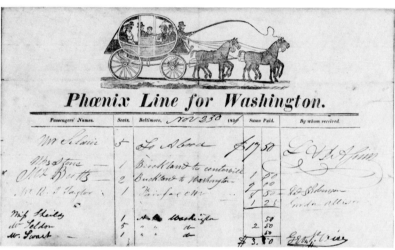

to Winchester was under the management of Mr. John Boyd. He informed the Alexandria public that: "having become the proprietor of the line from Alexandria to Winchester he has at considerable expense very much improved the Stages and Horses and is prepared to accommodate passengers comfortably. The stage leaves Mr. Clagett's (City Tavern), Alexandria every Monday, Wednesday and Friday at half past 3 o'clock, A.M. arriving to breakfast at Fairfax Court House at half past 6 (and in time for the Fauquier stage to Warrenton, Orange Court

House, etc.) dine at the Ball Tavern in Middleburg (kept by the subscriber) and arrive at Berry's Ferry early the same evening; lodge there, and arrive at Winchester next morning to breakfast, and in time to take the Stage to Staunton, etc. . . . The proprietor has also provided himself with active horses, sober, careful, and experienced drivers, so that passengers may rely on having every attention paid to their comfort and convenience . . . Fare through from Alexandria to Winchester, Va.—six dollars."
(Alexandria Gazette, May 29, 1827)

After being persecuted for their pacifism in the Northern colonies, members of the Society of Friends first emigrated to Alexandria during the American Revolution. An early meeting house was constructed on the 300 block of South St. Asaph Street in the mid 1780s and became inadequate for the membership who later purchased a lot at the southwest corner of Wolfe and St. Asaph streets in 1798. A new meeting house, which cost nearly four thousand dollars and was sixty by thirty-six feet and two stories high was erected at this site in 1811. During the War Between the States, the Old Quaker Meeting House was utilized by the Feder-

al authorities as a military hospital. After the war, the Friends Society in Alexandria being nearly dissolved, the meeting house was leased to John Beach in 1872 and 1873 as a school. Known as the Alexandria Academy, as shown here, it should not be confused with the old Alexandria Academy on Wolfe Street which was constructed in 1785. The building in this print was later sold to a Negro church and during one Sunday service its second floor collapsed, nearly killing several members, whereupon it was purchased by a Mr. Daingerfield who razed it in the 1880s.

This early view of the Bank of Potomac at 415 Prince Street is unique because it represents the earliest known print of any building in Alexandria. Although the bank was first organized in 1804, its building, pictured on a five hundred dollar bill, was probably not occupied until 1807. During an era when there was a significant shortage of specie, the bank provided much needed capital for domestic improvements. Not chartered until 1811, the Bank of Potomac continued in existence until it merged with the Farmer's Bank of Alexandria on March 20, 1847. It ceased banking operations on September 18, 1861. From 1863 to 1865, this building housed the governor and was the capitol of the so-called restored government of Virginia, covering those portions of the state which were in the hands of the Union Army.

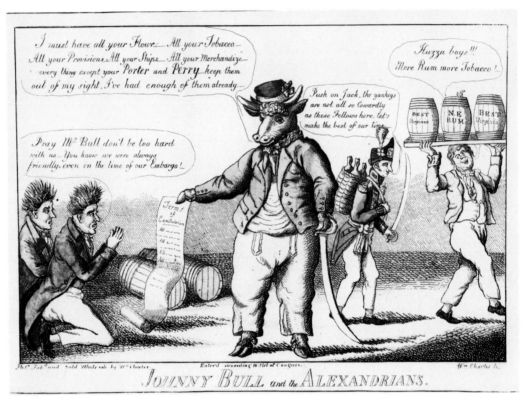

JOHNNY BULL and the ALEXANDRIANS.

During the War of 1812 a British squadron under the command of Capt. James Gordon sailed up the Potomac River and captured Alexandria on August 29, 1814. For the next five days the fleet occupied the town with no opposition from its seven thousand inhabitants. The British looted stores and warehouses of valuable flour, tobacco, and cotton. Alexandrians were severely castigated in the national press for surrendering their town and allowing the British to plunder their stores. Typical of this commentary was a salvo fired by the National Intelligencer on September 1, 1814: "The degrading terms dictated by the Commander of the British squadron below Alexandria, to the civil authority of that town, connected with the offer of the townsmen, before the squadron had even reached the fort, to surrender without resistance, and their singular submission to Admiral Cockburn while in this city, have everywhere excited astonishment and indignation." The local militia being absent, there was little use for the remaining townspeople to attempt to stand up to the armed squadron, for any apparent military confrontation would undoubtedly have resulted in at least a partial destruction of the town by bombardment to say nothing of the loss of life which might have resulted.

"Johnny Bull and the Alexandrians" is the title of this cartoon sketch which appeared shortly after the surrender of Alexandria. The cartoon shows Johnny Bull, the English national symbol, demanding of the Alexandria merchants, "All your flour . . . and your tobacco . . . all your provisions . . . all your Merchandise . . . Everything except your Porter and Perry (a reference to Oliver Hazzard Perry who defeated the English on Lake Erie) keep them out of my sight. I've had enough of them already" The merchants replying - "I pray Mr. Bull, don't be too hard on us. You know we were always friendly, even in the loss of our embargo." Two English soldiers carrying off stores from the city reply, "Huzza boys. More Rum; More Tobacco." The cartoon was drawn by one William Charles in 1814 and is now in the Library of Congress in Washington. (Thom Lammond, Alexandria Gazette, August 29, 1962)
Virginia State Library

A

B

C

Market Square, originally an open area surrounded by public and semi-public structures (a courthouse, an early Market House containing offices of town officials, a town (or school) house, several firehouses and a central area used both as a market site and a drill field for local militia) was gradually built up as the growing town's requirements demanded. A new Market House (circa 1784) faced Cameron Street from its corner with Royal and this building was apparently incorporated in a still newer Market House facing Royal Street running between Cameron Street and Sharpshin Alley. Both sides of this newer building (erected in 1817 containing a town clock and steeple attributed to Benjamin Henry Latrobe) are seen in these three views.

A. Looking south on Royal Street, the 1817 Market House appears in the cen-

ter, the small frame structure just to its right being the very early Rainbow Tavern which was destroyed in the fire that consumed the Market House in 1871. The steeple in the distance is St. Mary's Church.

B. A photograph taken from the Mansion House hotel shows the backside of the 1817 Market House (the top of Gadsby's tavern or City Hotel appears to the right of the steeple and to the right of that is the probable roof and cupola of the Liberty Hall in the 400 block of Cameron Street). With its three-story galleries the open area of the square is filled with covered market stalls and the roofs and partial facades of smaller buildings on Fairfax Street including a firehouse.

C. A wartime (circa 1864) drawing by a presently unknown artist shows same area as B. The Market House in combi-

nation with earlier buildings is now ell-shaped, the Hydraulion Engine House appears on the left while the old Town Hall and schoolhouse (corner of Fairfax and Cameron) sits on the right, leaving the rest of the Fairfax Street side of the square open to the market area. This was not closed off till the building of the new U-shaped City Hall in 1872, following the destruction of most of these buildings by fire on May 19, 1871. One of Alexandria's ubiquitous street pumps stands on the sidewalk (center of view). The Masonic Hall which had been located in numerous sites throughout the city was later housed in the 1784 Market House building.

Collection of Government Services Savings and Loan, Bethesda, Maryland

59

Although taken in 1911, this view of the 600 block of Cameron Street could closely compare with the same scene a hundred years earlier (except for the Christ Church steeple which was erected in 1818). There had been an earlier steeple of unknown dimensions built in 1799. The Yeaton-Fairfax house (right foreground at 607 Cameron) is considered to be possibly the finest house of the Federalist period in Alexandria and was built around 1800 by William Yeaton, who had moved to Alexandria from New Hampshire five years earlier and who later designed the enclosure which houses the tomb of George and Martha Washington (built 1835). His family occupied it for many years, and it was later purchased as a townhouse in 1830 by Thomas, ninth Lord Fairfax, whose family resided there until the war period. The property was condemned by Federal authorities in

1864 and sold at auction. Next door (609-611 Cameron) were twin houses constructed by John Bogue between 1795 and 1800 for John Irwin and himself. Number 611 Cameron has become

known as the General (Lighthorse Harry) Lee House because he moved in with his family, including his young son, Robert Edward Lee, for a short time during 1810. *Library of Congress*

St. Paul's Episcopal Church (220 South Pitt Street, shown during the war), designed by Benjamin Henry Latrobe and built in 1817, resulted from a split in the congregation of Christ Church in 1809. Of Gothic Revival style it has been stated that "as Gothic, the church is a naive example belonging much more to the "Gothick" manner of the eighteenth century than to the true Gothic Revival." (Denys Peter Myers, Alexandria—A Towne in Transition 1800-1900) Although Latrobe was unhappy with the congregation for certain changes made in his plans, it was completed with considerable monetary help from one of the founders, Daniel McLean, a successful merchant of Scottish ancestry who had moved to Alexandria from Burlington, New Jersey, and who operated a sugar refinery next to his residence at 111 North Alfred Street. He was the father of Wilmer McLean whose residence in Prince William County was virtually at the center of both battles of Manassas (1861 and 1862) and who then moved his family away to a quiet country location named Appomattox Court House, only to have Generals Lee and Grant meet in his parlor to arrange for the surrender of Confederate forces on April 9, 1865.

The Rev. William Holland Wilmer (serving from 1812 to 1826) was a vital force in both his church and his community. He was a founder of the Theological Seminary and St. John's Church, Lafayette Square, Washington, leaving Alexandria to become President of the College of William and Mary. On Sunday, February 9, 1862, the Rev. Kenzie J. Stewart was conducting services here when, upon ignoring demands by soldiers in the congregation to recite a prayer for the president of the United States, he was

arrested, hauled from the pulpit and made to walk in his clerical robes to a military installation on Washington Street. The military governor stated that

since the order for the arrest had not come from Washington, the action was to be condemned. This calmed the excitement and Mr. Stewart was released.

The cornerstone of Mechanics Hall at 114 North Alfred Street was laid in 1818 in a Masonic ceremony for the Mechanic Relief Society of Alexandria and became a popular meeting place for political rallies. The Lyceum Company was organized here in 1838. The Alexandria Gazette on November 16, 1838, carried an appeal to all "Mechanics" to "help free the Society from its present difficulties" but this was apparently unsuccessful for the building was sold in 1842 to Hugh C. Smith who already owned considerable property in this block. It was after this date that it became a private residence and was owned and occupied by the family of Anthony McLean in the 1870s and 1880s. He was the son of Daniel McLean who had lived across the street at 111 North Alfred after 1815 and among other interests, had operated a sugar refinery at that location. The McLean family, bottom photo, with a few hangers-on are shown in the side yard about 1880.
Gift of William Triplett.

The young French hero of the American Revolution, the Marquis de Lafayette (1757-1834) was certainly no stranger to the town of Alexandria. After landing in North Carolina in 1777, it is believed that he took lodging at Mrs. Hawkins' tavern (Gadsby's) on his way north to Philadelphia. Other visits included a brief stop here in April 1781 on his way south to assist in the defeat of Cornwallis at Yorktown and an August 1784 reception at Lomax's Tavern. At a grand celebration given the Marquis in October 1824, thousands of Alexandrians took to the streets to welcome the French here to American shores. The city council feted him one last time in the summer of 1825 before his departure for France.
Courtesy of the Library of Congress Print Division

The Lafayette House at 301 South St. Asaph Street was built for Thomas Lawrason in 1815-1816 (he died in 1819) and must have been considered one of the town's finest residences because it was offered by Lawrason's widow and accepted for the use of Marquis de Lafayette during his month-long stay as a guest of the town of Alexandria in October 1824. This fine example of Federal architecture has been known as the Lafayette House ever since and its doorway is unusual and unique in Alexandria.
O'Brien/Hulfish Collection, circa 1900

Located at 403 North St. Asaph Street, the old Alexandria Jail was demolished in July 1987 and a row of pseudo-federal and Victorian townhouses constructed on its site. Only its facade was preserved.

The Fairfax County Jail originally was housed at Spring Field near current Tyson's Corner and moved to Market Square in Alexandria in 1752 to 1753 along with a pillory and stocks. In 1816, the prison was located in a building at the foot of Wolfe Street and in 1826 to 1827, this structure costing ten thousand dollars was erected on North Saint Asaph Street. It was designed by Charles Bulfinch and housed Confederate prisoners during the War Between the States, its prison population fluctuating between two and three hundred men. Surrounded by a high wall, the main structure and outbuildings were neatly whitewashed. Many of the internees were nearly destitute of clothing and it was advised that two stoves be placed "in the corridor around the cells to make the building more comfortable." This facility was vacated by Union military authorities in May 1865. During the nineteenth century, its yard to the north was witness to several hangings. Despite its age and many remodelings and additions over the years, it continued to serve its original purpose until the very end. Alexandria was long known to have something less than the most modern of conveniences for its jailhouse population.
Milton Grigg Collection

The genesis of the Protestant Episcopal Theological Seminary dates to a meeting of the clergy and laity of Washington, Georgetown, and Alexandria in June 1818 when an organization called "The Society for the Education of Pious Young Men for the Ministry of the Protestant Episcopal Church" was established. Among the early trustees were the Reverend William Holland Wilmer, rector of St. Paul's Church, Edmund J. Lee, and the renowned Francis Scott Key. By 1823, the Seminary met in the upper rooms of a building located at the southeast corner of Washington and King streets. In 1827, the founders purchased a beautiful sixty-five acre tract three miles from Alexandria because of its "healthiness of the atmosphere, the beauty of the prospect and its many conveniences. The property, half cleared, was covered with field grass and forest trees." Sunday services were held in the prayer hall of the old three-story Seminary building in this print. Constructed circa 1835 it remained in situ until it was replaced by Aspinwall (1858), Bohlen (1859), and Meade (1860) Halls. Currently Aspinwall Hall with its pagoda-like spire is most familiar to local Alexandrians and tourists alike. Because of the large number of missionaries sent out from the Seminary in its early years, some local citizens, not looking upon the Aspinwall spire as a thing of beauty, referred to it as "China's Revenge."
National Archives, Brady Collection
circa 1864

Razed in 1960, this beautiful Greek Revival building at 414 North Washington Street with heavy modillioned cornice and an ionic entrance portico, was constructed circa 1830 and was probably Alexandria's finest example of that style. During the War Between the States, it was converted into the Grosvenor House military hospital with Edward Bentley, surgeon, in charge. After the conflict, Brig. Gen. Montgomery D. Corse (C.S.A.) and his wife Elizabeth Beverley resided here. General Corse (1816-1895) had raised a company of Alexandria volunteers for service during the Mexican War. When the War Between the States erupted, Corse was commissioned as colonel of the seventeenth Virginia Regiment and after the Battle of Sharpsburg he was promoted to the rank of general. Corse fought to the bitter end of the conflict and was captured at the Battle of Saylor's Creek; then sent to Fort Warren, Massachusetts as a prisoner of war. He retired to Alexandria after the conflict and entered into business with his brother, Wilmer, trading as W. D. Corse and Company. The banking firm specialized in the exchange of securities. (William Hurd, "Montgomery Dent Corse," Alexandria History, volume 4, 1982.) Until its destruction, Dr. Clarence Leadbeater and his family occupied the building beginning in 1905. A pharmacist, Dr. Leadbeater, was the last operator of the Leadbeater Drug Company which descended from the original Stabler Apothecary shop, established in 1794. Gift of Robert G. Whitton

The northwest corner of Duke and Payne streets shows buildings used as a military prison when this photograph was taken. The large structure on the left was built about 1812 and was the home of Brig. Gen. Robert Young, of the Second Militia of the District of Columbia, for a short time. By 1828, a newspaper advertisement stated "The Subscribers having leased for a term of years the large three-story brick house on Duke Street, formerly occupied by General Young, we wish to purchase one hundred and fifty likely young negroes of both sexes between the ages of eight and twenty-five years.—Franklin & Armfield." This building with additional structures thus became a slave trading pen, Alexandria's largest, until 1861 when, under the name of Price Birch and Company, Dealers in Slaves, it was closed. Interior photographs of heavy-doored cells, purported to be those in which slaves were incarcerated, were actually built by Federal authorities at the time of the conversion of the building to a prison. The main structure radically altered, still stands at 1315 Duke Street.
National Archives

Benjamin Hallowell's school (called "Brimstone Castle" by students and others) was Alexandria's foremost and best known educational facility during the 1830s and 1840s and appeared as shown here in a contemporary catalog. All during this period, however, numerous private schools, seminaries, and academies were established, all having varying degrees of longevity and success. This complex was located on the west side of the 200 block of North Washington Street.

Tradition states that through his friendship with Col. John Fitzgerald, George Washington contributed toward the construction of the first Roman Catholic Church located on South Washington Street, built in 1796, whose original cemetery still exists in that location. By 1809, the old Methodist Meeting House on Chapel Alley (which runs south from Duke, midway between Royal and Fairfax) was purchased, additional land added in 1817, and a new church (shown in this 1858 print) was consecrated on March 4, 1827. Located on the east side of the 300 block of South Royal Street, St. Mary's is the oldest Roman Catholic parish in Virginia. The flounder house in the back of the Presbyterian Meeting House cemetery appears to the right of the church.
(Ballou's Pictorial Drawing Room Companion, 1858)

The Second Presbyterian Church was formed after a split in the congregation of the First (Old Presbyterian Meeting House) in April 1817 and this handsome Greek Revival structure was erected in 1840 on the northwest corner of Prince and South St. Asaph streets. After nearly fifty years of use, Glenn Brown, Alexandria's first professionally trained architect, was engaged to modernize and enlarge the church, so in 1889 the style was advanced from Greek to Roman (esque), a decided retreat from the attractiveness of the earlier facade. Interestingly enough, the left hand (west) wall was not changed except for restyling the windows and it appears today much as the right side did in the earlier photograph. Mr. William Leadbeater, who gave the writer a similar picture, said that he attended Sunday School in the basement of this church, before its remodeling, and that it always had a dank, musty smell which he could never forget.
U.S. Army Military History Institute, circa 1864

The Green family were cabinetmakers and furniture manufacturers for a period of seventy years in Alexandria. William Green, an Englishman, arrived in 1817 and immediately set up shop in his already established trade in buildings located first on King Street, later on North Royal and still later on South Royal, where a fire which started in his shop in 1827 destroyed his and fifty-two other stores, warehouses, and residences, probably Alexandria's most disastrous fire of all time. William was succeeded by his son, James, who in 1834 purchased the brick building on the southeast corner of Prince and Fairfax streets from John Ricketts, owner of Cameron Mills and who used it for the storage of grain. This remained the furniture manufactory for as long as the Greens remained in business. James expanded his interests in several directions, particularly real estate, and turned over the business to his son, John W. Green. This was a highly profitable and successful operation up to the War Between the States. John and his brother, Stephen, had joined forces just before the war, then it was closed down for five years. Reopened in May 1866, business flourished for a time, but competition from larger, and probably more sophisticated, manufacturers in other cities, particularly Washington and Baltimore, caused a downturn in the enterprise till finally the last Green brother, Stephen, was forced into bankruptcy in April, 1887. The building still stands and it has housed several automobile dealerships and garages, ultimately being remodeled into a condominium about 1980. The cupola, with its familiar bell ringing the beginning and the ending of the days' activities, has been long since removed.

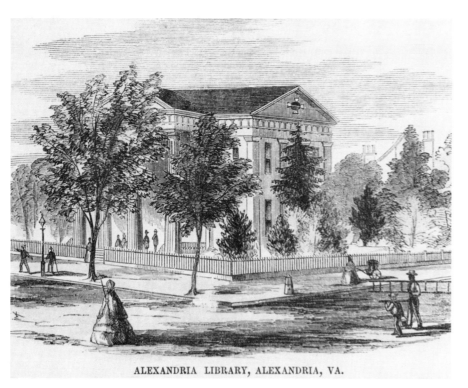

ALEXANDRIA LIBRARY, ALEXANDRIA, VA.

The Lyceum Movement began in America in the 1830s and was an attempt to provide for the opening and broadening of citizens' minds by exposure to literary and scientific knowledge through lectures and debates. Such a society was promoted and founded by Alexandria's prolific Quaker pedagogue, Benjamin Hallowell, and a few friends in about 1835. By 1839, funds were sufficient to allow for the erection of this Greek Revival structure at the southwest corner of Washington and Prince streets, which provided a second-story lecture hall, and occupancy of part of the first floor by the collection of the Alexandria Library Company, an organization which has survived to the present day in conjunction and cooperation with the city's Alexandria Library system. A report on the town in 1835 stated that the library was incorporated in 1797, (it had been founded in 1794) and contained about four thousand volumes. Ballou's Pictorial Drawing Room Companion, *1858)*

The District Courthouse for Alexandria, D.C., was designed by the well-known Robert Mills, who held the title of Architect of Public Buildings, appointed by President Andrew Jackson in 1836. After inspecting the recently failed Bank of Alexandria Building (southeast corner of Cameron and North Fairfax streets) for use as a courthouse, he decided a new structure was called for. This Greek Revival edifice was the only one in Alexandria to be designed by Mills and was constructed in 1838 on the west side of the 300 block of North Columbus Street, it and its surrounding grounds occupying the entire block. Court days were announced by the ringing of a bell which hung in its cupola. It was of fireproof construction and its facade had a two-story Doric portico above a high basement and a gracefully curved double stairway rose to the main floor level. In March 1841, the Alexandria Gazette stated: "It may be regarded as rather 'small potatoes' by some . . . (but) it is by no means to be sneezed at, unless you have a particularly bad cold." In its later years, it was virtually abandoned being used for little more than a polling place and was finally demolished in 1905.
Alexandria Library

The prohibition of digging private wells after 1810 for health reasons led to the creation of deep public wells and pumps on street corners throughout the town and these remained the principal source of water for most townspeople for sometime after the establishment of the Alexandria Water Company in 1851-1852. Reminiscing about "The Town Pump" on April 24, 1890, the Alexandria Gazette stated: "Lonely, neglected and useless, its formerly busy iron handle that loudly creaked with every movement, now hanging idle, the drip stone that bears the marks of the cooling drops of water that in the olden time slaked the thirst of the former residents, and the wood work gradually rotting away, 'its occupation gone'—such is the picture of the only pump left on King Street ... owing to the convenience of the river, for the water was pure and sweet before the contamination of more modern days, no pumps were placed east of Lee (or Wa-

ter) street ... The town pump was 'the King.' Life, pleasure and the pursuit of happiness depended on the uniform looking and uniform giving of the flowing water from these popular resorts. There were generally two on each block ... they were eagerly sought after and patronized both day and night ... especially about the noon hour (for we were dreadfully old fashioned in those days), when the servants would go for a pitcher or bucket of cool water for the dinner table ... what a place it was for gossip ... Going to the pump in those days was the 'summum bonum' of a child's existence—a reward held out to the good; a deprivation was a punishment to the bad. Besides the 'nigh pumps' as they were vernacularly called, were those in the suburbs, and as the water was better and purer they were much sought after." These pumps supplied "water carts"—"a large hogshead laid on its side, carried on a framework with shafts and supported on two wheels ... a

big brass spigot at the rear end regulated the filling of the buckets at one cent for each bucket ... A string of bells on an iron frame fastened to the harness gave notice of the approach of these vehicles ... The familiar cry of 'Wart!' was frequently heard in those days when the tardy servant failed to hear ... the bells ... but the cry of the driver in his stentorian tones seldom failed to arouse one to a sense of duty ... The pumps not only supplied the water ... for drinking and cooking ... but, away from the river, were the dependence for the extinguishment of fires, for after the introduction of the suction fire engine, each pump was provided with the half of a water tight hogshead placed beneath the drip spout, and which was kept filled with water and which proved to be not only convenient for watering horses, but exceedingly useful to the firemen. Those were the days of hand engines and volunteer firemen." Brien/Hulfish Collection

A

B

C

Alexandria's origins came about as a direct result of its being located on a navigable stream. It was relatively easy for needed supplies to be brought to the early settlers (mostly wandering Scots) who in turn established commercial enterprises to provide needed services for the community's residents. Its location guaranteed its importance to inland and up-country farmers who wished to use the nearest port from which to ship first their tobacco and later their grain and related products to buyers in other parts of the country and the world. It was quite natural, then, for the earliest known views of the town, however crude and amateurishly done, to be depictions of a port

town having a great variety of shipping and boating activity.

A. The oldest appeared on a one hundred dollar bill issued by the Bank of Potomac after 1810 and was a scene depicting a sailing vessel with a town in the background. This may have been merely a representative view of a town like Alexandria, although the bank did include, in the same monetary issue, an accurate engraving of its headquarters (415 Prince Street and still standing).

B. This scene appeared in an anti-slavery broadside, published in New York in 1836, and shows a boatload of people, presumably slaves, being rowed to an awaiting vessel which would carry them

to Southern ports for sale. It is difficult to pick out any specific building in the background as belonging in the town, but other scenes on the sheet contain very accurate pictures of Alexandria structures.

C. This engraving which appeared in an English travel book, A Stranger's Guide, in 1845, gives the impression that the artist really tried to show the town as it appeared at that time. Artistically it is superior to the others, but again, this might be the result of a final work done at home, based on a very rough sketch made at the time of his visit. Still, it definitely has the feel of Alexandria.

70

This view, circa 1910, of the Strand between King and Prince streets shows large warehouses, most of which were built in the first third of the nineteenth century. All were related, in their uses, to the waterfront and shipping activities. River traffic appears to be in the doldrums (which it probably was). Brick structures such as these, spread out over seven or eight blocks on Union and the Strand, replaced the eighteenth century wooden warehouses that were removed by fire or old age. One of the first public buildings erected was a one-story frame warehouse built by John Carlyle for the Trustees of Alexandria in 1755 on Point Lumley (foot of Duke Street) which was one hundred feet by twenty-four feet and covered by an attic with dormer windows. *Columbia Historical Society*

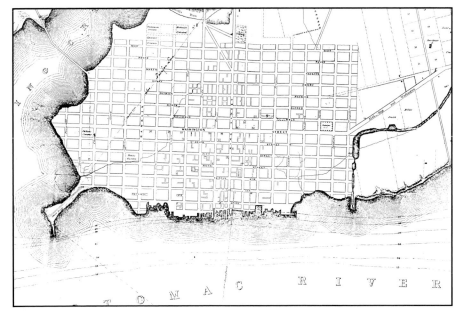

On October 15, 1840, Maskell Ewing, assistant engineer of the Alexandria Canal Company, was authorized by the Alexandria City Council "to extend the topographical survey of the town about to be commenced . . . and that a complete map thereof be made at the expense of the corporation." (*Alexandria Gazette*, October 17, 1840). Completed in 1845, this detailed map of the city shows the location of twenty-six points of interest including the Alexandria Canal on the north, a rope walk on Jones Point, and the early cemeteries on the western fringes of town.

Born on April 30, 1781, George Washington Park Custis, a talented playwright, author, and painter, was the grandson of Martha Washington. Upon the death of his father, John Custis, at the Siege of Yorktown in 1781, young "Wash" Custis as he was known left his home at Abingdon (a portion of the present site of National Airport) and went to live with his grandparents, General and Mrs. Washington at Mount Vernon. For a time, young Custis was a student at the College of New Jersey at Princeton and St. John's College in Annapolis, Maryland. Upon Martha Washington's death in 1802, he moved to Mount Washington, a lovely eminence overlooking the new Columbia District. In 1804, he married Mary Lee Fitzhugh, daughter of William Fitzhugh of Ravensworth, at a wedding ceremony held at 607 Oronoco Street in Alexandria. Custis subsequently took his bride to Mount Washington which he later named Arlington (now Arlington Cemetery) for the ancestral Custis home on the eastern shore of Virginia. Having grown up in the shadow of George Washington at Mount Vernon, "Wash" Custis literally idolized the memory of the first president and he subsequently purchased a large number of Washington relics and memorabilia for his personal estate. On June 30, 1831, the Custis' only surviving child, Mary Anne Randolph Custis, married Robert E. Lee at Arlington. Although General Lee never owned Arlington, he considered it his home until the mansion was illegally seized by the Federal Army during the War Between the States.

Universally known and respected in Alexandria, Mr. Custis was a frequent visitor to town and was called upon to address audiences on the Fourth of July and other holidays at the Market Square and Lyceum. A brilliant orator, he never failed to attract an enthusiastic crowd. Of medium height and fine complexion, Custis displayed great personal charm until his death at Arlington in 1857. Source: *Harper's Weekly*

The Alexandria Canal designed to extend the Chesapeake and Ohio Canal from Georgetown, D.C., to Alexandria, commenced at groundbreaking ceremonies attended by a large and orderly crowd of officials, citizens, and strangers, on July 4, 1831. Although the canal opened in 1843, the Alexandria Gazette, announced the arrival of the first two boats in the canal basin on October 19, 1850, "laden with coal from Cumberland." Further, "we hail with joy and gladness an event so intimately connected as we conceive with the future growth and prosperity of our good old town. For many years we have had our attention steadfastly directed to the completion of this work as the sure harbinger of better and more prosperous days." Business was brisk in the following decade but the operation of the canal was terminated when Union military authorities drained it following the occupation of Alexandria in May 1861. It was reopened in 1867 but never achieved anticipated profitability and the town, which had invested heavily in the canal's construction, was saddled with an enormous debt which cast a pall over its economic recovery. The use of the canal was abandoned in 1887. This view is the only known photograph of the outlet from the first lock into the Potomac River and indicates a less than active maintenance program for its upkeep. National Archives, circa 1864

"BEFORE THE STORM"
THE ANTEBELLUM STAGE
1848 to 1860

pon its retrocession to Virginia in 1847, Alexandria entered upon a new phase of economic prosperity and nascent industrialization.

As early as 1847, Lewis McKenzie, a wealthy Scottish entrepreneur, had spearheaded efforts to construct a railroad into the Shenandoah Valley. Known as the Alexandria & Harper's Ferry Railroad, this enterprise was not well received by the conservative business community and subsequently failed. However, by 1848, the Orange & Alexandria Railroad had been organized. Its charter stipulated that the company's track would be laid from Gordonsville to Alexandria via Orange Courthouse and Culpeper. In April 1851, rails were laid on Wilkes Street and on May 6 of the same year, the first locomotive belched smoke and cinders and the shrill sound of its whistle could be heard as it chugged down Union Street to the Wilkes Street tunnel. On May 30, the *Alexandria Gazette* reported that:

> Yesterday forenoon, our citizens on the wharf were delighted with the sight of 3 carloads of flour, meal and shipstuffs, from the Central Mills, owned by Messrs. J.J. Wheat & Brothers. The cars came in with flags flying and amidst the shouts of the assembled crowd. Mr. John Tatspaugh . . . claims the honor of taking off the first barrel of flour received by the railroad.

During this epoch Alexandria was also served by three other railroads. Incorporated in 1854, the Alexandria, Loudoun & Hampshire operated between the city and Leesburg to the west while the Manassas Gap Railroad, chartered in 1850, was primarily controlled by agricultural interests in Fauquier County. Initially the road was scheduled to run through Manassas Gap to Harrisonburg. However, by the terms of a lease agreement, freight and passenger service was extended to Alexandria via the Orange & Alexandria Railroad. Friction soon developed between the two companies and the Manassas line complained bitterly about the exorbitant freight rates it was charged. Thus in 1852, the rail company received permission from the state of Virginia to construct a parallel line beside the Orange & Alexandria branch all the way to Alexandria. By 1855 the town had purchased seven thousand shares, worth $350,000, in this new enterprise. With the outbreak of the War Between the States, this line which was supposed to terminate at Jones Point was never completed. Sections of Route 95 East to the Wilson Bridge, however, currently traverse the uncompleted roadbed. Another major antebellum railroad was the Alexandria & Washington. Owned and operated by the dynamic James Strange French, this short line ran from its turntable at Princess and Fairfax streets northwesterly to the east side of the Alexandria & Washington turnpike until it reached the Fourteenth Street Bridge. From there the passengers alighted, and took a horse drawn vehicle to Washington proper.

In addition to these four railroad facilities, Alexandria was fortunate to be home to the Smith and Perkins Locomotive Works. Located on the south side of Wolfe at Union Street, the manufactory covered 51,500 feet of ground fronting on the Potomac River. Besides the machine shop, there was a foundry building, a blacksmith shop, boiler shop, and car shop. In 1852, the firm was building railroad

During its early history Alexandria's water resources were supplied by wells and pumps located in private homes and at street corners. Frequently the local water was contaminated by raw sewage and bacteria which seeped into the underground water supply from the presence of the large number of privies which dotted practically ever city block. No doubt this undesirable situation contributed to the outbreak of typhoid, malaria, and dysentery. To correct this health hazard, the digging and use of private wells was suspended after 1810 and deep public wells

were dug on street corners. It was the astute Quaker teacher, Benjamin Hallowell, who first suggested that a public reservoir be constructed atop Shuter's Hill. In a letter to his good friend and colleague, Robert Miller, Hallowell described the genesis of the Water Company and how the reservoir site was constructed near Shuter's Hill. "When on a visit to my sister at Morristown, New Jersey while this subject (water) was occupying my thoughts I met there with James L. Halme of Mt. Holly and in conversation, I ascertained that his mill had recently

been brought into requisition, as a means of supply the town of Mt. Holly with water . . . This idea was at once transferred to the Cameron Mill and on my returning to Alexandria and mentioning the subject to some of my friends there . . . they encouraged me . . . if I would make a speech upon the subject in favour of using the Cameron stream . . . In my remarks, I spoke of the feasibility of having 'the clear and pure water of the Pebbly Brooke (Cameron Stream) conducted through all our houses on its way to the Potomac' . . . The subscription got on

Benjamin Hallowell

finely and meeting of the stockholders was soon called to elect officers. . . . I was unanimously elected with the exception of my own vote. I accepted the office upon two conditions. First I was to have no salary. Second, that I was to have the privilege of selecting a competent Engineer who had constructed similar works . . . Frederick Erdman . . . was of course elected by the Board, our engineer."

Hallowell continued to serve as president of the Water Company for many years and ground was broken for the project in early 1851: " . . . this took place

on the lot recently purchased of Peter Tressler, in the rear of Shuter's hill. The venerable Benjamin Hallowell, spade in hand, and with a degree of vigor and enthusiasm . . . took the lead . . ."

Mr. Hallowell made a very neat and appropriate address. The work of laying the pipes into town and construction of the reservoir was finished by 1852 and water let into town June 15. During the War Between the States, the reservoir seen in this photograph (circa 1930) was pumped dry by Federal forces who occupied Alexandria. With the city's increased

demand for water, a large dam was constructed which formed Lake Barcroft, circa 1915, and it served as the city's main water supply until the 1960s when the reservoir on Occoquan Creek, under the Fairfax Water Authority, assumed that important role.
Reservoir from the Alexandria Library; portrait from the Alexandria Association

Ames W. Williams Collection, Alexandria Library

Lewis McKenzie occupies an unusual place in Alexandria's history in that, as a native of the city, he was very active and prominent in the business development of the community before the War Between the States, chose to side with the Union during the war, then lived to reap the benefits of such actions from his Southern-oriented fellow townsmen. Born in 1810 he first clerked for one of the major shipping and commission firms in town, Fowle and Daingerfield, but by 1830 he had entered into partnership with Benjamin H. Lambert for the purpose of establishing a similar business and this was a highly successful operation until 1853 when the partnership was ended. McKenzie continued in the same line until the 1880s. He was the moving power in the building of the Alexandria, Loudoun & Hampshire Railroad, became its president, later served as president of the First National Bank and before the war "commanded the respect of friend and foe and was foremost in nearly all of the most important enterprises conceived for the aggrandisement of his native city." Upon the commencement of the war in 1861, his sympathies for the federal government led to his serving for a time as acting mayor, member of the leg-

islature, presiding justice of the magistrates court and brigadier general of the local militia. He ran for the House of Representatives in 1865, was defeated, ran again in 1869 and was elected as the least objectionable of those nominated but served about one year, being defeated in 1870. Being a Republican in a fast developing Democratic stronghold, he was defeated again for public office but was appointed as postmaster of the town in the early 1880s, removed in the Mahone Readjuster era and finally was elected to the Board of Aldermen shortly before the end of his life at the age of eighty-five. The Alexandria Gazette and Virginia Advertiser of June 29, 1895, in trying to cover all aspects of his life stated: "The deceased . . . never seemed to possess the true elements of greatness . . . regarded as unstable . . . little of the serious in him" yet "a man of good heart and dispensed his charity liberally . . . Like many prominent men, he had his peculiarities, paradoxes, inconsistencies and freaks . . . No matter who his political bedfellows may have been—and they were sometimes of the menagerie type—he never fell into the growing sins of his associates." So much for one, most of whose fellow citizens considered to be a turncoat.

Constructed in 1826 by Abijah Janney, this interesting building had been enlarged to forty rooms by 1859 and housed the Alexandria High School. This institution was conducted by Caleb Hallowell, nephew of Benjamin Hallowell, before the outbreak of the War Between the States. It then became one of Alexandria's many hostelries, the Magnolia House, located at the southeast corner of Duke and Columbus streets and boasted that it was: "the place for all lovers of good things in life. Here you can eat and grow fat—drink and be merry. The Larder is always plentifully supplied with the best of everything. All kinds of Liquors; Ale and Porter on draught, Weiss Berr, choice Segars, etc. always on hand. This is also the most convenient House for travellers, being only two blocks from the Railroad Depot. The proprietor also takes pleasure in announcing that his new, elegant and COMMODIOUS HALL, is now finished, and can be engaged for Parties, Balls, Concerts, Lectures, etc. at the most reasonable rates. For terms apply to R. FREDERICK, Proprietor." (Alexandria Gazette, November 3, 1865)

The hotel also promoted its gas baths and charged its customers the following rates: "Transient Boarders $2 per day, Permanent Boarders, with single rooms, from $7 to $10 per week, according to the size and location of the room, Room

with double bed for two gentlemen, from $6 to $7 per week each. (Alexandria Gazette, January 5, 1866)

In September 1884, St. John's Military

Academy, established by Richard Carne, occupied the building and remained here until its demise in 1892. It was converted into a condominium in the early 1980s.

The two buildings in the immediate foreground (601 and 603 Queen Street) were constructed by Robert L. Brockett and for many years served as his "Alexandria Academy." The structure in the immediate foreground (601 Queen) was built in 1842, and as his school became more popular, he needed room to expand his enterprise. Thus, in February 1853, Brockett purchased a lot on the west and erected this enormous three-story edifice which was described in 1858 as being "fully supplied with gas and water, and thoroughly heated by flues." (Alexandria Gazette, February 15, 1858) During the War Between the States, 603 Queen Street was seized by Federal authorities and converted into the Queen Street Hospital. Capt. A.W. Bartlett, a doctor on duty there with the Twelfth New Hampshire volunteers penned a poignant description of the scene: "This building is situated in the city of Alexandria Va. and is distinguished from the many other Hospitals of the place by the name of the street upon which it stands. It was built and used for a Female Boarding Seminary ... The room in which I am now writing was once filled up with study desks and was used as the study hall of the delicate Southern beauties who were wont each day to spend a portion of their time within its high and smooth polished walls.

Now as then is written in printed capitals over the door the words "Study Hall", but alas how changed the interior. The long rows of desks are gone and their places filled with narrow iron bedsteads covered with ticks of straw and blankets each supporting its daily lessening weight of suffering flesh. In place of mirthful minds and merry hearts of careless and bright eyed maid youth conning impatiently over the irksome page is now seen the aching-hearted, soul stricken victims of disease and death. Where once sat the rosy cheeks of smiling faced innocence, may now be seen the pale & cadaverous features of the dying soldier about to appear before the Great Governor of the

Universe and Judge of all living . . . Stranger, come with me into this study hall. For such it still is and learn greater lessons than the dead letters of science can ever teach. Come with men and learn what the bed side witness of an expiring soul alone can teach. . . . I know of no place where one can seem to look beyond the reach of him and catch a faint glimpse of the unfathomed mysteries of eternity as he can by the bed side of the dying Christian. It is here that doubts turn into faith." (Cox, Street by Street; Alexandria Archaeology Center; Edward T. Wenzel)
Milton Grigg Collection

The Trinity Methodist Church housed the original Methodist Episcopal congregation in Alexandria and was located on the east side of the 100 block of South Washington Street. Early stirrings of Methodism began in the 1770s and by 1791, a meeting house was built on Chapel Alley, now the site of St. Mary's Roman Catholic Church. A new church was erected on the Washington Street site in 1803-1804 and became the "Alexandria Station" from which, following internal strife for various reasons or by agreement, at least three new churches emerged: The Methodist Protestant Church in 1828, Roberts Chapel (later Roberts Memorial United Methodist Church) in 1832 and Washington Street Methodist Church in 1849. In 1883, the building was remodeled by B. F. Price, one of Alexandria's premier architects, into the structure seen here. In 1939, when most of the fractured Methodist churches in the United States were reunited, there were three churches of the same denomination within one block of each other on Washington Street. Trinity, in a weakened condition at the time, moved to Cameron Mills Road in 1942, demolished this structure, and incorporated parts of it into its new church where it has grown anew and continues to thrive.

engines for the Manassas Gap Railroad, Baltimore & Ohio, and Hudson Valley Railroad. Indeed all the cars utilized on the Manassas Gap Railroad and the Orange & Alexandria Railroad were constructed at this establishment. Smith and Perkins employed between 160 and 200 men and expended from twelve thousand to fifteen thousand dollars per month. (Alexandria Gazette, December 1, 1852). Unfortunately the firm declared bankruptcy in 1857.

From the years 1850 to 1860, Alexandria experienced unprecedented growth. Its population increased from 8,795 to 12,652 and more than five hundred houses were constructed in the five year period from 1850 to 1855. "The stagnation and dullness which had prevailed here before had given way to economic prosperity. Houses which erst went begging for occupants were filled to overflowing . . . The miserable skeletons of antiquated buildings are metamorphosed into large, neat and substantial edifices which are useful and ornamental."

Writing in 1853, a correspondent of the Rockingham Register noted that "the animation and occupation which enlivens her railroad depots, her wharves and canal basin, as well as the bustle and hum of her streets, prove that this worthy daughter of the Old Dominion is in a fair way to rank, ere long, among the most prosperous cities of the land." (Alexandria Gazette, November 2, 1853).

Among the many internal improvements which ornamented Alexandria during this era were a new gas and waterworks. The gas plant was situated on the southeast corner of Lee and Oronoco streets and was completed near the end of 1851. Underground pipes supplied local denizens and street lamps with gas as Alexandrians were ushered into a new epoch of illumination.

Through the years Alexandria had been visited by many typhoid and dysentery epidemics so it was decided in 1850 that the town should construct a public waterworks. In an effort to eliminate these maladies, Benjamin Hallowell, a prominent Quaker teacher, proposed that a public reservoir be built atop Shuter's Hill. Subequently, a water company was established and Hallowell was named its first president. The work of laying pipes and constructing a reservoir was finished by 1852 and water let into town on June 15th of that year.

As iron horses hauled their precious cargoes of grain from the Valley of Virginia, it became clear that Alexandria needed a first-class flour mill. Therefore, in 1852, the Alexandria Steam Flour Company erected a splendid facility at the foot of Duke Street along the Potomac River. Known as Pioneer Mill, it was six-stories high, had twelve run-of-burr millstones and a 250 horse power engine capable of turning out eight thousand barrels of flour per day and consuming four thousand bushels of wheat. During its peak period of operation, it was considered one of the largest flour mills in the United States.

Another important business in town centered around the importation of guano. Years of planting tobacco had leached the fertile Virginia soil. To remedy these conditions, tons of guano were imported from Peru and discharged upon the wharves at Alexandria where it was mixed with phosphatic materials and offered for sale as fertilizer to local farmers.

In the field of education, Alexandria was fortunate to have a number of academies and private schools. There was the Alexandria Public School; the Female Seminary, James Hallowell, principal; St. John's Academy; La Valle Seminary; Brockett's Academy; and Mrs. A. K. Evans School at the cor-

Pioneer Mills

The Alexandria Steam Flour Company have now erected their splendid Steam Mill in this place, and it being nearly completed and ready for the commencment of operations, we have taken great pleasure in going through it, and examining its capabilities.

The Mill, built of brick of the best and most durable materials, slate roof and fire proof, is situated on the Strand at the foot of Duke Street. It fronts on the Potomac River 122 feet - the main building being 80 feet deep - and the engine room 32—making a total depth of 112 feet. It is six stories high, and the roof 77 feet above high water mark, or 73 feet from the first floor. It has 12 run-of-burr mill stones and splendid steam engine of 250 horse power. The Mill is capable of turning out eight hundred barrels of flour per day, and of consuming, per day, four thousand bushels of wheat. Attached to the Mill is an elevator for taking grain from the holds of vessels, and carrying it directly into the building. Large vessels can be loaded directly at the door of the Mill. A wharf has been constructed on the north side of the building on which a switch from the track of the railroad on Union Street will be laid - so that grain from the cars will be brought, also, directly to the Mill.

This establishment is the largest Steam Flour Mill in the United States - and second only in extent to the Gallego Mills in Richmond. All the appurtenances and machinery are of the best kind, and the most modern improvements have been introduced.

Mr. William H. Fowle, is the General Agent, Mr. James C. Nevett, the Clerk and Treasurer, and Mr. R. F. Roberts, Chief Miller. This view shows the ruins of the Pioneer Mill after a terrible fire swept the Strand area of the Alexandria waterfront in June 1897 at which time the mill was totally destroyed. Alexandria Gazette, March 11, 1854, page 3.

Milton Grigg Collection

of Washington and Duke Street. By far one of the most successful of these institutions was the one conducted by Benjamin Hallowell, called by students the ''Brimstone Castle'' on the west side of the 200 block of North Washington Street.

For entertainment, Alexandrians could enjoy theater performances at Serepta hall on King Street or attend lectures at the Lyceum by renowned orators including George Washington Parke Custis, John Quincy Adams, or Caleb Cushing. In addition, silver-tongued orators mesmerized audiences as they debated leading political questions of the day at American and Liberty halls which were situated near the northwest corner of Cameron and Royal streets. During the hot sultry summers, Alexandrians would also promenade to Jones Point where they enjoyed the luxuriant foliage and visited the newly constructed Federal Light House (1855).

The late 1850s dawned propitiuously for Alexandria. The Aqueduct of the Alexandria Canal over the Potomac River at Georgetown was considered one of the engineering feats of the century. Dozens of canal boats descended the C&O Canal, crossed the river and delivered their cargo of black gold to town. From the coal wharves at Alexandria, many tons of the product were transshipped to San Francisco and South America.

In 1850 the assessed value of property in the city was $2,850,000. By 1859 it was $5,306,000, an increase in nine years of $2,455,000. ''In church property alone there (had) been an improvement to the extent of $50,000. Four new churches (had) been built . . . fourteen first class warehouses and an extensive flour mill had been put up on the River front and twenty-six large warehouses for the accommodation of merchants . . . Since 1850 there have been built six hundred brick dwellings, a greater portion of them first class. The lands around Alexandria have increased in value 100%.'' (*Alexandria Gazette,* July 27, 1859).

However, this spirit of revitalization and renewal was shattered by John Brown's raid on Harper's Ferry on October 16, 1859. An ardent abolitionist, Brown's attempt to incite a slave revolt inflamed regional passions. The Alexandria Riflemen left town on October 18th and were among those who reinforced the garrison at Harper's Ferry. Brown's raid was a catalyst which fueled the controversy over slavery. Coupled with the furor over state's rights, nullification, and tariffs, the federal ship of state broke asunder when South Carolina seceded from the Union in December 1860. A conflagrant wave of death and destruction swept across the land as America became embroiled in a fratricidal Civil War. Virginia, which seceded on April 17, 1861, subsequently voted in a public referendum on May 23rd to remove itself from the Union. Alexandria, because of its strategic military importance, became one of first victims of this terrible conflict. The town would never be the same as the *ancien regime* was replaced by an occupation army.

The Jones Point Lighthouse, built on the southeastern tip of Alexandria in 1855-1856 is possibly the oldest inland waterway lighthouse in the country. It stands almost atop the original cornerstone for the District of Columbia and was in active operation from May 1, 1856 (first illumination) to December 1919. The job of lighthouse keeper throughout the country was subject to a notorious "spoils system" and a writer in 1874 complained that "The politicians of a base sort have often defeated the intentions and desires of the (Lighthouse) board and ousted a good man to put in one 'useful at the polls.'" Of the several lighthouse keepers, the one who managed to serve longest was Benjamin Greenwood, appointed after October 1861 and whose tenure ended at his death in 1906. Being an accused Republican, several efforts were made to remove him but each attempt

failed. He apparently was faithful to his duties and to his wives, it being said that he sired 17 children by them (the first being eliminated by death). The last keeper, Francis Wilkins, had little to do since the need for manned light had been virtually eliminated by a drastic change in the shoreline (a tidal flat, sometimes called Battery Cove, which had bordered the north side of the narrow Jones Point peninsula had been filled in after 1910) and the erection of a large shipyard within a few hundred yards of the lighthouse, so at his death in 1919, no replacement was named. A sixty-foot tower with a permanent electric light was built in 1926 and operated into the 1940s. The light house structure itself was placed in the hands of the Mount Vernon Chapter of the Daughters of the American Revolution for preservation in 1926 but at the approach of World War II, the entire area

was fenced off due to the placement of a sensitive armed forces communications facility there. Since the only approach was by water, few of the ladies had much desire to visit, knowing that to do so might have resulted in being arrested as suspected saboteurs. The quaint building suffered much from vandalism during and after the war, but the National Park Service stepped in, contained its deterioration and, it is to be hoped, has plans for its eventual restoration. This view of the lighthouse is dated 1929, and shows the enclosure built in 1912 surrounding the original cornerstone of the District of Columbia.

(National Archives)

The Alexandria Custom House and Post Office, was built in 1858, having been designed by Ammi Young, an architect and Federal office holder who produced many public structures between 1849 and 1860. Located on the southwest corner of Prince and St. Asaph Streets, it was a completely fireproof structure, made of granite with cast iron door, window frames, and stairways. The Post Office was on the first floor, the customs rooms on the second, and a courtroom was housed on the third. Original construction consisted of three bays on each street facade, but it was later enlarged on the St. Asaph Street side to five bays. A description of the Post Office room stated: "as elegant a room for the purpose ... as we have ever seen. The ceiling of this room is to be beautifully frescoed and the design for the vestibule, in three parts, the centre representing the coat-of-arms of Virginia, surrounded with the United States flag ... is beautiful, original and appropriate." (Penny Morrill, Who Built Alexandria?) The Building was demolished to provide parking spaces for the new U.S. Court House, erected facing Washington Street about 1930. O'Brien/Hulfish Collection, before 1900

This 1860s view shows the First Baptist Church in the 200 block of South Washington Street, recently reconstructed (1858-1859) within the walls of the existing Meeting House which had replaced an earlier building which burned in 1829. This building, considerably longer than its predecessor, is an early example of Romanesque Revival, attributed to Thomas Tefft, a well-known architect from Providence, Rhode Island. As with the Methodist Society, many black residents of Alexandria were drawn to the Baptist Society and both black and white members worshiped in the same building until about 1818 when by agreement, the black congregation moved to separate quarters, ultimately building the first and oldest black church in town, the Alfred Street Baptist Church. The major portion of the congregation of the First Baptist Church moved in recent years to a larger building on King Street extended, but a movement immediately took place which resulted in the formation of the Downtown Baptist Church, occupant of the old edifice to this day. To the left of the church may be seen the side yard of a house facing Prince Street and owned at various times by S. F. Beach and Judge J. K. M. Norton. This was demolished in the early 1930s to provide space for the U.S. Court House and Post Office. To the right of the Baptist Church are the Schofield/Lloyd buildings, the two closest of which were torn down in 1926, being replaced by a modern Sunday School building for the church. The brick sidewalks, granite curbstones, and cobblestone street surfaces are clearly evident. The farthest two-and-one-half-story house (220 South Washington) besides being Judge Cranch's residence in the early nineteenth century, was later owned by R. W. Avery, who was courier to Gen. George Pickett who led the famous Pickett's Charge at the Battle of Gettysburg in 1863.

Grace Church (200 block South Patrick Street), consecrated in October 1860, had its beginnings in 1856 when a dedicated group decided that a new church needed to be placed in the western part of town where no other churches then existed (with the possible exception of the black congregation located in the Alfred Street Baptist Church). The Alexandria Gazette and Virginia Advertiser (December 9, 1856) under Local Items read: "We may state that it is for a part of our town, in which there is no house of worship of any kind. The gospel must be carried to the people. It is in vain to expect people to come to it . . . It is in vain to talk about room in other Churches, if the churches are so far off, the people will not go. Now this Church is to go to the people—going as a missionary—a pioneer—to bring in those who are wandering away." Within a short time after the start of the war, Grace was closed for use as a hospital (what's new?). It reopened after the occupation ended and remained Alexandria's "high" Episcopal church, as opposed to the "low" services conducted in Christ and St. Paul's Churches. The low form had evolved as a sort of protest to the very formal service of the Church of England (Anglican) (in which bells and incense were used, considered popish by many) during and after the Revolution. Grace, however, stuck to its guns and has remained, even after its removal in the early 1950s, to far Russell Road, as Alexandria's "high" church, a service which satisfies many. This view, showing soldiers on crutches, was obviously taken while it served as a hospital. After its congregation moved, it was remodeled and spent a blessedly short time as a teen-aged night club, and has since been converted into condominia.
Rebecca Ramsay Reese Collection

General Haupt, third from right, inspects the stockades erected by his Construction Corps around the entire Orange & Alexandria Railroad complex. They were constructed to offer protection both to personnel and equipment from anticipated Confederate lightning raids, such as those conducted by Col. John S. Mosby and his men throughout the Northern Virginia area. These palisades were similar to those built in the river front area. This view facing north toward Duke Street shows the upper stories of two houses in the 200 block of South Payne Street which are standing today.

THE OCCUPIED CITY
ALEXANDRIA DURING THE WAR
BETWEEN THE STATES
1861 to 1865

ark war clouds hovered over Alexandria during the early months and spring of 1861. By January, Mississippi, Alabama, Florida, Georgia, and Louisiana had followed the course of South Carolina and seceded. Virginia, although not a deep cotton state, called a secessionists' convention on February 4, 1861. After much debate, it withdrew from the Union on April 17, with the proviso that a public referendum on secession be taken May 23, 1861. Alexandria with its strong Federalist heritage was initially opposed to disunion however. During the election campaign of 1860, the town had cast a majority of ballots for John Bell—the Constitutional Unionist candidate. The *Alexandria Gazette* of September 28, 1860, announced:

> ... the Union men of Alexandria made the most imposing demonstration ... last night, which had ever taken place in this city. If there has ever been a doubt of the intense enthusiasm which the Union cause and its candidates have erected in their good old town, that doubt must have been dissipated by the outpouring of popular sentiment last night.

In an effort to see that Virginia remained in the Union, Alexandrians elected George Brent, an opponent to secession, to the February conclave in Richmond by a margin of 638 votes. However, when South Carolina fired on Fort Sumter on April 12, 1861, and President Lincoln subsequently called for seventy-five thousand troops to crush the rebellion, the town's sentiments dramatically changed. On April 17, 1861, James Jackson, the local proprietor of the Marshall House hotel raised a Confederate

flag at that hotel to the huzzas and enthusiasm of a local crowd. Charles H. Taylor, a native Alexandrian, had solicited funds to have the flag made by two local ladies.

As war fever swept the city, militia units composed of the town's youth drilled at the old Catalpa Lot on the west side of North Washington Street between Pendleton and Madison streets. On May 23, 1861, Virginians went to the polls to voice their sentiments for the articles of secession. By a vote of 958 for and 106 against, Alexandrians gave their approval for secession. Almost immediately the next morning, Union troops under the command of Maj. Gen. Charles W. Sanford of the New York State militia invaded Alexandria by sea and land. The main expeditionary force composed of New York militia troops crossed at the old Long Bridge while the First Michigan Volunteers marched into Alexandria from the north along Washington Street. Another regiment of New York Fire Zouaves led by Col. Elmer E. Ellsworth landed at the foot of Cameron Street. With a few recruits, Ellsworth proceeded up King Street where he noticed the Confederate flag which fluttered in the breeze over the Marshall House hotel. The colonel and his retinue entered the hotel, clammered to the roof and seized the banner. Upon descending the staircase, Ellsworth was met by the proprietor, James Jackson, who fired a shotgun blast into his chest and who was subsequently shot and bayoneted by Union Corporal Brownell. As the blood of these two men trickled down the steps, each became a celebrated martyr to his cause. As President Lincoln's former law clerk and close friend, Colonel Ellsworth's body was transported to the

This 1863 Bird's Eye View of Alexandria by Charles Magnus of New York depicts the town during its occupation by the Union Army. The harbor is a formidable forest of warships and steamers while the outlying environs are occupied by dozens of armed Federal camps. Occupied on May 24, 1861, Alexandria suffered the longest military occupation of any town during the War Between the States. With the large influx of soldiery, the town became a logistical supply center for the Union Army. Hundreds of oxen and cattle were butchered daily and an enormous bakery occupied the entire northeast block of Princess and Fayette streets. Daily, over two hundred employees used twenty ovens to produce over ninety thousand loaves of bread at this facility. Fort Ellsworth is visible at the head of King Street on the crest of Shuter's Hill while the distinctive U.S. military round house traverses Henry between Duke and Wilkes streets to the left. When the last vestiges of the Union Army departed Alexandria in the fall of 1865, the local populace began the long process of restoring their shattered lives.

White House where the first family mourned his loss. Jackson's corpse which had been turned over to his family was buried without fanfare near Langley, Fairfax County, Virginia.

The invasion of Alexandria by 2,100 Union troops would forever change the fabric of the old seaport community. A conflagrant wave of death and destruction surged over the Southland as the old order was swept away by a tidal wave of change. For four long years Alexandria was occupied by foreign forces and suffered under the yoke of Northern oppression. Indeed the town endured the longest military occupation by Union troops of any town during the conflict. Undoubtedly with the influx of so many soldiers, there was great excitement and pandemonium. General Slough, the Union military governor of the city wrote in 1862:

... there had been for days previous, a reign of terror in Alexandria. The streets were crowded with intoxicated soldiery; murder was of almost hourly occurrence and disturbances, robbery and riot were constant. The sidewalks and docks were covered with drunken men, women and children and quiet citizens were afraid to venture into the streets and life and property were at the mercy of the maddened throng—a condition of things perhaps never in the history of this country to be found in any other city.

After order was restored Alexandrians literally walked their streets as strangers. They were not permitted to go out at night, their mail was intercepted,

and passes were required to travel to Washington and outlying environs. Those who failed to swear obedience to the United States Government were suspected of treason and arrested on the slightest pretext. In addition, violators of the occupation ordinances were hauled before a military provost. Some were fined, others sent to the slave pen jail at 1315 Duke Street or the old Capitol prison which occupied the site of the present U.S. Supreme Court building.

Alexandria was then transformed into a huge logistical supply center for Federal Armies fighting in Virginia. Private homes, churches, and local public buildings were commandeered for military barracks, hospitals, and prisons. The U.S. quartermaster department constructed substantial warehouses along the bustling waterfront and barricades were erected across the streets to thwart possible Confederate Cavalry sorties against these facilities while the U.S. Military Railroad command occupied a twelve-block area on upper Duke Street near Henry.

Various newspaper correspondents visited the city throughout the conflict and penned impressions of the war-torn town. One journalist remarked:

August 8, 1863—This ancient city has now become a centre of commercial importance, being the great warehouse as it might be termed, for supplies of the Army of Potomac. Miniature mountains of hay and pyramids of oat bags, high up in the air, meet the gaze as one approaches the city from the river. Spacious and

In January 1861, James W. Jackson, an ardent secessionist, moved to Alexandria and reopened the old hotel, originally built about 1785, shown here on the southeast corner of King and Pitt streets. On April 17, 1861, a Confederate flag, perhaps Alexandria's first, was flying from the flagpole of the Marshall House. Before dawn on the morning of May 24th while the town was being invaded by numerous Federal Army groups from the North, Col. Elmer Ellsworth, leading his Eleventh New York Fire Zouaves, was transported by boat, landed on the waterfront, and began occupation from the east. As he and his troops marched up King Street, he saw the Southern banner atop the Marshall House, decided to remove it and accompanied by several soldiers, entered the building. He hauled down the flag, and while descending the stairs, was met by the proprietor of the hotel, shotgun in hand. Jackson had

claimed publicly that the flag would be removed only over his dead body and thus, after shooting and killing Ellsworth, flag in hand, he was instantly shot and bayoneted by Corp. Francis Brownell. This ended the lives of the first Union officer killed in the fast approaching conflict and that of a Southern citizen defending his personal property against newly foreign invaders. Two of the wars' earliest martyrs were enshrined that day. The writer recalls talking with a very elderly Miss Kroes Ficklin, daughter of one of Alexandria's first public school superintendents, in the early 1950s and being told that her older sister had attended an early service at Saint Mary's Church on May 24, 1861, and that upon leaving the church, found great confusion and turbulence on the streets, the shootings of Ellsworth and Jackson having taken place only a short time before.
National Archives

This is James W. Jackson shortly before his death.
Ames W. Williams Collection, Alexandria Library; courtesy of Mrs. Arthur J. Mourot

85

The Royal Street side of the Market House (built 1817) appears in this drawing shortly after occupation by Union troops in May 1861. The small building to the right is one which had formerly housed the early Rainbow Tavern while behind it looms the cupola on Green's Mansion House, through the block on Fairfax Street. On the left may be seen the steeple (or bell tower) which sat atop the Hydraulion Fire Engine House at 209 North Royal Street. This print appeared in Frank Leslie's Illustrated Newspaper on October 5, 1861.

antiquated storehouses along the wharves are filled to repletion with all kinds of stores for the use of our brave army, hordes of contrabands are busily at work unloading vessels . . . Alexandria for the past two years can boast of more shipping at its wharves than any other city of its size in the Union . . .
The old residents of Alexandria have mostly departed. Not one third of the original inhabitants now remained and the places of the absent ones are filled by traffickers and dealers in military goods . . . (Extract from the *Philadelphia Inquirer* in the *Alexandria Gazette,* August 10, 1863)
George Alfred Townsend, a correspondent with the *New York Herald,* visited Alexandria in 1863 and remarked that:

Many hamlets and towns have been destroyed during the war. But of all that in some form survive, Alexandria has most suffered . . . Its streets, its docks, its warehouses, its dwellings and its suburbs have been absorbed to the thousand uses of war.
Alexandria is filled with ruined people; they walk as strangers through their ancient streets, and their property is no longer theirs to possess. I do not know any Federal functionary was accused of tyranny, or wantonness, but these things ensued as the natural result of Civil War.

By 1864, Alexandria had changed from the old town that it had been prior to the war as its outskirts and vacant lots were filled up with shanties and contraband houses. "These houses, huddled together, with no conveniences for drainage, swarmed with a mass of men, women and children. Little neighborhoods called Petersburg, Contraband Valley, Pump Town and twenty other locales existed within the midst of the city." (*Alexandria Gazette,* August 25, 1864)

When General Grant launched his 1864-1865 offensive against the Confederate capital at Richmond, thousands of wounded Union soldiers poured into Alexandria hospitals. A soldier's cemetery was established on Wilkes Street extended. Isabel Emerson, a young girl, who resided at Henry and Duke streets wrote in her diary:

Funerals of the Federal soldiers are constantly passing en route to the military cemetery. Sometimes just a company of soldiers with drum and fife and the body of their poor dead comrade on a caisson wrapped in the flag in whose defence he fell, with no friend or relative to shed a tear. Sometimes there is a band and a battalion or regiment. The sound of the Dead March will ring in my ears long after this war is over. It seems a tragedy upon grief, the slow marching with bayonets reversed going to the grave and the lively jig or quickstep as they return. (Diary of Isabel Emerson, in *Pen Portraits of Alexandria,* page 242)

With mounting casualties, a mortuary industry soon flourished in town and over sixteen hundred Union soldiers were embalmed and sent North.

The killing and suffering came to an end on April 9, 1865, when General Lee surrendered his army to General Grant at Appomattox Court House. For native Alexandrians it was a day of despair and gloom. Union soldiers and sympathizers, however,

The Construction Corps of the U.S. Military Railroad was organized and developed into a highly efficient force under Gen. Herman Haupt who in early 1862 had been called to head the effort of reconstruction and operation of all railroad activities under the Army of the Potomac in Northern Virginia, with headquarters in Alexandria. It was the responsibility of the Corps to repair trackage and rebuild bridges destroyed by Confederate raids and accidents. This is a view of the Corps' lumberyard on the river front where stacks of railroad ties and planks are being dressed with hand planes. This is the approximate site of the later Agnew's Shipyard. The houses at the top of the embankment are those in the 400, 500, and 600 blocks of South Lee Street, most of which are still standing, but those on the flats below, including a number of flounders, have long since dis- appeared. The large structure in the left background, built about 1800 by Thomas Vowell, Jr., was the home of Edgar Snowden and his family from 1842 till the second decade of the twentieth century. Snowden was the editor of the Alexandria Gazette. The house was purchased in 1939 by Hugo L. Black, justice of the U.S. Supreme Court, and remained his residence till his death.
National Archives

The two major staging and supply areas on the Potomac River used by the Union Army were located at Alexandria and Aquia Creek, about twenty-five miles downriver. Because of numerous obstructions in the form of wide creeks and swamps, no railroad connection had been completed between the two before the war, so it was necessary to transport loaded boxcars and locomotives by water. Gen. Herman Haupt's Construction Corps solved the problem with car floats created by tying four Schuylkill barges together, covering them with long timbers and laying tracks atop these, sufficient to haul sixteen cars and/or locomotives. Such a float is shown in this view to the right of the wharf which had three adjustable ramps at its end. Cars to be transported to Aquia Creek were shoved up these ramps and onto the float, which was then pushed downriver by a tug-like steamboat. This dock was located near the outlet of the Alexandria Canal.
Photograph by Capt. A. J. Russell, National Archives

This fascinating view of Alexandria's waterfront, looking north towards Washington, was taken in 1864 from the town's largest building, the Pioneer Mill. It shows all the buildings, mostly warehouses, facing the Strand from Duke Street and gives an idea of the large variety of vessels to be seen during the period of occupation, including the large white side-wheeler docked at the foot of Prince Street. Local residents, unless they had proven their loyalty to the Union, were forbidden in this area, and palisades in the form of high timber fences with gates were constructed a block or so inland across all the streets leading to the waterfront. It is interesting to study this photograph with a magnifying glass and to pick out the activities taking place on the boats and ships and on the docks, including what looks like an old man sitting in the morning sun in front of the building on the lower left corner.

celebrated wildly in the streets as a victory parade formed at the end of North Washington Street and wended its way through the city. In a letter to his wife, Capt. R. D. Pettit, Union inspector of prisons, described the plight of returning Confederate soldiers and the unsanitary conditions which prevailed in the city that torpid summer:

June 5, 1865—Large numbers of the rebels have returned here and taken the oath—Some of them are minus legs, arms, etc.—for my part I wish it was their heads they lost for in truth I do not put much faith in their oaths. The city is full of troops and stragglers and some excesses have been committed.

August 9, 1865; . . . This city as you know has not a single sewer—all the filth is allowed to drain itself into the gutters and thence to the river. Many streets are so nearly level that the filthy green water and garbage from kitchens may constantly be seen in the gutters and as a rule in hot weather not a drop of filth reaches the river—it all being evaporated or absorbed by the hot paving stones . . . It is quite sickly there—many deaths occur daily—one undertaker told me that he had sold the last week 108 coffins. ("Prison Life in Civil War Alexandrian" by T. Michael Miller in *Northern Virginia Heritage*, October 1987)

The social fabric of old Alexandria would never be the same. While a hundred or more of its young men had died in defense of the Confederacy, an influx of Northern merchants had established many new businesses in Alexandria. Returning refugees discovered that new faces and firms greeted them upon their arrival.

By July 1865 the U.S. War Department had abolished the office of military governor and during the summer months, outlying forts, blockhouses, and army camps were dismantled and sold at public auction. Alexandria, which had been a major Federal supply depot during the conflict had received, issued, and transferred from

1861-1865, . . . more than 64,000 pounds of wood, 81,000,000 pounds of corn, 412,000,000 pounds each of oats and hay and 530,000,000 pounds of coal . . . (James G. Barber, *Alexandria in the Civil War* (Lynchburg, Virginia: H. E. Howard, Inc., 1988, page 103)

Indeed, U.S. military railroad property alone in the city was valued at more than two million dollars. Eventually Alexandria returned to normalcy as the town's residents tried to rebuild their shattered lives. It would be many years, however, before the ugly scars of the Civil War would heal. Besides the personal losses suffered by its citizens, Alexandria's economy was devastated and it entered a period of malaise from which it did not totally recover until World War II. In addition, the surrounding landscape was totally denuded of trees, the harbor lay in ruins with its wharves rotting in the sun and hundreds of decrepit buildings were in desperate need of repair. As 1865 drew to a close, Alexandria's future certainly was not bright as it entered the Reconstruction Era.

This is a wartime view of the residence of Gen. John P. Slough (209 South St. Asaph Street), military governor of Alexandria from August 1862 to July 1865. The double brick structure (209-211) was originally composed of separate brick (211) and frame (209) dwellings. The lot at 211 was purchased by John Janney in 1809 and the house he built remained his home until his death in 1823. It was purchased in 1847 by William McVeigh who then bought the frame tenement next door (209) in 1851, tore down the frame, erected the present structure and remodeled the adjoining house to match it. (211 South St. Asaph was restored about 1960). Just beyond is the Custom House which also housed the Post Office (erected in 1858) and across Prince Street is the facade of the handsome Greek revival Second Presbyterian Church dating from 1840.

From the latter part of 1862 till the end of the war, Alexandria had a military governor in the person of Gen. John P. Slough, an eccentric and bellicose man. Born in Cincinnati on February 1, 1829, he was expelled from the Ohio legislature at the age of twenty-one for striking another member with his fists. He then moved to the Kansas Territory and later to Denver in 1860 where he became actively engaged in military affairs and was made a colonel of the First Colorado Infantry. His troops were sent to New Mexico where, in direct defiance of explicit orders by his commanding officer, he engaged Confederate units and defeated them. He immediately went to Washington where President Lincoln appointed him brigadier general of volunteers and became military governor of Alexandria where he had numerous unpleasant confrontations with other army commanders who served within his sphere of influence. Following the war he was named chief justice of New Mexico Territory where "his imperious temper rendered him very unpopular." He confronted a member of the Territorial senate who sought to censure Slough for unprofessional conduct and, in the affray, Slough was shot and died on December 17, 1867. The Alexandria Gazette on December 28, 1867, in noting his demise, stated that he "was at one time in command in this place, where he was well known." While in Alexandria he occupied either as a residence or as headquarters both the Francis L. Smith house at 511 Wolfe Street and the McVeigh house at 209 South St. Asaph Street. Photographs show General Slough and his staff and the members of his military band. Portrait courtesy of Alexandria-Washington Lodge No. 22; Band courtesy of Marie Goods Flynn, Alexandria Library

The depot of the Alexandria, Loudoun & Hampshire Railroad Company, located on the northeast corner of North Water (Lee) and Princess streets, was taken over by the Federal Quartermaster Department during the war. A part of the wood palisade, sealing off the waterfront from Alexandria citizens and possible Confederate raids, is seen to the left. Parts of the Canal basin and locks may be seen to the rear. An article from the Rockingham Virginia Register quoted in the Alexandria Gazette November 7, 1859) stated that this railroad is "putting a new face on the ragged and unsightly part of the city selected for its depot . . . a large and commodious building, and admirably suited to the purposes for which it is intended. The workmen are driving ahead with the spirit of railroad activity, and soon this important interest will be felt in the commercial life of the city." Eighteen months later, the city was occupied, thus bringing to a halt virtually all business activity owned or operated by the local citizenry.
National Archives

The Orange & Alexandria Railroad, headquartered in Alexandria, was chartered in 1848, laid its tracks to the southwest as far as Gordonsville, and by 1859 had extended its service to Lynchburg. On the outbreak of war, the line was in a very hazardous and exposed position so President John S. Barbour, member of an old and distinguished Virginia family and a former U.S. congressman, organized crews to move nearly all the sixteen locomotives and a great majority of the rolling stock then in use to south of Manassas Junction to keep them out of Federal hands. The roundhouse, located near the crossing of Duke and South Henry streets, was a circular brick structure with a turntable in the middle surrounded by stalls in which engines could be housed, cleaned, and repaired. The open cupola and clerestory windows afforded light in the center of the building but one wonders how much light actually could penetrate the glass of the windows considering the enormous mounts of smoke produced by the locomotives. This view is looking east toward the center of town.
National Archives

A somewhat later view of the east side of the roundhouse, with newly installed platform on top of the cupola, shows USMRR locomotive Lion, built in New Jersey in 1862 (which appears to be moving, but not likely since two men are standing on the track in front of it) and the yards and administrative offices of the Orange & Alexandria Railroad. It is interesting to note the discarded wooden locomotive cab and stave pilots (cow catchers) in the right foreground. Engines which were damaged by raid or accident were constantly being repaired and/or rebuilt in the railroad shops. It may well be assumed that the story-and-a-half structure (with dormers) on the left, predates the laying of the yards and erection of railroad buildings by many years. Southern Railroad

This series of photographs from the Brady Collection in the National Archives gives a fascinating panoramic view of the area surrounding the yards from the cupola of the Orange & Alexandria Railroad roundhouse, circa 1863.

A. The shops for the O&ARR where maintenance and repair work were performed on the rolling stock, are shown here in their entirety and these original brick buildings, unique in their unaltered state, remained standing until the late 1970's when South Henry Street was merged with Patrick Street in an effort to alleviate the ever increasing traffic problem caused by residents of the eastern part of Fairfax County traveling through the city on their daily trips to and from Washington, D.C. The writer recalls visiting the Alexandria Lumber Company which occupied these structures for a number of years and, on the right, looking at the rafters and roof supports (in the right-hand long shop structure) which had become blackened and soot covered more than a hundred years before by the smoke of locomotives chuffing in and out through the large entryway into the building. The large structure to the left of center (above the long, low, building in the southeastern view) shows the backside of the Hill House (The Shadows) located at 617 South Washington Street and the small white building to the left of the square smoke stack is the Village Chapel Sunday School organized by the Methodist Episcopal Church, South, in 1857 and located on Gibbon Street.

B. In this southern view a part of the O&ARR shops appears, and to the left of Henry Street (center) stand several much earlier structures which had become surrounded by the expanding yards and activities of the railroad. The dormered house in right foreground stood just to the east of the O&ARR offices and served as a hospital. Above it is the old Makley House (corner of Henry and Wilkes streets) which was replaced by the Southern Railway test shops in the 1920s. The mouth of Hunting Creek, flowing into the Potomac River, is seen at the top, behind which is the eminence on which the present day Belle Haven residential development is located.

C. The administrative offices of the O&ARR are shown in this southwest view. Across Hunting Creek is seen the almost totally denuded land rising above and behind the stream, the removal of virtually all trees being considered a necessity to prevent hiding places for possible Confederate infiltrators as well as providing much needed fuel for railroad locomotives. One of the largest of the

forts in the defenses of Washington chain, Fort Lyon, may be seen in the distant hill to the right of center. It commanded a fine overview of the Southern sympathizing but Northern-occupied town and fortunately for the inhabitants no shots were ever fired in her direction.

D. Now facing west, we see the yard rails merge into the O&ARR single track route to Manassas and ultimately to Gordonsville and Lynchburg. Trackage and bridges were constantly being destroyed, mostly by Confederates in order to slow down any movement by the U.S. Military Railroad into territory controlled by the South, and the Construction Corps was kept busy repairing or replacing these vital parts of the railroad program.

E. Practically every kind of rolling stock including engines, may be seen in these photographs: hospital cars, box cars, cattle cars, flat cars, gondolas, and passenger cars. The twelve hundred to fifteen hundred blocks of Duke Street cross from right to left and in the immediate center partially hidden by trees is the old Price and Birch Company slave pen which by the time of this picture, was serving as a military prison housing mostly drunken and criminally inclined Union soldiers, unrepentant townspeople, and some hangers on. Shuter's Hill rises in the background on top of which sits Fort Ellsworth, named for the first Yankee martyr. Fort Ellsworth was another in the series of forts established mostly in Virginia to protect Washington from possible raids or attacks by Confederate forces. Other major forts within Alexandria were Battery Rogers, Fort Ward, and Fort Worth. The burned house (right hand edge) was rumored to have been destroyed by contrabands since this building stood in a whole city block which contained housing for them. Contraband was the name applied to recently escaped or freed blacks, most being former slaves who migrated from all over the countryside to the nearest town where they thought they might be taken care of. Their ever increasing number in Alexandria during the war period created many problems. While many obtained jobs working on the waterfront as stevedores, teamsters, or in the railroad yards, many others were drifters. In addition to housing, heroic efforts were made to provide schooling for their children, classes being set up in the Lancastrian School building on Washington Street. This northwest view shows the area of town which was to some known shortly as "West End."

F. The final picture looking north with Duke Street (1100 and part of 1200 block) forms the edge of the yards. The

B

handsome brick house (center) still stands even though it has seen better days and there are other buildings which may be picked out which are in existence today. The walls of the burned house (lefthand on Duke) were subsequently used in rebuilding and it stands today much as it did as reconstructed shortly after the war's end. The distant view indicates the large number of Union encampments surrounding the town on the virtually treeless field. The large structure in the upper right corner is "Colross," home of the Masons and Smoots for several generations.

All photographs except B, National Archives Photograph B, Ansco Collection

A

C

D

E

F

Battery Rodgers was located nearly one-half mile below the wharves and populous portion of Alexandria along the waterfront block bounded by Jefferson, Union, Lee, and Green streets. Initially, it was referred to as the Water Battery but on September 17, 1863, it was renamed "Battery Rogers after Fleet Captain G. W. Rogers, U.S. Navy, killed August 17, 1863, on a naval attack upon Ft. Wagner, Charleston Harbor, South Carolina." The fortification included a hospital, slaughter houses, and barracks. Of particular interest however, were the five 200-pound Parrott rifles and an enormous fifteen-inch Rodman gun which were mounted at the Battery. The Rodman was the heaviest cannon utilized in the defenses of Washington and it alone weighed twenty-five tons and could project a 302 pound shell a maximum range of 4,680 yards. This photograph shows a lone sentinel standing guard above the 15" Rodman gun; and the battery with its bomb proofs.
National Archives, Brady Collection

Located on the west side of the 700 block of North Washington Street, the Catalpa Lot long served as a drill field for the local Alexandria militia. Its name was possibly due to a prevalence of catalpa trees in the vicinity and its use probably became necessary when the open area around the Market Square was gradually taken over by new buildings. A young private, Edgar Warfield, remarked in his A Confederate Soldier's Memoirs that: "... we were required to drill for an hour each afternoon and the ladies of the city both young and old, congregated to witness our evolutions ..." On May 20th, 1861, Judith McGuire, a resident of Seminary Hill, Fairfax County, Virginia, recorded in her diary: "Yesterday evening we rode to the parade ground in Alexandria; it

was a beautiful but sad sight. How many of these young, brave boys may be cut off, or maimed for life!" (Judith McGuire, Diary of a Southern Refugee During the War, page 16).

The troops in this etching are not Confederate but an occupation force of the Seventy-first New York Regiment.

The building in the background is the Mount Vernon Cotton Factory and the house to the right was called Dundas Castle because it was owned by former Alexandria merchant John Dundas. After the war, the house was abandoned and was considered for many years to be haunted.

The Thin Grey Line
Standing in front of the R. E. Lee Camp Hall at 806 Prince Street, these survivors of the seventeenth Virginia Regiment are proud of the role they played in trying to secure Southern Independence. After the War Between the States, the R. E. Lee Camp of the United Confederate Veterans was organized in 1884 with the purpose of establishing a fraternal organization to provide for the welfare of their comrades, widows, and families and to promote an interest in Southern heritage

and the late Confederacy. During the early years of the organization, they met in a room in the former Green Furniture Factory at the southeast corner of Prince and Fairfax streets. In 1903 the veterans purchased the old DeLagnel estate at 806 Prince Street. This beautiful edifice had been constructed by the Reverend James T. Johnson, rector of St. Paul's Church, shortly after 1850. A man of wealth from Savannah, Georgia, Parson Johnston built his palatial home utilizing many architectural details reminiscent of his native city.

As the membership of R. E. Lee Camp dwindled, the veterans decided to deed their home in 1922 to the ladies of the Mary Custis Lee— Seventeenth Virginia Regiment Chapter, United Daughters of the Confederacy. The building is currently owned by this organization and houses a fine museum of Confederate relics including the famous camp chair used by General Lee during the late unpleasantness.
Gift of Courtland L. Warfield

CONFEDERATE VETERANS.

806

The mammoth building in the foreground at the southeast corner of Wolfe and South St. Asaph streets was constructed by renowned Alexandria lawyer, Francis H. Smith. Previously, John Vowell, a wealthy Alexandria merchant and Smith's father-in-law, resided in a two-story frame building on this corner. The house, one of the largest in old Alexandria, was subsequently seized by Union military authorities and converted first into military Gov. John Slough's headquarters and then into U.S. military hospital. It contained room for one hundred beds and there are reports that sol-

diers carved their names on the back of the structure. General Robert E. Lee visited his lawyer, Francis Smith, at this house in 1870 in an attempt to regain possession of Arlington House.

The handsome tuscan villa (beyond the Smith residence) had formerly served as a ward of the first division general hospital. Notice the barriers placed around the young saplings in front of the fence. These were erected to keep horses and roaming cows from eating the bark off the trees, thus killing them.
Alexandria Library

95

Erected in 1851-1852, this Greek Revival building at the northwest corner of Prince and Lee streets housed the Bank of the Old Dominion before it was seized by the Union Army and converted into the Chief Commisary's office. The rather self-satisfied group of men has Federal Army officers as well as a number of civilians who, one is led to think, just might include a Northern-sympathizing local scalawag or two.
National Archives

B-5238

These silent rows of tombstones are testimony to the thousands of Union soldiers who died in Alexandria military hospitals. Frequently the bodies of officers would be embalmed and sent to grieving relatives. Others, the majority of whom were enlisted men, were interred in the Soldiers'

Cemetery on Wilkes Street extended. The Alexandria Common Council leased the property to the federal government for 999 years on June 1, 1862, for eight hundred dollars. A deed of release giving the U.S. government clear title to the land was executed in April 1875.

In August 1876 the pinehead boards which marked the soldiers graves were replaced with stone slabs. Confederate soldiers who died in Alexandria hospitals were initially interred in the Soldiers' (National) Cemetery until December 1879 when their bodies were exhumed by the Southern Memorial Association and reinterred in Christ Church graveyard on North Washington Street.

Besides the National Cemetery on Wilkes Street, Union soldiers were also buried at the Union and Penny Hill cemeteries early in the war. Whether their remains were moved to the Soldiers' Cemetery is not known.
National Archives, Brady Collection

As the north geared for war, the topography and quietude of Shuter's Hill was dramatically altered. After the Union invasion of Alexandria, New York Zouaves immediately began digging trenches and fortifying Shuter's Hill on May 25, 1861. This strategic fortification would be called Fort Ellsworth in honor of Col. Elmer E. Ellsworth, the fallen Northern hero. Located several hundred yards behind the current George Washington Masonic Memorial, it was one of sixty-eight forts which by 1863 would make Washington the most secured capital in the world. President Lincoln and his retinue visited the fort in 1862. This photograph shows a fine interior view of the citadel.
National Archives

This is the Mansion House Hospital on the east side of the 100 block of North Fairfax Street. After 1848, James Green, noted Alexandria furniture manufacturer, added on to the old Bank of Alexandria (southeast corner of Cameron and North Fairfax Street), thus transforming the building into the Green's Mansion House hotel — one of the premier hotelries on the East Coast. When the War Between the States erupted, this fine old building along with many others in Alexandria was confiscated by Union military authorities for use as a hospital. The Mansion House Hospital, as it was called, was headquarters for the first division General Hospital and was until 1864 the largest medical facility in Alexandria. "A very convenient arrangement, in this structure was the presence of a sort of dumb waiter, by which not only provisions were transported from one story to another with dispatch and promptitude, but also by which the wounded were more easily raised or lowered on stretchers from one floor to another." In March 1864 a tragic accident occurred at this facility. One of the patients who was insane, managed to get through a window in his ward and catch hold of the eaves of the building. There he hung for a short time and finally "fell upon the balustrade below, injuring himself so seriously as to die in a few hours."

The barricades in the street to the left were erected to prevent surprise Confederate cavalry attacks against the vast quartermaster depot along the waterfront. In the far background to the right, one can see the cupola of the James Green furniture factory which was situated on the southeast corner of Prince and Fairfax streets.
Library of Congress

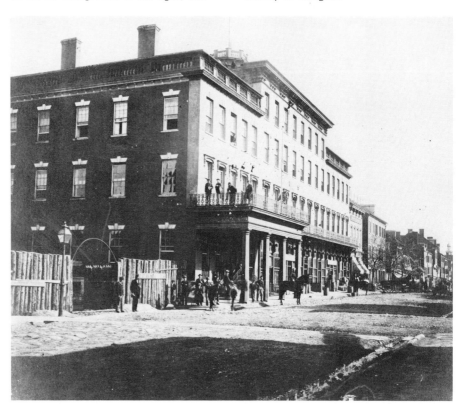

Two articles in the Alexandria Gazette give a concise history of this establishment. "The Soldiers' Rest, designed for the accommodation of U.S. troops arriving and remaining temporarily in this place, recently built at the upper end of Duke street, near the O&ARR depot, is said to be the largest and most complete establishment for the purpose contemplated, in the U.S., or any where else. It has sleeping apartments, bathing rooms, reading rooms, etc., etc. The estimated cost of the whole establishment is $50,000." (October 31, 1863) "The building and fences on the property at the upper end of Duke Street, belonging to Geo. Kephart, and known laterly as the Soldiers' Rest, were disposed of on Saturday morning last, at public auction, by officers of the United States government, to gentlemen of this city, at comparatively cheap rates, and the buildings will be speedily removed."(Alexandria Gazette, November 12, 1866). It was located on the south side of Duke Street, at the end of West Street and nearly opposite the Slave Pen.

A fascinating panorama of Alexandria, facing generally east, was taken from the top of Shuter's Hill in 1864, when the Forty-fourth New York Infantry was encamped on the hill. In this scene from the panorama, Hunting Creek flows into the Potomac and is crossed by a bridge (containing a block house at its center) carrying the King's Highway south towards Fredericksburg and Richmond. Catts' (Drover's) Tavern appears in the group of buildings at the foot of the hill. National Archives, Brady Collection

A circa 1864 view of Duke Street is this photograph taken from atop the Pioneer Mill on the waterfront. Facing west, one quickly observes the stockade fence across the street at its junction with Union. While most structures east of Union Street (foreground) are now gone, many existing buildings may be seen beyond including the Presbyterian Meeting House belfry, the steeples of both St. Mary's Catholic and First (Downtown) Baptist churches and the upper story of the recently erected custom house (flat-roofed white edifice just to the right of center, slightly below the horizon). Courtesy of the U.S. Army History Institute

When the market had an overabundance
of country folk bringing their wares into
town for sale, especially at holiday times,
the area expanded out onto the sidewalks
of Royal Street. This circa 1895 scene is
presumed to be before Christmas because
of the presence of greens (particularly
running cedar) for sale. The west side
of the 100 block of North Royal is seen
in the background with the fine jewelry
shop of Henry R. Wildt on the left and
Gadsby's Tavern at the far end of the
block (on the right)
O'Brien/Hulfish Collection

A Map of Alexandria showing numerous places of interest. Taken from the 1877 Hopkins City Atlas of Alexandria, Virginia.

liquor dealers, 4 dentists and 1 distiller. Politically, by the terms of the new 1869 Virginia Constitution, Alexandria and every political entity within the Commonwealth with a population of 10,000 or over became an independent city.

Tragedy befell the city in 1871 when its venerable City Hall and Market House was totally destroyed by fire. In the portion of the building on Royal Street:

> there was a fine brick building, from which rose a splendid steeple constructed in 1817 . . . Shrouded in a sheet of fire the steeple bent downward and hung suspended until it was consumed carrying with it masses of mortar, bricks and timber. . . In the third story of this building was the Alexandria museum in which were deposited many relics of the early days of the city which were of great interest and value associated as they were with the Revolutionary War. (*Alexandria Gazette,* May 19, 1871)

Fortunately many of these relics were saved and are now housed in the George Washington Masonic National Memorial. In 1872, Adolph Cluss, noted Washington architect, submitted plans for a new city hall which was constructed by E. H. Delehay, builder. Funds for the steeple on the new building were donated by John Daingerfield, a town citizen and philanthropist.

It was during the 1872 presidential election that Alexandrians were once again able to exercise their franchise for the first time since 1860. Surprisingly the election resulted in a tie vote locally between President Grant, the sitting Republican and Horace Greeley, the Democratic challenger.

During the 1880s Alexandria began to acquire modern conveniences with the introduction of the telephone in 1881, rural free mail delivery in 1887, and electricity by 1889. For the most part it was a quiet town with a modest amount of industry and commerce. Gone however were the halcyon days of the golden epoch when Alexandria's harbor brimmed with ships, its merchant princes quaffed madeira at a local coffee house, and lines of wagons parked on Commerce Street waiting to unload their precious harvest of wheat and grain. Overshadowed by its neighbors Washington and Baltimore, Alexandria exhibited a charm of its own. One writer commented in 1887 that:

> he enjoyed the town's quaint old buildings with their arched doors, old knockers, latticed and dormer windows and immense chimneys. The situation of the town is beautiful. It rises from the harbor like "Genoa the Superb." The expanse of the river is like that of a fine bay. In every direction there is charming scenery and

the air is wholesome. One can live much cheaper than in Washington . . . I hope Alexandria will never lose its mature and leisurely way . . . Even now many in Government employ reside in the ancient town. (*Alexandria Gazette,* October 27, 1887)

Although the future appeared propitious, Alexandria suffered a severe setback in 1889 when a devastating flood caused considerable damage to business houses along the waterfront. More destructive than the flood of 1856" all along the Strand from the lower shipyard to the old American coal company, several feet of water were on the first floors of every building, while Union Street from Prince to the cove above Fishtown was an unbroken canal, suggestive of a scene in Venice . . ." (*Alexandria Gazette,* June 3, 1889)

Initially the Gay Nineties was an epoch of economic prosperity but ended on a sour note of financial decline and depression. The town's population had advanced relatively slowly after the war with 13,570 inhabitants in 1870; 13,659 in 1880; 14,339 in 1890 and 14,528 in 1900. Although several new businesses were established including the Potomac Shoe Company by Frederick Paff in 1890, the end of the century witnessed a general economic malaise. Some of the reasons for the decline can be attributed to the large number of flour mills which were constructed within a hundred mile radius of Alexandria — thus curtailing the grain trade. In addition the sugar trade, once a very lucrative business, was dislocated by Baltimore's importation of cheap European sugars. In June 1897, Alexandria was visited by one of the most destructive fires in its history as flames devoured the old Pioneer Mill at the foot of Duke Street and the entire Strand east of Union from Duke to Prince Streets. The conflagration left a ruinous path of tottering chimneys, burnt walls and charred wharves "which in times past were the receptacles of shiploads of West Indies sugar and molasses and upon which direct importation of articles from nearly every clime had been deposited." (*Alexandria Gazette,* June 3, 1897)

In 1898 the Alexandria Light Infantry heeded President McKinley's call for troops to fight the Spanish in Cuba. War fever once again pervaded the town as Alexandria troops gathered at the Washington Southern Railroad depot in anticipation of their departure for Richmond on May 14, 1898. Few, however, saw active combat before the war was concluded by a peace treaty between the United States and Spain in December 1898.

As Alexandria prospered and became more populous, housing developments and suburban communities sprang up in the environs surrounding the

This interesting winter scene, taken circa 1864, from the roof of Green's Mansion House hotel takes in the northeast quadrant of the town, an area seldom photographed, probably due to the fact that it was heavily industrialized, containing the city gas works as well as many warehouses and mills and possibly because the section had a rather unsavory reputation and numbers of its houses were considered to be "sporting" or bawdy in nature. The large building to the left is the back half of the Jonah Thompson House (facing 209-211 North Fairfax Street) while the three-and-one-half story structure on which is a painted sign "Delahay & Kemp Manufacturers of Sash Doors & Blinds" housed the building and contracting business of Edwin H. Delahay. He had moved to Alexandria in 1856 from Maryland and remained here until 1874 when he left for Baltimore. While a resident of this town, probably during the period of occupation, he served on the Common Council and later was the contractor for the building of the new City Hall in 1871-1872. This building was later occupied by the Hill Bakery Company. The large building directly to the east (across Lee Street in the 200 block north) had been home to the Jamieson Cracker Bakery until purchased by George R. Hill who moved his bakery operation across to the Delahay and Kemp Building. The large structure on the waterfront (near the right side) is the "Globe" or Ladd's Mill.
(U.S. Army Historical Institute, Carlisle Barracks, Pennsylvania)

An interesting octagonal house, located on Leesburg Pike (King Street extended) about a mile from the western limits of town, was taken over for use as the Seventh Brigade Hospital, General Slocum's Brigade 1861-1862. The Theological Seminary appears in the background to the left of the structure. The Alexandria Gazette on November 22, 1866, reported the burning of the "Octagon House" under rather mysterious circumstances. The accused arsonist was a man from Philadelphia who was known to have been connected with the Provost Marshall's office during the late war. We have been unable to determine whether or not he was convicted of the dastardly crime.
Perkins Library, Duke University

A sight, seldom seen today, is an ox with its cart, resting in the shadow of Gadsby's Tavern, the wood cover of the sidewalk opening of the underground ice-house appearing in the foreground. The three buildings in the center background (400 block Cameron, north side) occupy the site of Liberty Hall, Alexandria's first theatre, built in 1799. It burned in 1872 and some of its walls may be incorporated in these structures. The building to the right, housing the Harlow and Brothers grocery and feed store which just happened to sell liquors, too, replaced the old George Tavern which was demolished in 1870.
Gift of Deborah Cooney

city. As early as 1892 a consortium of businessmen from Philadelphia and Alexandria established a community called New Alexandria across Great Hunting Creek on sixteen hundred acres. This venture failed in 1924 when the New Alexandria company declared bankruptcy and sold all its acreage at public auction. George Washington Park, Rosemont, Del Ray, and Braddock Heights were other enclaves which soon became bedroom communities for Alexandria's middle and upperclass residents.

The Alexandria of the early twentieth century was a town of many manufacturing industries and commercial enterprises including the Robert Portner Brewing Company, the Bel Pre and Old Dominion Glass works, and the Potomac Yards, the nation's largest railroad classification yard at that time (1903).

When the United States entered World War I in 1917, Alexandria was still a small southern town of approximately sixteen thousand inhabitants. From the very first days of the conflict there was a great display of patriotism in the old seaport town. In March 1917 the city was bedecked in holiday attire with "Old Glory" fluttering from many residences and places of business as townspeople signaled their support for President Wilson's actions against Germany. Throughout the spring and early summer, elements of the Alexandria Light Infantry could been seen drilling hard throughout the city as "the officers and non-coms took little groups of rookies daily and instructed them in various maneuvers." On July 31, 1917, the Alexandria Light Infantry was mustered into federal service and by September the troops of Company G, First Regiment of Virginia had been ordered to Anniston, Alabama, for basic training. As the city's young men went to fight at the Marne and other famous battlefields in France, Alexandria was transformed into a workshop for the war effort. Demand for housing and real estate soared as workers flooded the city and new industries were created. On December 7, 1917, the U.S. Shipping Board Emergency Fleet Corporation negotiated a contract with the Groton Iron Works of Connecticut to construct

twelve metal vessels each costing $1,504,000 at Jones Point. Alexandria was also home to other war-related industries including the Briggs Aeroplane Company which commenced operation in the 600 block of North St. Asaph Street in 1917 and the Atlantic Life Boat Company, charged with manufacturing a thousand steel life boats for the U.S. Government in 1918. Perhaps the city's best known munition facility was the Torpedo Plant at the foot of Cameron Street. A contract for the erection of two buildings, a four-story machine shop and a two-story storage building, was let on October 14, 1918, but the war had ended before the first torpedo came off the line in November 1920.

With the signing of the Treaty of Versailles in 1919, it was not long before Alexandria's fighting men returned home to a victory parade and pageant staged in their honor the week of June 11 to 14th 1919.

> As the heroes marched through the court of honor erected on Washington Street between King and Prince about 1,000 public school children strew flowers in their paths, . . . The boys made an excellent showing and were given a rousing ovation as they marched by. Thousands of people lined King Street and cheered the passing pageant . . . The soldiers participating were marched with a firm step and were the synacure of all eyes . . . The fire apparatus was bedecked with flags, pennants, bunting and flowers and showed conclusively that the fire laddies had spared no pain in preparing for the event . . . Hundreds of soldiers, civilians, their sweethearts and others enjoyed the block dance which was later staged in the court of honor.
> (*Alexandria Gazette*, June 11, 1919)

Thus as the terrible conflict drew to a close, Alexandrians were duly proud of their soldiery and the role they had played in defeating the Central Powers. As Alexandria entered the Roaring Twenties, it basked in the sunshine of peace and relative economic prosperity.

A little known and even less publicized aspect of Alexandria's business community was the presence of certain "working girls" who occupied some of the town's more historic buildings, particularly in the waterfront area. The establishments where these ladies worked were scattered through the older part of town and one of the last, and best known "sporting houses" was that which made use of the three white buildings in this 1924 photograph located on the northwest corner of Queen and North Lee streets. The writer, while trying to identify these buildings in the mid 1950s (they had long since been torn down), knocked on a rooming house door across the street which was answered by a middle aged gentleman who, when shown the photograph, laughed and said, "That's Rosie Moore's." He explained to the innocent questioner that Miss Moore had been the proprietress of a rather extensive organization, occupying the three buildings in question and who,

on Sunday afternoons when business was either slow or illegal would hire a carriage to transport her "girls," dressed in white for purity or, maybe, innocence, around the town in order to regain some fresh air which was not always available during the business week. Capt. Fred Tilp, the late expert on all things concerning the Potomac River, is known to have stated that some of these ladies even occupied houseboats on the river's edge, but the writer, being young, cannot attest to the accuracy of his statements. An article in the Alexandria Gazette on June 12, 1914, described the city's planned closing of the "red light district" and included a short history of prostitution in Alexandria. It seems that it had always existed to a certain extent but that during the War Between the States "an army of lewd men and women followed the (occupying) soldiers to this city. They roosted in every section, some of which now form the residential neighborhoods where the most disgraceful orgies were conducted. There were five brothels on Prince Street, between Royal and Fairfax, and equally as many more on Prince Street, between Lee and Union and on Wolfe Street, between Fairfax and Royal . . . At the close of the war the work of eviction began, and in a few years the undesirables gradually took up their abode in the most undesirable quarter of the city, where they have remained until their nests have been disturbed by the orders of the court." Photograph by W. P. Gray, Valentine Museum

The southeast corner of Cameron and North Alfred Street was purchased by William S. Moore who operated a sugar refinery on the southern portion of this quarter-acre lot. In 1810, Alexandria ranked third in the nation as a major producer of sugar and this was one of three refineries in town. Circa 1808, Moore constructed the house (right) at 111 North Alfred Street and later conveyed it to Daniel McLean in 1815. McLean, a former baker, continued to operate the refinery and was also a successful wholesale and retail merchant. He was instrumental in establishing Saint Paul's Episcopal Church, having given the money to purchase the original church property at 216-220 South Fairfax Street in 1810. McLean's wife Lucretia was known for the beautiful flowers which grew in her garden at 111 North Alfred. Upon Daniel McLean's death in 1823 his executors sold his home and real estate to Hugh C. Smith. Smith was a son of the prosperous Alexandria china and glass merchant, Hugh Smith, who resided at what is now 105 North Alfred Street.

The large Victorian edifice in this photograph with the big bay windows was

owned by Mrs. Mary Marshall Foote in the 1870s. Wife of William H. Foote, she had previously resided at a plantation called Hayfield on Telegraph Road in Fairfax County. At one time this farm was owned by George Washington who later sold it to his nephew Lund Washington circa 1783. One of the most respected members of Alexandria society,

Mary Foote died in 1880 and her home was resided in by a number of inhabitants until it became a Scottish Rite Club in the 1930s. Unfortunately the house was razed in the 1950s and the site is now a parking lot.
Gift of William Triplett

Hidden from the view of most tourists, this unique Italian loggia as it appeared in 1924, in the rear of 209-211 North Fairfax Street was possibly designed by architect Benjamin Latrobe for Jonah Thompson, erstwhile mayor of the town from 1805 to 1808, merchant and later president of the Bank of Alexandria in 1819. The entire structure is monumental in scale and consists of two houses joined by a hyphen and entrance court. The front entrance is graced by two unusual arched doorways made of Aquia stone. Upon Jonah Thompson's death in 1834, his heirs sold the property to Benjamin Hallowell for $4,650. Hallowell's nephew, James, also a school teacher, purchased the building from his uncle four years later for $9,000. For many years he operated the female seminary at this location until its operation was interrupted by the War Between the States. After the conflict the Roman Catholic Church purchased the dwelling in 1868 and converted it into the first site of Saint Mary's Academy. The school continued in operation here until it moved to the Swann-Daingerfield Mansion at 706 Prince Street in 1905. Photograph by W. P. Gray, Valentine Museum

Located on the southwest corner of South Fairfax and Duke streets, this fine old eighteenth century house served as: (1) a Catholic school operated by the Sisters of Charity; (2) the residence of Dr. Francis Murphy; (3) the site of the Alexandria Infirmary. While operating a school in this building in the 1830s, the Sisters of Charity enrolled a young girl named Mary Jenkins. She married John Surratt in 1835 and later operated a tavern and post office at Surrattsville, now Clinton, Maryland. Widowed, she moved to Washington where she ran a boarding house which was used by John Wilkes Booth and his band of conspirators to plot the assassination of Abraham Lincoln and members of his cabinet. Upon Lincoln's murder on April 14, 1865, Mrs. Surratt, who was probably totally innocent of the plot, was arrested and subsequently hanged on July 7, 1865, along with three others whose complicity was certain.

Dr. Murphy (1812-1877) also resided in this house for many years and practiced medicine in Alexandria until his retirement circa 1874. Having grown infirm, he spent his last days being cared for by Mrs. Melissa Wood at her home, the Shadows, at 617 South Washington Street. Upon his death on May 24, 1877, he was buried at St. Mary's Catholic cemetery.

Shortly after the death of Dr. Murphy, his home became the first location of the Alexandria Infirmary. The brainchild of Julia Johns, the facility was opened here

in March 1873. The Alexandria Gazette of March 6, 1873, reported its opening: The Alexandria Infirmary . . . opened for the reception of patients on Monday last. (March 3). Dr. Powell is the resident and Drs. Lewis and Gibson the consulting physicians. Mrs. Timberlake, formerly of Fredericksburg, is the matron, and the services of excellent nurses have been engaged. The original construction of the building . . . was such as to make it easily divisible into two separate and distinct divisions, and this has been availed of with reference to the accommodation of male and female patients. Each division contains several rooms of different size and though all are furnished neatly and comfortably, and supplied with all the necessary conveniences of a sick chamber, those for pay patients present probably a more elaborate appearance, and those who occupy them can be attended by any physician whose services they may desire. The managers have made arrangements with the government for taking care of and treating all sailors arriving at this port who may require medical or surgical attention. (Alexandria Gazette, March 6, 1873)

The infirmary remained at this location until 1874. The house was razed about 1953.
Photograph by W. P. Gray, Valentine Museum

Founded in 1839 as a preparatory school for the Theological Seminary, the Episcopal High School was established on adjoining grounds purchased from the Howard family who had owned and occupied the land for a number of years. The school had its ups and downs in the early years, and it soon became a preparatory school for college rather than the Seminary itself. After being closed for four years while it served, along with the Sem-inary next door, as a hospital during the War Between the States, its reopening in 1865 began a climb to pre-eminence as an academically strong boys' "prep" school, drawing students from all over the country, particularly the Southern states, under the long tutelage of Head-master Lancelot Minor Blackford. This view shows the school buildings as they appeared in 1900.
Courtesy of Episcopal High School

The Royal Street side of the newly built City Hall and steeple (1872-1873) appears in this view taken shortly before the removal of the cobblestoned street surface. The two three-storied buildings to the right of Sharpshin Alley were also new since the very old structure which had housed the Rainbow Tavern had burned at the same time as the Market House fire in 1871. These were occupied for many years by representatives of two of Alexandria's oldest and highly respected families: Richard H. Wattles who ran a farm implement and hardware store and J. C. Milburn who had his grocery business next door. The ground floor of the City Hall was occupied by commercial enterprises such as groceries and butcher shops.
William A. Moore Collection, circa 1890

From the earliest times, one of the great fears of all citizens in a newly developing town (which consisted of mostly frame structures) was that of fire which, when out of control, could destroy vast numbers of buildings and their contents. This was no exception in Alexandria and by 1774, its first fire company, the Friendship, was formed. Within a few years, more fire companies were organized: the Sun (1776), the Relief Society (1788), the Star (1795) and the Hydraulion (1827). Several of these companies exist today.

Friendship was long ago deactivated and is today a museum operated by the

city; the Sun died shortly after the War Between the States; the Relief (one of its organizers was Justice Bushrod Washington) is now known as the Relief Truck and Engine Company, No. 1 (300 block Prince Street); the Star changed its name to the Columbia Steam Fire Engine Company when a new steam fire engine bearing that name was purchased and assigned to it by the city in 1871; the Hydraulion was dissolved around the turn of the twentieth century after which some members reorganized into the Reliance Company, now known as Engine Company No. 5.

Before the War Between the States, all

firefighting apparatus in Alexandria consisted of hand-drawn and hand-operated pumps (on wheels) and hose reels. The first two steam engines introduced locally were brought by Federal troops during the War Between the States when most firefighting activity was handled by the military. For the most part, the remaining remnants of the local companies were not allowed to respond to or to fight any fires but the equipment was used by the occupying troops in such a rough manner that most of it was destroyed or made useless by war's end, in addition to which the engine houses were left in bad states of repair. The U.S. government later paid

B

C

for repairs to the houses but paid little heed to claims for destroyed apparatus. The city managed to purchase one of the steam engines (its first) from military authorities after the war, and thus began the slow, agonizing movement toward a more modern and partially paid city fire department. The era of the horse-drawn ladder truck and the steam pumper, with all the excitement brought on by their appearances both when racing to fires or when clanking along in a parade, began to fade when the mechanization of the now consolidated department began with the purchase of an American LaFrance Triple Combination Pumper in 1915; by the early 1920s the entire Fire Department had been equipped with gasoline motor driven apparatus. The photographs show (A) a finely polished steamer pumper in front of the Columbia Engine House No. 4, prior to 1900 when it was located at 109 South St. Asaph Street and was probably prepared to enter a parade celebrating the Fourth of July. The engine company was moved some years ago and the firehouse is now occupied by a restaurant. (William A. Moore Collection); (B) the Friendship Fire House, built in 1855 in the 100 block of South Alfred Street, taken about 1900, which now houses a museum of firefighting equipment and memorabilia. (C) the Hydraulion Engine House built in 1856 with modification in 1872, in the 200 block of North Royal Street; it originally had a bell tower or steeple. This view was taken around the turn of the twentieth century after the demise of the company and removal of the tower. It now serves as a residence.
Milton Grigg Collection

1. Pate Haynes
2. William Bontz
3. Steven Taylor
4. Gil Simpson
5. James McEwen
6. William Price
7. Sam Ticer
8. Cudge Grady
9. Chief Wm Webster
10. Stephen Nightingale

Feb 22, 1883

11. Mayor C. E. Downham
12. Lieut James Smith
13. Frank Betts
14. Keith Davis
15. Rolley Henry
16. George Jones
17. Banner Young
18. Joshua Sherwood
19. Cash Brenner

This 1883 photograph of Alexandria's Finest was taken in front of the old Police Department situated on the west side of the 100 block of North Fairfax Street. Mayor E. E. Downham (gentleman wearing the stovepipe hat), Chief Webster (bearded officer) and the members of the Alexandria police force appear to enjoy posing before the cameraman's lens.

During its early history, Alexandria's police department was modeled after the British constabulary-nightwatch system. The constables who patrolled town and enforced order were a distinct organization from the night watchmen. In June 1858, with the passage of "An Act Concerning the Night Watch" these officers were also empowered to carry out their duties during daylight hours. Twelve years later on July 15, 1870, the dual system was abolished and a police board was created to supervise the activities of the twenty-one-man force. Each policeman was uniformed at his own expense and ordered to wear "a badge in the shape of a star."
(Edward Perlman, "Fire and Police Protection" in A Towne in Transition, 1977)

Born in Westphalia, Germany, on March 20, 1837, Robert Portner first came to the United States when he was sixteen years old. Before settling in Alexandria, he was engaged in the wholesale tobacco trade in New York City. During the outbreak of the War Between the States, he moved to Alexandria and established a small grocery business selling supplies to sutlers of both armies. After the conflict, Mr. Portner "organized three building and loan associations in Alexandria, of which he was president; he originated the Alexandria shipyards for the building and repair of vessels; he organized the

German-American Banking company, of which, also, he was made president . . . He was president of the Capital Construction company, president of the German Building association and a director in the following corporations: The American Security and Trust Company, of Washington; Riggs Fire Insurance Company of Washington, National Bank of Washington; Virginia Midland Railway company, National Bank of Manassas, etc." (Robert Portner, Men of Mark in Virginia, volume 5, page 350)

Robert Portner commenced the brewing business in Alexandria in 1864-1865. By 1883, a stock company had been formed with Robert Portner, president; Paul Muhlhauser, vice president; C. A. Strangman, secretary and treasurer. The output of the concern in 1883 was twenty-six thousand barrels and subsequently increased to sixty thousand barrels by 1890. The company's main facilities covered two acres bounded by Washington, Pitt, Wythe, and Pendleton streets with a railroad side track on St. Asaph Street. The main building was 160 by 60 feet, three stories high, of brick

and was used for storage of beer. A brew house five stories high of brick, 60 by 40 feet contained the most advanced equipment for brewing and the copper kettle had a capacity of 350 barrels. Adjoining the brewhouse was a barley elevator and storage room with a capacity of fifty thousand bushels of barley which was purchased from Canada and the West. A bottling house 40 by 60 feet two-stories high was also part of the brewing complex. During the late nineteenth century the old Mount Vernon Cotton Factory at 515 North Washington Street served as the company's bottling house. Known for their special brews called Vienna Cabinet and Tivoli, the Portner Company also owned part interest in fifty railroad cars and had branches in North and South Carolina and Georgia. For many years Alexandria's largest enterprise, the Portner Company was virtually destroyed when Virginia adopted Prohibition in 1915. It managed to continue, in operation producing soft drinks until 1920 when it closed down for good. Most of the buildings which comprised the two acres were demolished in the 1930s.

"Toonerville Trolley"—The story of developing railroads and their effects on Alexandria is yet to be written. Railroads in Alexandria were born, died, merged, went bankrupt, and were swallowed up by larger corporations, much of this brought about by the rivalry between the Pennsylvania Railroad and the Baltimore & Ohio Railroad for control of unbroken rail trackage between the North and the South. Alexandria was the geographical center through which all such East Coast rail activity had to pass. As a result, tracks ran the length of Union Street, and half the length of St. Asaph, Henry, and Fayette streets. It was not until the building of the elevated consolidated tracks west of the town proper (crossing at upper King Street) that, one by one, the downtown street tracks were abandoned, Union Street lasting until 1976. This unusual photograph taken about 1897, shows the "Toonerville Trolley"—a small locomotive, coal car, and single passenger car—which ran between Alexandria and Washington, standing in the 200 block of North Fayette Street beside its freight and passenger depot, following a heavy winter snowstorm. An 1890 consolidation of the Alexandria & Fredericksburg Railroad and the Alexandria & Washington Railroad had resulted in a new corporate entity called the Washington Southern Railway Company and it was under this title that the pictured train operated. Subsequently this line was acquired by the Richmond, Fredericksburg & Potomac Railway.
Gift of Mrs. David Abshire; from Frank Carlin

Potomac River fisheries were a major industry in the economic life of Alexandria as thousands of tons of shad, herring, and sturgeon were brought to town to be cleaned, cured and packed. With the approach of the fishing season (March through June), the fish wharves in Alexandria would be rented by the superintendent of police in January or February to the highest bidder. One region on the east side of Union Street between Princess and Oronoco, was known throughout the nineteenth century as Fishtown.

During the spring, rude huts constructed of ill-fitting lumber would be thrown together for the workers, mostly slaves, who frequented this shanty town. Some of the tenements were utilized as salting houses but the major portion were eating establishments with a large number of drinking facilities attached. Fights and brawls were common and many citizens forbade their children to ever frequent this unsavory area.

As soon as a schooner came alongside the wharf, its catch would be quickly sold and two men would go into the hold of the vessel and fill large buckets which would be hauled ashore and dumped. Almost immediately, negro women as shown in this photograph were busy at work cutting and cleaning the fish. Meanwhile a fish agent with his book and the agent of the wharf would settle their accounts. The scene of several fires, Fishtown was again destroyed by a blaze in 1896 and this scene probably dates prior to that time.

O'Brien/Hulfish Collection

Shipbuilding has been a part of Alexandria's heritage from its earliest days although her various boat and shipyards probably did considerably more ship repairing and maintenance work than actual building. There was a public yard during the Revolution which constructed government vessels to be used against the British naval forces in the Tidewater and Chesapeake Bay area. By 1800, Hunter's Shipyard had been established at the foot of Wolfe Street and it flourished for a considerable time along with other yards until the beginning of the War Between the States. Such activity for local purposes was shut down during the war and recovery was very slow during the Reconstruction period. During the 1870s there was a general economic slump in the shipbuilding industry and it was decided by some Northern builders (mostly from Maine) to move to the South where

ships' timbers were more readily available and monetary savings might be realized. This experimental maneuver led to the purchase of one of Alexandria's major shipyards, quickly named the Alexandria Marine Railway and Shipbuilding Company (at the foot of Franklin Street) by a relative newcomer, Robert Portner, who later made a fortune in the beer brewing business. The three marine railways were kept busy and a number of three-masted schooners were built and launched. Apparently Mr. Portner's other interests became paramount for he sold his business about 1881 to a local Potomac River coal dealer, John Parke Custis Agnew, who leased the yard to several New Englanders who, in turn, continued building large-sized schooners. The launching of a large ship was always a cause for celebration in Alexandria and this was particularly noted by large crowds at the christening on

Alexandria Marine Railway & Ship Building Company, ALEXANDRIA, VIRGINIA.

A unique work boat called the Potomac Long Boat *is shown under repairs at the Agnew shipyard, taken before 1900. O'Brien/Hulfish Collection*

July 21, 1883, of the largest ship built to that time. This was the William T. Hart *a 205 foot four-masted coasting vessel which was the seventh and largest class ship to be constructed in Alexandria in as many years. Her cost was estimated at forty-five thousand dollars, "she had four hatches fixed to work two at a time, and was provided with an engine to hoist the sails, anchors and cargo. The 'Hart's' cabin was handsomely fitted out with oak and red plush." (Donald G. Shomette, Maritime Alexandria, Alexandria Archaeology Center, 1985.) About this time the "Maine men" came to the realization that big ship construction in this area was not economically feasible since most of the fittings had to be manufactured elsewhere and shipped to Alexandria, so they abandoned their posts to return home to northern climes and large wooden shipbuilding in Alexandria came to*

an end. The Agnew Yard continued to operate, however, building small river vessels up to the beginning of World War I.

On December 7, 1917, following our entry into the First World War, the United States Shipping Board Emergency Fleet Corporation negotiated a contract with the Groton (Connecticut) Iron Works to construct twelve metal vessels, each costing $1,504,000, and since this enterprise was to be located on the newly filled land where Battery Cove had formerly existed, it caused great excitement in Alexandria. Although there were many top officers the strings seem to have been controlled by Charles W. Morse, member of an old and highly respected Bath, Maine, shipbuilding family. Mr. Morse had been caught up in the toils of the law before but had somehow managed to escape the claws of justice, so continued his questionable ways in the operation of

the Groton Iron Works subsidiary, the Virginia Shipbuilding Corporation. The keel-laying ceremony for the first ship was attended by President and Mrs. Wilson along with a large contingent of political notables from both Washington and Virginia. This same ship, a forty foot, 9,400 ton steel vessel named Gunston Hall, was the first down the ways when she was christened on February 23, 1919. Eight more ships were completed under the government contract, most named for members of the Morse family, but long before the final launching, the yard had become embroiled in a great controversy amid charges of fraud and misuse of government funds by many of the officials. Virginia Shipbuilding Corporation

Steam ferryboat service began as early as 1815 between Alexandria and Washington. It expanded over the years, various private companies being formed to provide this service, while other ferries were operated by railroads in conjunction with their rail activities. The Orange & Alexandria Railroad provided frequent trips from the ferry slip at the foot of King Street to the Seventh Street wharf in Washington. Just before Alexandria's occupation by Union troops in May 1861, the railroad sent one of its two ferryboats, the George Page, to the South where it was converted into a gunboat named City of Richmond by the Confederates. The Alexandria Steam Ferry Company, started in 1856, ran ferries across the river to Fox's ferry, Maryland, for many years, while other companies provided service to Oxon Run and Shepherd's Landing, Maryland. The Alexandria & Washington Steamboat Company, which had managed to survive the war, placed several new boats in service, two being double-ended sidewheelers, City of Washington and City of Alexandria built in 1868. By the time the latter vessel burned in 1892, it was said to have made more than seventy thousand round trips. With the advent of better railroad connections, the building of trolley lines, and finally the establishment of regularly scheduled bus lines, the need for ferryboats between Alexandria, Washington, and points on the Maryland shore decreased dramatically, even though one company managed to hold on till the early 1930s. This view shows the City of Alexandria tied up for repairs around 1888 at Agnews Shipyard located below the 600 block of South Lee Street.
(Gift of Ashby Reardon, Sr.)

While a good bit of riverboat service had originated in Alexandria prior to the War Between the States, the economic doldrums of the Reconstruction period left the town little chance to recover due to the fact that other larger coastal cities which had suffered little or no adverse effects from the war were able to continue their expansion programs. Baltimore, in particular, had succeeded in diverting much of the Shenandoah Valley grain to her mills because of rail extensions which entered the Valley from the north and she was able to control much of the shipping which continued to expand along all the tributaries flowing into the Chesapeake Bay. Numbers of shipping companies were set up to provide water transportation for both passengers and local produce for many years throughout the Tidewater areas of Maryland and Virginia. Regularly scheduled stops at local wharves provided, in many cases, the only way that rural people could ship their saleable products (usually farm produce) or could themselves get away to the big city, namely Alexandria, Washington, Norfolk, or Baltimore. Because Baltimore interests, especially the Old Bay Line, controlled much of this river traffic during the latter part of the nineteenth century and the early twentieth century, many a Tidewater Virginia countryman learned the gastronomic delights of seafood houses in that city rather than the seaport town to which they might more naturally tend to favor, specifically Norfolk. As better roads and truck transport began making inroads into the waterborne business and causing unprofitable runs, steamboats started cutting down on their scheduled stops and in 1934, the last Baltimore steamer visited Alexandria while the Norfolk and Washington Steamboat Co. continued to provide service to the early 1950's.

During the latter part of the nineteenth century the Washington Steamboat Company operated several ships on the lower Potomac run and this circa 1900 view shows the T. V. Arrowsmith leaving the dock at Alexandria to begin her many country wharf stops downriver. Gift of Melissa Lovejoy Hill

Recently sold for more than a million dollars, this quaint house at 322 South St. Asaph Street was referred to as a cottage in a late nineteenth-century court deposition. In 1877, Edward J. Evans (1826-1915) a veteran of the War Between the States, resided here with his family. His son, George H. Evans, was active in the civil and political affairs of the community. A member of the Alexandria-Washington Lodge, he was the first commander of the Alexandria American Legion Post and a founder of the musical association called the Sharps and Flats. Known as Captain Evans for his service in the U.S. Quartermaster Corps during World War I, George displayed a keen interest in Alexandria history. He once reminisced that "gutters in Alexandria were often 3 feet deep and during the summer months were rank with weeds. The odors were almost beyond belief . . . In my boyhood we had few of the conveniences which are now an accepted part of everyday living. Central heating was a luxury for a very few. Illumination was supplied by coal oil lamps and manufactured gas street lights had to await the evening round of the lamplighter in order to shed their feeble glow . . ." (Alexandria Gazette, April 15 and 16, 1954.) After many years of devoted service to his community, Captain Evans died March 14, 1954, in the eighty-eighth year of his life at his family home seen in this photograph.

Organized in the mid 1880s, by Capt. George H. Evans, and his sister Virginia Evans O'Brien, the musical group called the Sharps and Flats performed light opera and popular musicals in Alexandria until they were dissolved in 1923. Frequently their repertoire included the amusing and satirical operettas by the talented English composers and librettists Gilbert and Sullivan. Many of these performances were staged at Lannon's Opera House located at the southwest corner of King and Pitt Street. In reporting the activities of the chorus in October 1897,

the Alexandria Gazette indicated that: the honorary membership and chorus were limited to 50 persons each, the honorary members to pay 25 cents a month dues and those composing the chorus 10 cents each. A communication from the Hydraulion Fire Company was received requesting the club to reproduce the opera Pinafore for the benefit of that company. After some discussion it was decided to reproduce the opera for the benefit of that company two nights, the latter part of this month (October 1897) . . . It was decided to arrange for the op-

era "Patience" to be produced in January for the benefit of the Alexandria Library. Now that the organization is permanent much credit is due to Mrs. Virginia Evans O'Brien for her untiring efforts in bringing together and developing the vocal talent of this city. Much praise is also due Mr. John Herndon, the secretary of the club . . . Judging from the production of Pinafore last year much can be expected this season of the club . . . Alexandria Gazette, October 1, 1897)

This fine Greek Revival structure at the N.E. corner of St. Asaph and Cameron Streets was the home for many years of members of the Ramsay family. Particularly interesting was the fact that Mr. G.W.D. Ramsey died in this house, the residence of his son, G. William Ramsay and the Alexandria Gazette, in recording the death of the elder Mr. Ramsay on May 2, 1900, stated: "The deceased who was 91 years old, was born in this city in July 1809, in the frame building now standing at the northeast corner of King and Fairfax Streets (the Ramsay House). He was a son of Col. Dennis Ramsay, who was a son of Captain William Ramsay, who was among the incorporators of the town on July 18, 1749, both of whom served in the Revolutionary army. The deceased was the color-bearer of the Alexandria Independent Blues, and was the last Alexandrian who participated in the reception tendered Genl. Lafayette when he visited this city in 1824." Following the death of his son, the recently widowed Mrs. G. William Ramsay

found herself owner of a large house with very little money to maintain it. Common practice among the town's many widowed ladies in similar circumstances was to take in young gentlemen or married couples either as roomers or boarders in order to make ends meet. This activity was totally acceptable within the social structure of the town and was one of the very few means by which such ladies could actively engage in a money making enterprise. Mrs. Ramsay and her daughter, Rebecca operated a well-known boarding house here in the early decades of the twentieth century. Rebecca, after her marriage, became well known and respected throughout the community as Rebecca Ramsay Reece, one of Alexandria's earliest preservationists.

The writer's newly married parents moved to Alexandria in 1919 and they roomed at Mrs. Monroe's on Duke Street and had their meals at Mrs. Tackett's on St. Asaph Street and/or Mrs. Ramsay's on Cameron Street. There being virtually no apartment houses, this was the only

type of accommodation available to young working people until they amassed enough money to buy houses in George Washington Park, Rosemont or another residence in the downtown area. This house was demolished in the 1950's and the lot continues to serve as a parking lot.

One of Alexandria's most successful nineteenth-century businesses was the Hill Steam bakery located at the corner of Thompson Alley and North Lee Street. The firm was renowned for its cream wafers and family soda biscuits as well as an assortment of cakes. After being in operation from the early 1870s, a terrible fire struck the business on February 9, 1895. Although the firemen worked heroically and fought the blaze for five hours, the entire building was destroyed. The bakery was a three-story structure and was fitted with modern machinery and the loss was reported to be about sixty thousand dollars. Mr. Hill originally came to Alexandria from Baltimore in 1869 and purchased what had been the old Jamieson bakery. After the 1895 fire, Hill and Company set up temporary headquarters in a warehouse on the northwest corner of Lee and King streets. On July 29, 1895, a contract for a new cracker factory was awarded to Mr. T. H. Nelson. The new building would be ninety-two feet on Lee Street running back a hundred feet on Thompson's Alley. It was constructed of brick, three-stories high covered with slate and tin, and divided into four compartments with fire walls. Plans and specifications for the structure were drawn by W. Leon Clark, architect. By October 1895, the bulk of the work had been completed and the new ovens installed. Mr. Hill remained in business until the first decade of the twentieth century. This is a view prior to the 1895 fire.
Gift of Melissa Lovejoy Hill

Located just north of Queen Street on the east side of North Union, the Globe or Ladd's Mill was constructed by Joseph Ladd in 1827. Ladd had nearly completed his mill when a destructive fire struck on August 30, 1827: The newly built and valuable Steam Mill was yesterday morning nearly destroyed by fire, together with its contents of Flour and Grain. The loss cannot be estimated at less than Twenty Thousand dollars, perhaps Thirty, and not a cent of which was insured . . . How the accident occurred is unknown, but it is generally attributed to a defect in the upper part of the chimney. The Mill, though not entirely completed, had been in operation several weeks . . . . (Alexandria Gazette, August 31, 1827). On October 9, 1827, Ladd borrowed $7,000 from the Farmer's Bank and mortgaged the steam mills to John Hooff, cashier of the Bank. Unable to repay his loan Ladd defaulted. Benoni Wheat purchased the mill and wharf for $4,175 from Hooff on September 7, 1842. Wheat later conveyed the wharf and mill to his son John Jordan Wheat on September 15, 1847, for $1.00.

Subsequently the Wheat family leased their wharf to other enterprising businessmen. A correspondent of the Baltimore Sun wrote that: the Parker Vein Company of Boston have closed an agreement with an excellent fellow citizen, Benoni Wheat to lease his mill and wharf property for a term of five years at $1,500 per annum . . . The old frame boiler house, chimnies and machinery in the mill are to be removed . . . (Alexandria Gazette, November 3, 1851)

In 1898, Benjamin Wheat, Jr., sold the mill property to Mr. J. W. Emmert of Hagerstown, Maryland. Emmert agreed to start at once to introduce the most modern and improved roller machinery which would have the capacity of processing 100 to 125 barrels of flour daily. In September 1903, an incendiary attempted to set fire to the Globe Mill but was unsuccessful. Misfortune again visited the old mill, however, in September 1912 when it was totally destroyed by fire. Thereafter, the Alexandria Fertilizer and Chemical Company constructed a large storage warehouse on the property.
The Fireside Sentinel, *September 1988, Alexandria Library*

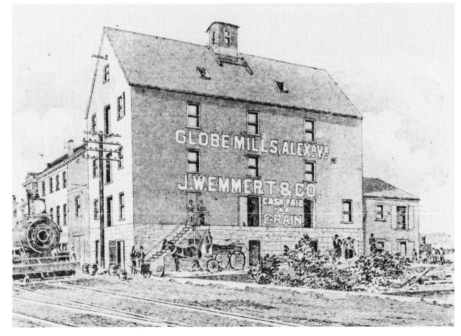

Dredged from the Potomac River and brought in as ships' ballast, cobblestones were first used to pave Alexandria streets as early as 1794. The committee on streets advertised in October 1793 that they would "give a half and a Dollar for every ton of stone suitable for paving, delivered upon such wharf in the town as shall be directed when brought into port. The stone shall be best calculated for paving of the oval kind weighing 60 pounds and upwards . . ." For the next hundred years, the clatter of carriage and wagon wheels could be heard as they rolled over the cobblestoned streets and alleys. Frequently the streets were in such a bad state of repair that they elicited angry commentary from local citizens. One native remarked: If I were long here I should feel mortified at the constant re-

marks of strangers and visitors for business and pleasure. They ask is Alexandria so poor that the citizens cannot afford to put in good order the main street, . . . I saw the stage pass over a part of it (King Street) this morning in my early rambles and really pitied the passengers whose heads were in danger as the stage bounced over the huge boulders with which the street is paved, and watched it progress and pitied the noble horses as they dragged along at a slow pace after staggering as they would put a foot by accident in some deep rut. It is worse, infinitely worse, than the old cause walk that used to be made in the country with split or round logs over marshy places in the road. It is a sore evil to the business men all along King Street . . . (Alexandria Gazette, June 18, 1858)

During the latter nineteenth century it became so expensive to repair the cobblestone streets that the city engineer suggested in 1896 that they no longer be used. Instead it was recommended that the cobbles be replaced with vitrified brick. This photograph shows that many of the stones, taken up in 1912 and 1913, were stored on a lot at Cameron and Henry streets where the city constructed a stone crusher to break up the rocks into smaller pieces for road work. Today, only portions of two cobblestoned streets remain of what was once a maze of such thoroughfares throughout the city.
Robert Truax, Columbia Historical Society

Until its destruction by fire in 1953, the Alexandria Armory was the scene of many important military and social functions in the town's history. For many years, it was home to the Alexandria Light Infantry organized July 2, 1878. At a meeting of the A.L.I., held January 27, 1880, it was decided to construct a new armory. Plans for the new building were drawn by Alexandria architect B. F. Price and William Vincent was awarded the contract to build the armory on March 19, 1880, having submitted a bid of $3,356.62. Completed by May the same year, the A.L.I. occupied their new armory for the first time on July 1st, 1880. There were those who considered the new edifice a true ornament of the city: The front was a castellated brick. The hall (was) of the Norman style 40 x 90 feet, with a gallery 8 x 40 feet spanning the west and just over the entrance. The seating capacity of the hall was about 700. In the Northwest is the ordnance room where were stacked (1880) . . . 60 breach loading Springfield Rifles and in the southwest corner (was) a large committee room. At the east end of the hall (was) a stage 30 x 25 feet . . . (Alexandria Gazette, July 3, 1880)

In 1887, Glen Brown received a commission to enlarge and repair the armory. During the next fifty years numerous trade fairs, exhibits, and banquets would be held in this facility. A soldiers' rest was established here in July 1898 for troops participating in the Spanish American conflict and in December 1899 there was a large gathering of townspeople who paid homage to the one hundredth anniversary of George Washington's death. In 1908 a skating ring was installed on the main floor of the building. Finally the structure was purchased by the City of Alexandria in the 1930s. In 1947, two airplanes collided near national Airport and the victims' remains were transported to Alexandria where the old armory became a temporary morgue.
Loeb Collection, Alexandria Library

Alexandria Light Infantry, Co. F, 3rd Va.
Capt. G. A. Mushback

This is the Alexandria Light Infantry going through various drills under the command of Capt. G. A. Mushbach. At a meeting of the A.L.I held on March 21, 1878, the company adopted a striking full dress uniform of bearskin shakos, dark blue pants, and red swallow-tail coats. The guard attended many celebrations and parades and in a spirit of national reconciliation they participated in the funeral of General Grant in August 1885. One ex-Confederate cavalryman said of the affair: "Bless, what are we coming to? . . . going with Union Major Generals to pay a last tribute at Grant's tomb! Well, the war is ended at last."
(Alexandria Gazette, August 10, 1885)

Smoot-Field Fire

A

Alexandria suffered its share of disastrous fires all through the years. Probably the last big conflagration before the entry of motorized fire equipment took place on May 12, 1909, when the W. A. Smoot and Company's planing mill and lumber yard were seen to be afire on the north side of Cameron Street between Lee and Union. Quick work by the fire department did not prevent the wind-driven flames from jumping across Cameron to additional stores of lumber and building materials piled on the south side of the street. Massive flames and intense heat made firefighting most difficult and it was soon decided that Alexandria's three steamer engines were not sufficient to prevent the spread of destruction to the rest of the block. Assistance was requested from Washington which im- mediately dispatched two engines sent by railway and one fireboat. Their prompt arrival helped save most of the Cameron/ King block and only a relatively small amount of damage was sustained by the adjoining Henry Knox Field Lumber Yard with no loss of buildings. The Smoot Company was virtually wiped out and the fire raged for about five hours. Fortunately the steam fire engines were placed

on piers at the river's edge and there was never a lack of water. Flaming embers flying through the air kept many citizens on the roofs of buildings for several blocks around putting out small fires with buckets of water thus preventing further damage.

View A looks north on Lee Street toward its crossing with Cameron and men may be seen on the roof of the Field Factory while smoke and flames rise from the Smoot yards just beyond. This was taken at the height of the fire. The two-and-one-half story brick house behind the Field sign was saved and it may be seen from the rear in view B, on the left side of the picture, with the old Mansion House hotel (later the Wagar Apartments in 1909) looming behind it on Fairfax Street. This scene, taken the next day, looks west on Cameron to its crossing with Lee and covers much of the burned district. Most of the buildings in the background (west of Lee) are standing today.

Over the years, the Potomac River has often overflowed its banks, particularly during rainy spells in the early spring when accompanying strong southeast winds cause the water to pile up below Great Falls and prevent its regular flow downstream. This view of the eastern terminus of King Street at the river (circa 1910) is a typical scene of such flooded conditions. Since the first block and a half of King Street is filled land and is a few feet above sea level it is the street most affected by high water, sometimes totally inundated to the crossing at Lee (formerly Water) Street. In the foreground, streetcar tracks are visible on their way to the end-of-line at the ferry building and slip from where passengers could ride to Washington for ten cents. The Fitzgerald warehouses (erected circa 1780) on the right and the later early nineteenth century buildings (left) flank the street down to the Strand, which became the three-block-long waterfront lane between Cameron and Duke streets after the completion of filling in the "sunken grounds" by the 1790s. Constructed in 1923, the old Dominion Boat Club now occupies the site of the ferry building which was consumed by fire on March 21, 1922.

COMMERCIAL ARTERIES AND THOROUGHFARES

KING STREET

hile Alexandria's original settlement, Hunting Creek warehouse, was located on an indentation still called Oronoko Bay, and her traditional first street was a tobacco rolling road which led to that settlement, it was not long after 1749 that the majority of commercial structures being erected were situated five or six blocks south of the original location, centered around Prince, King, Fairfax, and Cameron streets. Retail establishments expanded westward from the riverfront and by 1800, when a whole block had been added to King Street by filling in a marshy, tidal area, it had assumed the position of the primary shopping street in town and despite a certain amount of retail activity along the other streets, particularly Prince and Cameron, King Street has managed to maintain that position to this very day.

The presentation which follows attempts to give a picture of King Street as it was from its earliest days and, to a great extent, its appearance well into the twentieth century. Except for occasional disastrous fires, Alexandria's "main" street changed very little over two hundred years, the prevailing practice being to remodel an older building into a more up-to-date style rather than to follow today's action of bulldozing everything and starting all over. The procedure here is to stroll up King Street from the waterfront to Shuter's Hill, block by block, to experience a feel for the street both in its architectural appearance and for the people who lived and worked in these buildings.

Col. John Fitzgerald, "an agreeable, broad-shouldered Irishman," and the foremost Roman Catholic layman in Alexandria, served with Washington at Valley Forge, then returned home and purchased in September 1778, low-lying land on the south side of King, and east of Water (now Lee) Street. Since landfill operations were taking place following his purchase, this building was erected at King and Union streets about 1780 and was advertised in 1801 as "three brick warehouses . . . three stories high . . . a sail loft above the upper story seventy-three feet in length and forty-two feet wide upon the floor . . . all under one roof." This view, taken by Virgil Davis (circa 1940) shows the appearance following removal of a three-story wing on the east and before a later two-story wing was added. William Ketlands "Bill's Old Anchor" was one of a series of oyster house, barroom (before Prohibition), and beer joint (maybe during and after) operations to occupy this building over the years. The Seaport Inn restaurant (opened 1946 was one of only a handful of eating establishments in downtown (before liquor-by-the drink) to succeed to the present day.

These early to mid-nineteenth-century warehouses generally housed businesses which were related to river and sea-going traffic, the last occupants before destruction by a fire in 1925 being H. Kirk and Sons, Wholesale Grocers and Ship Chandlers. These buildings, including the one facing on the Strand (right side) were removed to extend the U.S. Naval Torpedo Plant to the north side of King Street, during the early part of World War II.
Loeb Collection

The 100 block of King (north side) taken by J. Harry Shannon (the Rambler) about 1910 shows a row of late eighteenth or early nineteenth-century warehouses which, with a few exceptions, were built on land filled in by William Ramsay and his heirs. The warehouse at 117 King was purchased by Anthony C. Cazenove, agent for Victor duPont, son of Pierre Samuel duPont, as a base for trading in Virginia lands. This plan was abandoned and the building sold in 1807. By the late 1850s the railroad tracks in the foreground had been laid in the middle of Union Street and remained there until very recent times. During the early morning hours of the 1950s to 1970s it was interesting to see a ten or twelve-car train on Union Street, hauling coal to the Braddock Electric power Plant (now PEPCO) on the north end of town, come to a stop in the middle of King Street, the whole train crew jump to the ground, and amble over to a popular sandwich and coffee shop, "The Snack Bar," and load up on their gastronomic necessities for the morning. At such times both upper King and Prince streets might be cut off from the waterfront but no one seemed to mind. The "Snack Bar" and the railroad tracks were moved or removed at about the same time, in the early 1980s.

The southwest corner of King and Union streets was the site of three brick warehouses, erected before 1796, which had been purchased by the federal government for use as a custom house in 1820. This triple building was demolished to make way for the handsome new Corn Exchange Building in 1871. The Exchange operation was not particularly successful and the premises were soon taken over by N. Lindsey and Company, a wholesale grocery concern which ultimately became the Lindsey-Nicholson Corporation, an automotive parts distributor continuing in active operation in an adjacent building until the 1980s. This circa 1890 view makes one wonder what might have been the reason for so many barrels in front of a wholesale grocer's. Could there have been a small, but discreet, barroom attached?
Gift of W. Robins Lindsey

127

This scene of the north side of the 200 block of King contains a group of warehouses (217-215 King Street) which were built in 1803 by Hugh Smith; repaired after a fire in November 1855, in which seven firemen were killed by a falling wall, and were occupied by Henry Baader's stove, tinware and paint business from the time of their purchase in the mid-1880s to the time of this 1924 photograph. The business finally failed during the depression of the 1930s. The nearest of the three-story buildings was erected after 1877 since an atlas of that date showed the building on that site to have been of frame construction. The two-and-one-half-story structure to its right was built by William Bartleman about 1810. He had come to Alexandria in 1784 as a young man and later participated in Washington's funeral procession in his position as senior deacon of the Alexandria-Washington Masonic Lodge No. 22. The narrow building was probably built between two existing structures, resulting in what is sometimes referred to as an "alley house." This seems to date

from the nineteenth century. The corner (right hand edge) building replaced a sizeable frame warehouse when it was built in 1851 by William Bayne. It housed the offices of the William H. May Company, dealers in farm implements

and fertilizers for many years and later by the Herbert Bryant Company, founded in 1868, which dealt in similar agricultural products. (1924)
Photograph by W. P. Gray, Valentine Museum

The Ramsay house is shown here at the northeast corner of King and Fairfax streets. Reputed to be Alexandria's earliest structure, it was the home of William Ramsay, a Scottish merchant and one of the founding trustees of the town, upon whose death in 1785, George Washington participated in the funeral procession. The building was converted into a cigar manufacturing establishment soon after

the War Between the States. In 1883, Steiner and Yoho employed upwards of thirty workmen and manufactured about two million cigars here per year. During the late 1930s the building was known as "Ma's Place" and under her motherly influence, many a young Alexandrian was introduced to the joys of 3.2 beer. Ramsay House fell into a deplorable state and was nearly demolished in the late 1940s.

After much effort on the part of preservationists, the city finally agreed to its restoration, or more accurately, reconstruction. It has since served as headquarters for the Alexandria Tourist Council and Visitors Center, a city funded agency.
Loeb Collection, circa 1920

This 1924 view of the south side of the 200 block of King Street shows three fine buildings in a state of decline. The corner (with Lee Street) was built between 1802 and 1810 by Jacob Hoffman; it remained intact until 1949 when a fire destroyed the upper floors and the fourth story was eliminated during repairs by the creation of a shed roof replacing the former hip one. The next two structures completed by 1798 were built by Bernard Chequire and Col. George Gilpin respectively and they contained living quarters above the shops located on the ground floor, much as they do to this day. Financial reverses forced Chequire to sell to Jonathan Swift in 1800 and the Union Bank was an occupant for some time around 1820. The photograph would indicate that beds were either plentiful or in great demand in 1924 and that the Torpedo Inn was a hold-over from the World War I days of torpedo plant activity.
Photograph by W. P. Gray, Valentine Museum

The southeast corner of King and Fairfax streets has long been occupied by the venerable Burke and Herbert Bank and Trust Company, founded in 1852 by partners John Woolfolk Burke and Arthur Herbert. It was located in several nearby buildings in its earlier days but finally settled in on this corner before the turn of the twentieth century. This structure built on the site of the home of Col. John Fitzgerald who owned warehouses at King and Union streets, was erected about 1904. It has been enlarged several times and the bank continues to be operated by descendants of the Burke founder. The Herberts, not being as prolific as their partners, had died out in 1940. This view was taken sometime prior to 1937.

This 1924 view of the northwest corner of King and Fairfax streets (300 block) gives a fair idea of the general appearance of Alexandria's primary commercial thoroughfare from the mid-nineteenth century until its demolition by urban renewal in the mid-1960s. An unusual sight is the frame building in the foreground which had obviously outlived its usefulness by 1924. It was one of the very few wood commercial buildings left on King Street at this time and, as a matter of fact, was replaced about ten years later by a brick structure of essentially the same dimensions and appearance.
Photograph by W. P. Gray, Valentine Museum

The Worth Hulfish and Sons Hardware Store (315 King Street) was an Alexandria institution of long standing. Founded in 1844 by James F. Carlin, whose name it bore, the business was changed to Carlin-Hulfish Company in 1906 and finally to the name listed above in 1919, when the final Carlin interests were bought out by the Hulfish family. The building is unique in that it was the first (and possibly only) cast iron front structure in Alexandria. The facade erected in the late nineteenth century was composed of pre-cast pieces bolted together, attached, however, to the front wall of a considerably older building.
Photograph by Victor Amato, 1965, Historic Alexandria Foundation

The Alexandria National Bank on the northeast corner of King and Royal streets was long a town landmark and was considered one of the handsomest establishments in the state. The site was previously occupied by several wooden houses which were destroyed by fire in 1857. In September 1866, Mr. M. W. Brown constructed a new building here which was later occupied by Mr. Kemp as a hardware store and by Capt. Charles W. Green as a fancy goods shop. In 1879, Isaac Eichberg purchased the real estate from H. C. Slaymaker and Company. Both men operated very successful clothing, wholesale, and retail dry goods stores here. Following its founding in 1904, the bank occupied the building and it remained its headquarters until 1961, when City Council allocated $135,000 to purchase it under the Urban Renewal Program. It was replaced by an underground parking building and a portion of City Hall Plaza, also known as Market Square. The handsome building to the right (fourth from the corner) was built by the Virginia Safe Deposit and Trust Corporation in the early 1900s, replacing the building which housed R. H. Miller and Sons, which supplied townspeople for many years with china, glass, and crockery; said earlier structure having been destroyed by fire. After the demise of the Virginia Safe Deposit, the Alexandria Gazette moved its office into the building where it remained until 1965, when a new facility was built at 717 North Saint Asaph Street. The earliest known newspaper in Alexandria was published in 1784 and the Alexandria Gazette was, at least, a collateral descendant of that. It was published by several generations of the highly respected Snowden family at 310 Prince Street. After its purchase by Dr. Robert South Barrett circa 1911, its office was moved to King Street. The Carlin family later bought the paper and operated it for a number of decades.

The southwest corner of King and Fairfax streets was photographed in 1929. Established in 1792 by Edward Stabler, this was Alexandria's oldest firm engaged in the wholesale and retail drug business until the early 1930s. The corner building served as a storage warehouse for drugs and supplies which were marketed throughout the Washington-metropolitan region. Mr. Lawrence Fawcett, an old employee stated while reminiscing that in "delivering wholesale orders, wagons were sent to the following locations: One wagon delivered in downtown Washington by going by ferry at the foot of King Street to the 7th Street wharf in Washington, then delivered in the downtown section of the city. One went to the wharves of the Potomac River steamboats in Alexandria and unloaded there for shipment to down-river points; one went to the station of the Washington and Old Dominion Railroads, at Fairfax and Princess Streets for places such as Leesburg, Falls Church, and Bluemont; another went to the Southern Railroad freight station at Duke and Henry Streets for shipment to points on its line between here and Culpeper, and onward to its Manassas branch ... Still another went to the R.F.& P. station, located near the present Alexandria passenger station. Finally, one covered all local shops in Alexandria." In the 1880s, Henry Strauss, clothier, was the proprietor of the store at 302 King Street (right of the light pole). He furnished his clientele with ready-made clothing, hats, and trunks. Henry Wade operated a printing shop there in the 1920s. These buildings were demolished during the 1962 urban renewal in Alexandria.
National Archives, 1929

Construction of the Washington, Alexandria, Mount Vernon Electric Railway commenced in June 1892. Tracks were laid from the Ferry Wharf at lower King Street west to Columbus Street, north to Cameron thence west to the Baltimore & Potomac Railroad Station at Cameron and Fayette. When completed the electric railroad ran from Washington, D.C., over the Long Bridge, through Alexandria, to Mount Vernon. Over two thousand people cheered the opening of the system in Alexandria on September 20, 1892. "Here she comes! was raised by hundreds of boys and people who rushed pell mell from all quarters of the compass to get a look at the cars. The cry, 'The electric cars are coming,' brought every branch of business on King Street to a standstill. Both shopkeepers and their customers, bolted for the doors, auction rooms were vacated, and in less time than it takes to tell it the street was the scene of a moving tide of human beings, jostling, colliding, treading on each other's shoes, surging, pushing, squeezing, and jamming in order to reach points of observation where the panorama could be scanned for all it was worth." The trolley car in this photograph is headed west with the north side of the 400 block of King Street in the background. To the immediate left is the early structure housing Swann Brother's department store. In order to expand their facilities, the company purchased the two buildings to the east in April 1912 (427-429). These properties had been occupied by the Postal Telegraph Company, P. G. Lawler, the Jamieson Studio, and S. H. Lynn and Company. Later the western facade of the Swann Building was remodeled so as to provide extensive show windows.
William A. Moore Collection

This rare 1866 photograph provides a panoramic view of the south side of the lower 400 block of King Street. Clearly visible in the background are the buildings and the interesting roof lines of the 300 block of King Street looking east from J.T. Creighton's emporium. In connection with the tall buildings in the foreground, an advertisement in the Alexandria Gazette in September 1866 announced that: "the new buildings in the course of erection by Mr. David Appich (408-414) on King between Royal and Pitt Streets, are fast approaching completion and will when finished be very handsome and elegant buildings . . . We learn that they have already been leased by Messrs. Rosenthal as a shoe store, & Mr. Simon Waterman as a clothing store."
Rebecca Ramsay Reese Collection

It must have been a hot, muggy summer day (circa 1900) when these street cleaners arrived in front of J. W. Arnold's store at 406-408 King Street, later the site of Tom's Garden, a longtime, lower King Street blue collar pub. Throughout the nineteenth century the condition of King Street left much to be desired. In 1852 it was noted that the situation on King Street, from Washington to Royal, was such that "the water trench is paved over and there is left on either side, a modicum of clay which as soon as the sun comes out hot, and by the travel over it of carts and other vehicles is converted into dust, which makes it, when any wind is blowing, almost impassable and causes serious damage to the goods in our stores." (Alexandria Gazette, May 21, 1852) Arnold was the proprietor of a hat store for many years on King. William A. Moore Collection

The northwest corner at Pitt Street (circa 1900) contained an early frame structure occupied for many years by Warfield's drug store. Adjacent to it was B. B. Smith, Cigar Manufacturer. These buildings along with four adjoining ones (501 to 513 King) were unusual in that most wood structures along main thoroughfares were replaced during the nineteenth century by brick. This corner was torn down in 1905 to provide space for the new Warfield Building of three stories with a drug store on the ground and probably Alexandria's first modern apartment house on the floors above. Edgar Warfield, Sr., father of the final proprietors of the drugstore, was Alexandria's last living Confederate veteran. He died in 1934.
Gift of Courtland Warfield

Looking east on the south side of the 400 block of King Street, the old Marshall House of War Between the States fame is visible to the immediate right. Early nineteenth century occupants of this block included Louis Beeler, a baker, who operated a confectioner's shop (1823) close to where a Baskin-Robbins now dispenses ice cream, and James

Kennedy, a noted book dealer. After Kennedy's death in 1820 his "dwelling house and 2 stores" were replaced by the brick building known as 416-418 King Street. During the twentieth century this block has been occupied by the Levinson clothing store (424-426), the Loeb Photo Studio (426), Gaines and Company Shoe Store (422), Dysons Book Store (420), a

steam laundry (416) and Howell's Hatter shop (412). Subsequently the entire block was demolished during the urban renewal process in the mid-1960s but many archaeological artifacts were rescued before the current Holiday Inn was constructed there in the 1970s.
National Archives, circa 1864

For many years, Alexandria gained the reputation of a town which used any excuse to have a parade. Flags and bunting were hung from every available window and marching groups, military, school, and social organizations, were in great demand. This view (circa 1900) of the north side of the 500 block of King with a naval unit in the foreground, shows the north side as it must have appeared during most of the nineteenth century. Only the Appich Building (525 King) has been modernized. The structures with dormer windows (507-513 King to the left of Warfield's) were demolished in 1908 to make way for the white marble edifice of the First National Bank. At about the same time, several buildings at the far end (northeast corner) of the block were replaced by an equally imposing Citizens National Bank Building. In 1954 the two banks were merged and today their existence lies deeply buried in the files of the Crestar Bank. This entire block (north and south sides) was destroyed in the 1960s by the Urban Renewal Program.

This handsome Classical Revival building (shown in 1864 while occupied as the office of the provost marshall for the Union Army during the War Between the States) was originally built circa 1812 as the Mechanics Bank. On its demise about 1819, the first bank failure in the District of Columbia, the bank house was acquired by the Fire Insurance Company of Alexandria and it housed this institution (with a break for the war) until 1871 when the property was sold to David Appich. He subsequently extended the front of the building fifteen or so feet to the sidewalk and placed his name and the date, 1886, on the facade. It served as a restaurant under the direction of George A. Appich and much later as Frank Howard's, then his successors, Jones and Pritchard, Grocers.
National Archives

North side of 500 block of King Street.

This view of the north side of King Street shows two early nineteenth century structures, the right hand one (515-517 King) having originally served as a residence for Edmund Jennings Lee. There is some evidence that it was built as early as 1776. The adjoining one was constructed between 1805 and 1816 and an early owner was Anthony Charles Cazenove. The facade of the two-story building to the left (525 King) was an extension, added in 1886 by owner David Appich, of the bank/insurance office shown in the previous view. The uses to which the first floors of these buildings were put, along with so many others on King Street, were varied retail enterprises but the upper stories often served as residences for the owners of the shops below or as rooms or apartments. After the turn of the twentieth century many of the buildings became dilapidated and could hardly be classified as first-class housing. A strong effort by the Historic Alexandria Foundation along with preservation minded citizens was made in 1963 to save this group but Urban Renewal won out.
Photograph by Russell Jones, April 1959, Historic Alexandria Foundation

136

Lannon's Opera House (southwest corner of King and Pitt) was erected by John Lannon, and completed in May 1883 on land which he purchased from Robert Miller, the son of Mordecai Miller, an early silversmith and successful merchant.

The second-floor hall was reported to be handsomely furnished but the seating arrangements must have been a bit tight since an 1883 notice in the Alexandria Gazette, stated that the capacity would be about seventeen hundred. The hall was the scene of numerous light operas, theatrical performances and lectures and its truss roof was the first example of that construction in the city. After a decline in popularity, the hall was converted into a bowling alley which continued to operate until the building's removal about 1970. The first floor was occupied by Louis Brill's "Opera House Restaurant and Pool Room, the Palace Saloon of Alexandria" (which led to the erroneous assumption that the upstairs hall was really Brill's Opera house) and by barber, clothing, and print shops along with J. Kent White's electrical contracting and supply store. Incidentally, Brill's bar was one of many in Alexandria. The Opera House appears on the left edge of this photograph taken about 1900.
Melissa Lovejoy Hill Collection

A general view of the south side of the 500 block was taken in 1928 by M. Loeb, whose studio was located in the 400 block for about 50 years. It is interesting to note that Bradshaw's Shoe Store on the left occupied a building (510-512 King) which housed a boot and shoe-making shop, started by William Morgan in 1822, followed by Peyton Ballinger, a shoemaker from 1850 to 1896, succeeded by Philip Bradshaw who ran a shoe shop under his and his successor's ownership in the same location until 1965, a total of 144 years. Bradshaw's continued in business at another location after Urban Renewal. Streetcar tracks would continue to be used until 1932 and the day of the horse, except at race tracks and horse shows, was not quite over.
Loeb Collection, Alexandria Library

The 600 block looking west, taken in the late 1930s by M. Loeb, is the first block not affected by Urban Renewal, but due to modernization and remodeling particularly after 1900, contains only one early building today. During the first half of the twentieth century, this block was perhaps the center of retail business activity in Alexandria for it contained two five-and-ten-cents stores (Woolworth's and Kresge's); a furniture store (under several owners beginning with James F. Muir); a drugstore (first Lennon's, later Bowman and Grubbs); several grocery stores (including Sanitary Grocery); two jewelry stores (Saunders and R. C. Acton), an ice cream parlor (Fred Birrell); a department store (J. C. Penney), a meat market (Weil Brothers); a number of insurance offices (Horner and Holden Company, among others); a piano and music store; at least two hardware stores (Hoy's and R. E. Knight which later expanded into toys and schoolbooks and supplies); a shoe store (H. Fedder); clothing stores

(M. Sperling for ladies and children, Worth's ladies' hats, Kaufmann and Blumenfeld for men); an office building (originally named Washington Hall, later renamed the Smith Building); and the

Ingomar Theatre, which specialized in westerns and grade B movies. During this period the upper floors of many of the structures were remodeled and converted into apartments.

The south side (to the left) of the 600 block in 1925 still contained two interesting early buildings. To the right of the drugstore was an imposing three-story building structure, erected in 1854, known as Washington Hall (622-626 King) and abutting it on the corner was the building in which the first classes of the newly established Episcopal Theological Seminary were held in 1823. On the opposite corner (north side, right hand) stand the Amos Alexander Building, built in 1800, and to its right is the R.E. Knight and Sons hardware business which operated on this site for over seventy years. Most of Alexandria's young schoolchildren in the 1920s and 1930s bought their first schoolbooks here and many of Santa Claus's gifts came from the second-story toy department. The wri-ter remembers the crusty, old bachelor, Dr. Warren Grubbs, who ran the Rexall Drug Store (616 King, south side) where several families' children gathered each Halloween to watch all the other costumed children, with parents, who thronged the sidewalks of King Street. Loeb Collection, Alexandria Library

An early 1920s view of the southeast corner (King and South Washington streets) shows the first home of the Episcopal Theological Seminary (1823) among whose founders were Francis Scott Key, author of the National Anthem, William Holland Wilmer, rector of St. Paul's Church and Edmund Jennings Lee, uncle of Robert E. Lee. Years later it housed another religious group. The days of the modern garage and gas station were still a few years off as evidenced by the gas pump in front of the Alexandria Auto Supply Company which occupied the entire ground floor for a number of years. Washington Hall (622-626 King) to its left, was purchased in 1919 by the owner of the Smith Motor Supply Company, converted into offices, renamed the Smith Building, and housed a number of real estate and insurance offices, Retail Merchants Association, as well as a ground floor grocery store.
Milton Grigg Collection

This 1924 view of the northwest corner of King and Washington streets shows several businesses along the north side of the 700 block of King. In the immediate foreground is the old drugstore operated by Dr. Richard Stabler during the nineteenth century and later by J. E. W. Timberman during this century. The writer recalls this corner in the 1930s and 1940s as being a favorite spot for local drugstore cowboys (not called teenagers then) to hang out, some of their numbers working for Dr. Timberman as soda jerks.

This corner building was torn down and replaced in the 1960s by a non-descript two-story structure which has since housed several eateries, including a waffle shop, often referred to as the "awful" Shop. The building to the left (703 King) served as a bookstore and a candy and toy shop. Its proprietor, William F. Carne, was a noted journalist and published the first systematic history of Alexandria. He opened a bookstore here in 1897. Subsequently, his daughters operated the business and in 1929 they

purchased many rare newspapers from Mount Vernon. Many of these including issues of the old Alexandria Gazette were sold to the American Antiquarian Society at Worcester, Massachusetts. The Carne sisters, with their sweet and gentle manners, operated this tiny shop well into the 1930s and, in the writer's opinion, had they lived a century before, would have been perfect examples of shopkeepers in Dicken's London.
Photograph by W. P. Gray, Valentine Museum

The row of buildings, 703 to 713 King Street, was probably built in 1816-1817, by the following owners: 713, Charles Bennett, Alexandria philanthropist who was living here when he died in April 1839; 709-711, Jacob Hoffman, an early mayor of Alexandria and sugar factory entrepreneur; 705-707, John Withers; and 703, Benjamin Baden.

The Service Drugstore opened at 705 King Street in 1924. The proprietor boasted of its being the original cut-rate drugstore. Here could be found drugs of all sorts, a varied line of candy, cigars, toilet articles, hospital supplies, novelties, and an up-to-date soda fountain (Alexandria Gazette, January 1, 1926) In 1886, Mr. Lewis Appich opened a well-known restaurant and Oyster House at 709 King Street. His son, George A., took over the business upon his father's death. Meals were served to order at all hours and the finest wines, liquors, and cigars were for sale to a discriminating clientele. This building was remodeled in 1919 by Samuel DeVaughan, a local contractor, and later occupied by the Hollywood Restaurant. 713 King Street was the home of E. H. Hawkins in the 1890s, a member of city council and a former Confederate soldier. In 1912, J. W. Devers converted the residence into a store. By 1917, M. E. Parker and Brothers, a grocery firm, was in operation here followed in the late 1940s by Brown's Men Shop.
Photograph by Russell Jones, November 1962, Historic Alexandria Foundation

Parker's Grocery (713 King, north side) was a popular dispenser of produce and foodstuffs. This 1917 view might well have been taken about February 22 since the bunting and flags were annually displayed by most business houses in celebration of the birth of George Washington and in anticipation of the street parade which regularly took place on King Street, and continues to this day. Owners of the store, M. E. Parker, center, and Clarence C. Parker, right, operated in this location for over thirty years.
Courtesy of Helen Parker Surina

700 King Street, on the southwest corner of King and Washington streets is McBurney's Hall. Among the old established and influential merchants of Alexandria was that of George McBurney and Son, established by him in 1850. About 1870 he formed a co-partnership with his son, Alexander. The building, erected by B. F. Price for the McBurney brothers in 1879, was a handsome three-story structure and well adapted, both in location and facilities, for the extensive wholesale and retail trade conducted by the firm in Alexandria and the state of Virginia. They made a specialty of imported and domestic liquors and wines, teas, and cof-

GEO. McBURNEY & SON,
WHOLESALE AND RETAIL
Grocers and Liquor Dealers,
South West Corner
King & Washington
STREETS,
ALEXANDRIA, VA.
——
Teas, Canned Goods, and Fine Liquors a specialty.

fee—especially roasted coffee which they personally superintended. George McBurney had immigrated to the United States from Ireland in 1846. On the second floor of the building was a large hall which was the scene of many fashionable nineteenth-century dances and festivities. (Alexandria Gazette, December 13, 1888, page 2) Later in the 1920s, Frank B. Howard was the proprietor of an attractive grocery store at 700 King Street which sold fresh meats and vegetables. The writer's mother dealt at Howard's Grocery and he recalls accompanying her on Saturday morning to cash in one or two empty ginger ale bottles for a rebate of five cents each. A great deal of time could then be spent at Woolworth's or Kresges' five-and-ten-cent stores in the 600 block searching for items (usually candy) which might sell for under five cents. This building was removed in the late 1950s and replaced by a one-story Whelans Drug Store. Several other businesses have occupied the site since.

This fine old building at 704 King Street next to McBurney's Hall has unfortunately been razed. On May 27, 1889, it hosted for one week only the World's Muse, the greatest of all ten cents shows. One could view a bewildering array of mechanical wonders, illusions, curiosities, and objects of interest. Included in the show were Jumbo, the monster alligator, the largest ever captured, and a spiritual expose showing the tricks used by so-called mediums, spirit rapping, table lifting, spirit handwriting, etc. (Alexandria Gazette, May 27, 1889) A number of restaurants have also occupied the premises: the Mount Vernon Dining Room (circa 1900) followed by the Silver Grey Inn which opened in October 1924 and which catered to the culinary delight of local Alexandrians. Twelve years later another restaurant, the New York Cafe, was in business at this location. The rear of the Washington Street Methodist Church, located on South Washington Street, may be seen behind the vacant lot.
Carne Collection

Peabody School Building, sometimes known as the Lee School, was situated on the northwest corner of King and Alfred streets. In 1874 the Alexandria School Board purchased three buildings at Alfred and King streets from C. C. Bradley with money provided by a fund set up by George Peabody, a northern philanthropist, whose aim was to encourage the furtherance of education in the south. These were later remodeled and made into a school in 1875 by Benjamin Franklin Price, prominent Alexandria builder and carpenter. The building contained a beautiful hall graced with columns, gilt moldings, and fresco paper. First utilized on February 9, 1875, for an exhibition of the St. John's Demosthenian Society, it later housed the Lee, Peabody, and part of the Washington Schools. "Water was piped into each room, there were faucets in the yard and under the stairs, water closets were built out of doors, there was a small yard behind the Washington School wing, and there were large dry basements which were put to good use." (Henry G. Morgan, "Education" in a Town in Transition)

For many years after 1876 books of the Alexandria Library, Virginia's oldest, were stored in the building. In September 1897, several ladies under the direction of Miss Virginia Corse revived the Library Association and used the second floor of the structure for its facilities. In 1909 the City of Alexandria sold the school for eighteen thousand dollars, to J. D. Rodgers, who converted it into an apartment house called the Cameron. Fire gutted the building in 1936.
Photograph by William A. Moore

This 1924 photograph shows a row of buildings at the southwest corner of King (800 block) and Columbus streets. The four-story structure, built about 1919, was the new Michelbach furniture store which was a leading retail firm for many years. It was established in 1902 at a different location. The corner building in which Lutheran Church members first met in 1868, was replaced by the Millers' Hardware Building. The next two structures (806-808 King) stand today, but altered, and that beyond housing the Virginia Bowling and Athletic Supply Company was soon to be modernized for Hopkins furniture. Other businesses located here in the 1930s were the old Mammy Pastry Shop (802 King) and

Shield's Plumbers (806 King).
Photograph by W. P. Gray, Valentine Museum

142

The residences at 915-917 King Street (with dormer windows) were constructed between 1798 and 1802 by William Myers. By November 1803, Myers had sold 917 to Mary Helena Rozier of Prince George's County, Maryland. 915 King Street was conveyed to John Mills in 1803 for three thousand dollars and then to Anthony C. Cazenove in 1816. Cazenove, of French Hugenot heritage, was a wealthy and talented Alexandria merchant. In the 1840s, he was the proprietor of one of the largest wheat import and export firms in town. Thomas Brown, a young apprentice who stayed with the family in 1803, wrote of them as follows: "His wife was a very accomplished lady of an American family but spoke French fluently . . . Mr. Cazenove . . . was visited by all the best French families in Alexandria . . . A rule at his table, allowed nothing but French to be spoken, unless strangers were present . . ."

W. E. Hinken and Son, established in 1896, sold an extensive line of household goods of all kinds at 917 King Street in the 1920s. A small boy who had to approach Mr. Hinken on several occasions in the mid 1930s was terrorized by his size and demeanor and forever after referred to the proprietor as Stinkin' Hinken.
Photograph by W. P. Gray, Valentine Museum

These three substantial Federalist buildings which were on the south side of the 900 block of King Street have been razed and replaced by a tasteless, flat-roofed structure, and a parking lot. The three-story building in the immediate foreground housed the Arlington Apartments.
Photograph by W. P. Gray, 1924, Valentine Museum

143

1007 King Street was constructed circa 1805-1806 by Bolitha Laws, a brick contractor. Phineas Janney, president of the Little River Turnpike Company was a tenant here between 1812 to 1814. In July 1814, Anthony C. Cazenove, wealthy merchant and importer, purchased the house for thirty-two hundred dollars. Upon his death in 1852, his executors sold the structure to Sarah W. Griffith in 1856. (Cox, Street by Street, page 72) Later, the property was conveyed to the Mahlon Janney family who owned it until April 1924. After having served as a single family unit, the building later housed several commercial businesses, most recently being converted into law offices in 1972.
Photograph by Victor Amato

The buildings in this row (1116 to 1122 King) were probably built at the same time, the two nearest ones being erected about 1804 by William Myers, who had purchased the land before for fifty pounds. They were subsequently sold to William S. Moore in 1813 for seventeen hundred dollars. The corner structure was occupied for many years by Entwisle's Drug Store while the Virginia Shoe Repair Company and King's Chinese-American Restaurant were housed in adjoining buildings in the 1930s. In spite of King's long standing location at 1114 King Street, the buildings in this and nearby blocks had entered a period of neglect and dilapidation after the turn of the twentieth century.

This view (circa 1900) looking east, shows the north side of the 1100 block. In the foreground is a town pump, one of twenty or more scattered throughout the streets of Alexandria. These provided water for those citizens whose residences did not have piped-in water from the Alexandria Water Company reservoir (1852) located near the top of Shuter's Hill at the head of King Street. Records do not tell us who Uncle Hez was and why he was coming, but we may presume that he was some sort of traveling showman, possibly the operator of a medicine show. This particular pump was referred to in an 1840 advertisement as the "old diagonal pump" and was located at the southwest corner of King and Commerce streets. *O'Brien/Hulfish Collection*

The south side of the 1200 block as it appeared in 1924, shows that the pump had been removed and King Street was now completely hard surfaced, while Commerce was still a cobblestone street. The first three buildings were of early nineteenth-century construction while the rest of the block contained three-story mid-nineteenth-century structures. As late as 1936 this one-and-one-half-block stretch of King Street contained three auto tire stores (Goodrich, Dunlap, and Goodyear) one auto agency, three groceries (A&P, New Virginia, and Sanitary), two meat markets, one seafood shop, one state ABC store, the Draft Rite Garden (beer dispensary) to say nothing of a ladies' dress shop, beauty parlor, used car lot (Aero-Auto), shoe repair, jewelry store, and several real estate and insurance offices. The writer recalls that about 1946, a Chinese laundry, operated by one Sam Moy, was housed in the building adjoining the small flatiron building shown here. When the corner building was torn down to the basement level, too little concern was given to the substructure of the house next door and it collapsed into the hole. Poor Sam Moy was observed poking about the ruins of his house and business now located in the crater one lot east, rescuing his many packages of laundry.

Photographs by W. P. Gray, Valentine Museum

The southeast corner of King and Payne streets (1222 King) as it appeared in 1965 was probably built in 1853-1854 by Gilbert S. Minor who sold it in the latter year for $1,500. George Bauer bought it in 1875 for $850 and very likely updated and restyled it after that date. It housed Alexandria's second state ABC store (the first being located on the southeast corner of the 400 block of King) opened in the 1930s following the repeal of Prohibition.
Photograph by Victor Amato, 1965, Historic Alexandria Foundation

This 1962 view of the northeast corner of King and Payne streets shows three early nineteenth-century structures, all of which were originally two stories but subsequently altered and enlarged. The corner building (1229 King) was serving as McGraw's Pioneer Sumac Mill in 1877, later as a Sanitary Grocery, most recently as an easy credit appliance center. After standing empty for a time, it mysteriously burned in 1986 and despite the efforts of preservationists to save the still standing walls, it was torn down as had been the adjoining building a few years before. A parking lot now occupies the spot.
Photograph by Russell Jones, Historic Alexandria Foundation

This view of 1317 King taken in the early 1960s for the Historic Alexandria Foundation's survey of old buildings, shows a structure probably erected in the first two decades of the nineteenth century in a neighborhood of buildings generally used for commercial purposes, dispensing food (to some extent) and drink (to a greater extent) until recent times. Rising land values caused by the opening of the nearby King Street Metro Station have brought about a change in environment and uses. Although some nearby locations are still restaurants, the aura of a disreputable past has nearly disappeared. This building is unusual in that the structure is set back a considerable distance from the sidewalk reflecting its early use as a "brick dwelling house" which was likely built by James Sanderson after 1808 when he purchased 101 feet of frontage on King Street, extending east from West Street. It probably originally had one and one-half stories since the

Flemish bond brickwork on the facade stops abruptly at the top of the first-story level and changes to a common bond, in addition to which the wooden lintels over the second-story windows do not match the jack arches over the lower windows. Most of these buildings were built or owned at one time by Francis Peyton, Sr., an extensive land holder who lived in a large residence called Peyton's Grove

(later Aspen Grove) at the head of Cameron Street just one block away. That residence was removed many years ago (1878) and the site was occupied by the old Alexandria High School, erected about 1913.

Photographs by Victor Amato and Russell Jones, Historic Alexandria Foundation

Most of the buildings of the 1400 block were constructed in the latter half of the nineteenth century and, except for the usual corner groceries, served as residential units, mostly rental; a 1902 Sanborn map lists the uses for them as "tenements." On the northwest corner of King and Peyton (1500 block) stood buildings listed in a 1852 "Virginia Directory and Business Register" as the "Virginia House Tavern" operated by W. Legg. This inn, along with Catts' Tavern, situated in the 2000 block of Duke Street (both considered West End, and on the

edge of town), catered to the hired hands who brought cattle (drovers) and produce (wagoners) from the western counties, specifically western Fairfax, Fauquier, and Loudoun, for all of which Alexandria served as a major market center. Rooms could be rented for fifteen cents and twenty-five cents (a suite?). As time passed, the name was changed to Hotel Jackson and it became a hostelry for black travelers. This ended in 1927 when a tornado tore through this section of Alexandria and the King Street facade fell to the ground. The writer remembers

passing by the site in the early 1930s, fascinated by the sight of beds and furniture still exposed to the elements. This source of interest ended when the building was removed in 1931 and replaced by a new Coca-Cola bottling plant. The corner portion of the lot contained a small park-like area with a fountain which appeared to be a birdbath with an extended arm whose hand held a Coca-Cola bottle pouring water into the basin. Expansion later eliminated this open space. (taken circa 1920)

This house on the north side of the 1800 block of King Street was long known as the Baggett House. Built in the early years of the nineteenth century, it was surrounded by a large tract of land covering several city blocks which were acquired by the Baggett family prior to the War Between the States. The Alexandria Gazette in referring to the death of Townsend Baggett on May 24, 1880, stated "for a number of years Mr. Baggett was a butcher and occupied a stand in the Market, but more recently had confined his attention to his truck farm near this city." In the early years of the twentieth century, the west end of this property housed a wooden stadium known as Baggett's Field, on which local athletic events, May Day performances by school children, and pageants were held. The writer recalls attending several exciting football games in the rickety old stadium as well as making a short cut through the yard of this house when walking each day to Jefferson School, several blocks away. The house was demolished about 1935 to be replaced by the grand, new Reed Theatre, (1937) which itself was torn down in the early 1980s in anticipation of business development of land in the vicinity of the nearby King Street Metro Station. Courtesy of Benjamin F. Baggett

Shuter's Hill (often spelled Shooter's throughout the recorded history of the town) is the eminence rising above the head of King Street to a height of about 187 feet. As early as 1784, John Mills owned the Mansion House (shown here by an unknown artist) atop Shuter's Hill where it was "well known for its beautiful situation and the absolute perfection of the plan." Ludwell, son of Richard Henry Lee and at one time president of the Virginia Senate, purchased it, then sold it in 1799 to Benjamin Dulany who also owned a fine residence in downtown Alexandria, still standing (601 Duke Street). Ludwell Lee's daughter, Matilda, was born in this house in 1790, and later wrote: "I would like to describe my home (on Shuter's Hill, Alexandria) as I knew it. The house was large and roomy. You entered a large passage; to the right was a spacious dining room, elegantly furnished. A large press with glass door held the silver, glass and china. We were waited on by three stately servants in livery which was blue turned up with white, with buckskin short breeches with shoes and stockings. Across the passage on the left was an elegantly furnished drawing room with mirrors down to the floor, before which I danced many a day. Beyond that was the chamber and nursery. My father

drove a chariot and four white horses, which were paraded out when I wanted to go to Alexandria to buy morocco shoes, of which I was very fond."

The house was destroyed by fire in 1843 and a smaller one built in its place. At the beginning of the War Between the States, Alexandria was quickly occupied by Federal forces on May 24, 1861, and shortly thereafter a large military fort was erected atop Shuter's Hill. Named for

Col. Elmer E. Ellsworth, one of the first Union officers killed, Fort Ellsworth was laid out by Capt. H. G. Wright several hundred yards west of the current Masonic Temple on May 25, 1861. It housed a large garrison including twenty cannon. President Lincoln visited the facility in July 1861 and during four years of war, thousands of Union soldiers bivouacked there "around the watchfires of a hundred circling camps."

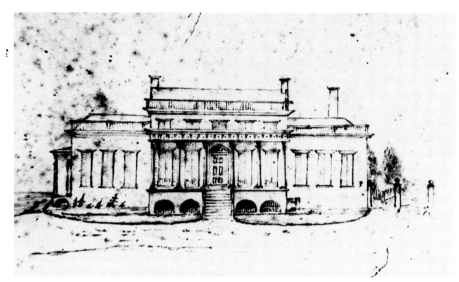

The commercial activity of King Street tended to die out along the 1500 block until the railroads, whose north-south tracks had run down the center of Fayette and Henry streets since the 1850s, were consolidated into a new, raised railbed, crossing King Street at about the 1900 block shortly after the turn of the twentieth century. At that time a new depot, Union Station, was

erected (1905) and it quickly became a popular spot for rail enthusiasts to bring their children to watch the giant locomotives, wave to engineers and conductors, and to dream of far away places where the trains ran usually on a daily basis; Atlanta, Memphis, and New Orleans. This 1918 view shows the station as originally constructed. In recent years it was allowed to deteriorate as passenger rail

traffic declined but it was restored and refurbished by the Richmond, Fredericksburg & Potomac Railroad in 1987. The shed-roofed overhang, protecting foot passenger walkways (shown in this view) was removed, causing the loss of a certain amount of the charm of the original building.

This view of Shuter's hill shows a portion of the Forty-fourth New York Regiment encampment in 1864, one of numerous Union military units which occupied Alexandria throughout the War Between the States. Leesburg Turnpike is seen on the right and Fort Ellsworth lies just behind the ridge. The occupying forces removed virtually all vegetation from the lands surrounding the city in order to prevent any surprise Confederate activity. (National Archives, Brady Collection)

There had long been a movement afoot to house the priceless relics of George Washington, owned by the Alexandria-Washington Masonic Lodge No. 22, of which Washington had served as worshipful master, in a safe, fireproof situation, particularly since many historically important items in the town museum had been lost in the burning of the Market House in 1871. This ultimately led to the erection of the George Washington Masonic Memorial whose cornerstone was laid by President Calvin Coolidge in 1923. The Memorial, as it appeared around 1930, was situated on the crown of Shuter's Hill facing east, down the entire length of King Street. Among other items housed here are a replica of the early lodge room and the original chair used by Washington.
Photograph by Virgil Davis

Alexandria as it appeared in 1864, looking east from Shuter's Hill. The occupying force of the Forty-fourth New York Regiment encampment sits in the foreground. At the upper end of King Street stands the Baggett House on the left with all its outbuildings and beyond it (to the left behind a white fence) is the Francis Peyton House. Both were large, commodious structures, occupying no less than a city block. The Baggett House was removed in 1935 prior to the building of the town's large new movie house, the Reed Theatre. Christ Church steeple may be seen above and slightly to the left of the Baggett House while the right side is dominated by the large circular roof of the Orange & Alexandria Railroad roundhouse.
Courtesy of the National Archives

This circa 1930 view, taken from the same spot as the previous picture, shows the newly terraced grounds of the Masonic Memorial as well as the RF&P Union Station, with the railroad tracks crossing King by way of an elevated overpass constructed in 1904. The Baggett House was still standing but the Peyton House was long gone, its site covered by the Alexandria High School. The roundhouse roof was no longer evident since about two-thirds of the building had been torn down some years earlier. The remainder, however, served for many years as the Southern Railroad Freight Office, and was finally burned during a period of racial unrest in the 1960s.

The 600 block, looking north toward the center of town, as it appeared in 1929, shows a portion of Roberts Chapel on the right (east side). Beyond it on the northeast corner of Gibbon and Washington looms the four-story commercial structure which housed the Paff Shoe Factory around the turn of the twentieth century and which later was used as a Sunday School annex by Roberts Chapel. Finally it was acquired by the DeMaine Funeral Home, founded in the 1800's, Alexandria's oldest. Across the street (west side, 500 block) may be seen the structure long known as the Old Club and beside it the French Lawler House. Actually Roberts Chapel, now known as Roberts Memorial United Methodist Church, is located just beyond the right edge of this view. It is the home of Alexandria's second oldest black church congregation, having been established in 1832.

National Archives

WASHINGTON STREET

ntil the 1890s, South Washington Street ended at St. Mary's Catholic Cemetery which had been established circa 1796. Beyond this point the land, which was still owned by a descendant of John Alexander, for whom the town was named, descended to Hunting Creek at a spot called Broomilaw Point. This name was undoubtedly derived from the passenger ship dock area in Glasgow, Scotland, known for several hundred years as The Broomielaw. In 1794, the area was leased to Robert Townsend Hooe, Alexandria's first mayor, and it was operated as a small farm for a number of years thereafter. Sometime after 1800, a tavern was constructed near a spring on the Point and this became the site of much warm weather entertainment since many of the townspeople would promenade in the area and would attend "fashionable dinners, dancing parties and festivities on public occasions." After Colonel Hooe's death in 1808, the farm and tavern continued in operation under the ownership of a Hooe kinsman and later of

William Fowle, a prominent town merchant who resided at 711 Prince Street. A writer in 1884 described Broomilaw as having once been "the principal pleasure resort of the city, a bowling alley, a dancing pavilion and other sources of amusement made the hilltop . . . a delightful place and its situation overlooking Hunting Creek and the river for miles away gave it an unusual pleasantness." The occupation of Alexandria during the War Between the States brought an end to such activity but in 1884 the Alexandria Brick Company was established on the Broomilaw tract and, despite several disastrous fires, remained in business until 1919. Two of its early major officials were Park Agnew and M. B. Harlow, both very active and successful businessmen. A requested subdivision of Broomilaw in 1893 included the construction of a bridge across the old railroad bed at Washington Street. The war had prevented completion of the railroad but the cut was widened and used for the Capital Beltway (I-95) when it was constructed in the early 1960s.

The Shadows (Hill House) was the southernmost elegant home built on South Washington Street (No. 617) in the nineteenth century. Built by Reuben Roberts about 1854, it was sold to Samuel B. Hussey, a Maine ship captain (master mariner) in 1857 and remained in the hands of his descendants (through marriages to Messrs. Wood and Hill) until it was disposed of about 1974. It remained intact in its large tree-shaded lot all through the years until destroyed to provide room for a sizeable commercial development comprised of numerous pseudo-Colonial structures. This view appears to have been taken around the 1880s. The writer recalls having attended the wedding reception of one of the Hill girls in the early 1940s and it was then still furnished very much as it must have been at the time of this photograph. It was truly a living museum.
Melissa Lovejoy Hill Collection

The northwest corner of Washington and Gibbon (No. 523) was occupied by this house around 1900 when the photograph was taken. The lot was purchased in 1804 by Thomas White, a prominent local merchant, and it remained in his family until about 1925. His son was for many years clerk of the city-owned Gas Company and later clerk of the Common Council, while his grandson, Thomas W. White, served as General Lee's chief headquarters clerk during the War Between the States. The original part of the house (north end) was said by family tradition to have been moved from Broomilaw Point but there is no evidence to verify this interesting theory. The structure as seen here was virtually unchanged from the early nineteenth century until the 1940s when, having become a very successful restaurant named the Old Club, from modest beginnings as a candy shop, it was remodeled into a large rambling building having a Mount Vernonesque portico.
O'Brien/Hulfish Collection

During most of the second half of the nineteenth century, the site on which this house stands contained the residence of George E. French, proprietor of a well-known book shop. Shortly before his death in 1890, his house was pulled down and replaced by two large and similarly styled structures, one brick (as seen here) and the other frame (long since demolished and replaced by a service station on the southwest corner of Washington and Wilkes streets). This fine Queen Anne-style house became the home of the Lawler family, whose initial member in the community, Martin Lawler, had come from Ireland at the age of twelve years, worked at the Smith and Perkins locomotive works in the 1850s, and later worked at Thomas Jamieson's machine shop at the southeast corner of Wilkes and Royal streets. After the war, he entered the grocery business and remained in this successfully to within a few years of his death in 1916. His son Nicholas J. Lawler succeeded to the ownership of this house and served for a time on the City Council. Most of the fixtures and woodwork remain in the house as when originally constructed.
Morrill Collection, 1979, Alexandria Library

On the southeast corner of South Washington and Wilkes streets stood the office of C. C. Smoot and Sons, leather manufacturers, better known as Smoot's Tannery, which had been established in 1820. It was a successful business for many years, having a capacity in 1907 of over sixteen thousand hides per week at its two major tanneries in Sperryville, Virginia, and North Carolina. It specialized in packers' hides. This view shows the headquarters building as it appeared around the turn of the century; the tanning operation occupied the rest of the east side of the 500 block of South Washington and covered at least two-thirds of the city block. A spectacular fire occurred here on May 29, 1889, which destroyed all the buildings in the tannery lot except for the office shown here, but the business continued for several more decades in Sperryville, Virginia and in North Carolina.
Loeb Collection

On the east side of the 400 block of South Washington Street stands the Alexandria Academy whose purpose was to provide a "permanent and respectable school" for the children of Alexandria and whose cornerstone was laid "on September 7, 1785 by Robert Adam, Esquire, Master of Lodge No. 39, Ancient York Masons, in an imposing Masonic ceremony." With funds contributed by George Washington, a member of the Board of Trustees, a free school for poor children, as opposed to the regular students of the Academy, was established in 1786 and occupied the third-story classroom until 1812 when the Lancastrian School was erected on a corner of the Academy lot. The Academy itself had among its students two nephews of George Washington, several Fairfax children, and Robert E. Lee. With neverending financial problems it continued in operation until about 1823 when the building was sold and somewhat remodeled as a residence by Samuel Arell Marsteller. It then changed hands several times over the next sixty-one years when in 1884, the owner, Joseph M. Howell and his family conveyed the old building to the Alexandria School Board and it once more became an active school used for that purpose until 1952. It is owned by the city to this day. This view was taken circa 1885 and probably shows Richard F. Carne or Theodore Ficklin, early School Board superintendents, standing before it with the students, all boys, peering from the windows.
Virgil Davis Collection

The Lancastrian School, also known as the Washington Free School, was built in 1812 for two thousand dollars provided by the Common Council. The Lancastrian method of teaching, popular at that time, allowed for the instruction of larger numbers of students with fewer teachers by having older students drill younger ones under the supervision of a single instructor. It seems that once the free school had moved here from the Academy building (seen in the left background) it became a school for black children, originally taught by the Reverend James H. Hanson, a white minister from the Methodist Episcopal Church. It is possible that some white children attended the school while Alexandria remained a part of the District of Columbia but after the retrocession of the city to the state of Virginia in 1847, black children were prohibited from receiving an education. For a short while during the occupation of Alexandria by Federal troops, classes were held here for the children of contrabands, a term used for blacks who escaped from Confederate territory and moved to areas under the control of the North. About 1887, this building was torn down and replaced the next year by the Washington School for boys.
Milton Grigg Collection

The Washington School, built in 1888, was originally the public school for boys (girls attended classes in the Lee School, later Prince Street School), subsequently became coed, then School Board offices and finally sold to the Alexandria Community Y to serve as its headquarters. At the present time the old Academy building stands empty but the Historic Alexandria Foundation is heading a drive to ensure its restoration and preservation. This view shows the Academy lot as it appeared in 1918.

This scene taken in 1960 shows the southeast corner of Washington and Duke streets shortly before its demolition, to be replaced by a structure housing a bank, which later became the First Virginia Bank. The facade was actually at 620 Duke Street but its two-story veranda, a very common appendage throughout Alexandria, and its side yard faced the 300 block of South Washington. It was occupied by the Whittlesey family in the late nineteenth century and a notice in the Alexandria Gazette (February 14, 1896) of the death of Miss Sarah J. C. Whittlesey, indicated that she was "an educated lady and possessed of a literary taste," for she wrote several books which were published in the 1850s, in addition to which she composed poetry, "some of her production showed . . . the spark of genius." She had moved to Alexandria from North Carolina with her father who taught for a number of years at the old Lancastrian School.
Photograph by Russell Jones, February 1960, Historic Alexandria Foundation

Jonathan Janney had this house (700 Duke Street) built about 1820 on the southwest corner of Washington and Duke streets and it remained in his possession until its sale in 1839. It served as a residence for several owners over the years including the T. J. Mehaffey family in the 1870s, finally becoming a rooming and tourist home until the early 1960s when it was converted to the main office of the First Commonwealth Savings and Loan Association, more recently changed to First Commonwealth Savings Bank. It still retains its interesting "widow's walk" and is an excellent example of making an adaptive use of an early structure for business purposes. Taken in the 1950s.
Photograph by Virgil Davis

This 1860s view gives a good idea of the appearance of Washington Street from the 200 block south, looking north. On the right side, the end of the Schofield/Lloyd Row is evident as well as the facade of the Downtown (originally First) Baptist Church, built on this site about 1805 and rebuilt in 1830 following a destructive fire, and finally enlarged to its present size in 1858. Beyond it is a light colored three-and-one-half story brick building, later replaced by the George Mason Hotel in 1929 on the northeast corner of Washington and Prince streets. All of the buildings on the left (west) side remained standing until the 1950s or 1960s when hospital expansion necessitated their destruction.

Many changes had taken place in the previous seven years when this 1936 photograph was taken. Still facing north in the 200 block of South Washington, only the McGuire House (Lyceum) and the Confederate Monument remain in the immediate foreground. Beyond the columned Lyceum (west side) stands the new Virginia Public Service Building (built in 1929 and predecessor to VEPCO or Virginia Power) while across the street the equally new U.S. Court House and Post Office and the George Mason Hotel, one hundred rooms—count 'em— all extremely small it might be noted) are visible. The greensward around the base of the monument has been removed due to a heavy increase in traffic, partially brought on by the inclusion of Washington Street as a part of the Mount Vernon Memorial Boulevard (1931) and angular parking has ceased altogether.
Loeb Collection, Alexandria Library

The west side of the 200 block of South Washington (at Duke) appeared this way shortly after the new Alexandria Hospital was erected in 1916-1917. Most of this entire block was owned and resided on by the prominent Daingerfield family, the large residence facing Washington Street being the home of John Daingerfield. This was the first of numerous residences on the street to be demolished as needs for the expanding hospital demanded.
Loeb Collection, Alexandria Library

This structure was long owned and lived in by Dr. R. H. Stabler, son of the founder of the Stabler-Leadbeater Apothecary Shop and later by members of the Snowden family who were publishers of the Alexandria Gazette, whose beginnings went back to at least 1800. This oddly shaped house, common to Alexandria, was called a flounder house because its eyes (windows) were on one side of the structure while the opposite wall, built on the lot line, contained no windows at all. This allowed the adjoining lot owner to build directly against the house without obstructing windows and provided maximum use of the remainder of the lot. The house was normally built back from the street to allow a later, more formal addition to be erected between it and the street. The origin of the flounder possibly goes back to the necessity of building a structure within a certain specified time on a newly purchased lot; some owners simply never got around to adding the front portion to their houses. A recent study by Christopher Martin indicates that the flounder style is an expression of vernacular architecture and is not specifically endemic to Alexandria. This house stood on the west side (No. 211) of South Washington Street and the photograph is dated about 1930.

Following the destruction of the Snowden (flounder) House, the rest were soon to follow so that by 1965 all but the corner Lyceum Building had been demolished, and it was preserved only after a long, hard-fought battle involving resolute preservationists and equally strong-willed business developers. The taller of the two houses in the foreground was the home of Edward Daingerfield and after 1911 of Thomas Clifton Howard, whose wife, Minnie Howard, organized the first Parent Teachers Association in Alexandria in the 1920s. It was Mr. Howard's great-grandfather's residence on the heights west of town which was purchased and became the nucleus of the Episcopal High School, founded in 1839.

The Lyceum on the southwest corner of Washington and Prince streets was built in 1839 for the Lyceum Company, a literary and mind-broadening society, which sponsored lectures by prominent people of the day. The building housed a large second-floor meeting hall, as well as smaller ones below, one of which was occupied by the Alexandria Library, founded in 1794, and which developed into the present library system for the city. Benjamin Hallowell, one of the founders, described the structure as a "fine building with a pediment front supported by four fluted columns, with a triglyph cornice ... surrounded with an iron railing and a beautiful yard of flowers and ornamental shrubbery." It served as a hospital during the War Between the States, as seen in this circa 1864 photograph, and was purchased in 1868 by John B. Daingerfield who remodeled it into a residence for his daughter's family. Gen. Fitzhugh Lee, Robert E. Lee's nephew and later commander of Confederate Cavalry, was married in this house. It was purchased in 1900 by Mrs. McGuire, whose husband was the son of Hunter McGuire, renowned personal physician to Stonewall Jackson, and it remained the office and residence of the popular Dr. Hugh McGuire until about 1940. It was then converted into offices, became derelict, and was saved from demolition by a determined Historic Alexandria Foundation and a helpful City Council, then became in 1974 the Northern Virginia Bicentennial Center.

The center of Washington and Prince streets shortly after the 1889 dedication of John Elder's "Appomattox," erected to the memory of Alexandria's Confederate soldiers who died during the conflict. In the background looms the Lyceum Building, then the residence of Philip Beverley Hooe, son-in-law of John B. Daingerfield, and behind it stands the handsome Victorianized home of Henry Daingerfield, who had purchased it in 1832 from Thomas Swann, a prominent attorney and probably builder of the house before 1803.

O'Brien/Hulfish Collection

PRINCE ST.

An additional view of the north side of the 600 block of Prince Street about 1900 reveals an interesting row of mostly mid-nineteenth century residences, occupied by well-known families, among others J. D. H. Smoot, F. A. Reed (an early importer of ice), and Dr. George Klipstein. The residence of the latter (the large, taller building to the left of the dark brick church on the next corner) had been purchased in 1853 by William Klipstein and it remained in his family's hands for nearly one hundred years. A portion later became the church office for the Second Presbyterian Church next door which had been modernized in 1889, thus destroying a handsome Greek Revival facade originally built in 1840. William A. Moore Collection

This view of Trinity Methodist Church in 1918 (with army trucks parked in front— World War I was not yet concluded) gives an idea how the large building dominated the entire east side of the 100 block. The first Methodist Meeting house was built about 1791 in Chapel Alley, on the south side of the 300 block of Duke Street, at the approximate location of the present St. Mary's Roman Catholic Church. The building on this site was erected in 1803-1804, considerably enlarged in 1883, and dismantled in 1942 when the congregation built a new sanctuary in the Beverly Hills section of Alexandria, incorporating some materials from the older church in the new.

The cornerstone of this Greek Revival building was laid in 1850 by members of the new Methodist Episcopal Church South, directly across the street from the original Methodist congregation, from whom they had split about a year earlier. It was built on the west side of South Washington and was confiscated for use as a hospital during the occupation of the town by Union troops. This circa 1864 view indicates that there was little else located on that side of the street other than the two-and-one-half story building located on the corner with King Street.
U.S. Army Historical Institute

167

The west side of 100 block of South Washington Street shows the new facade on the Washington Street Methodist Church, rebuilt in 1876. It was designed by John Lambdin, described as a "Master builder and architect," who practiced in Alexandria from 1853 to 1889. After unification in 1939 of the various fragments of the Methodist Church, there remained three churches of the same persuasion within one block of each other: Trinity (old northern), Washington Street (old southern) and the Methodist Protestant Church in the 100 block of North Washington Street. Two moved to suburbia leaving only the original Methodist Episcopal Church South, which despite serious parking problems, has managed to thrive and continue its active life in spite of the congested area in which it is located. The old George R. Hill Educational Building sat well back from the street. Erected in 1907, it was superseded by the much newer building located to the left of the church, and the Virginia Public Service Building, long since vacated by the successor to the power company still stands on the corner at Prince Street.

This 1925 view of the intersection of King and Washington streets (looking north) shows a street sufficiently wide to allow angular parking and an early example of the Alexandria Barcroft & Washington bus fleet. At about this time, Robert L. May, founder of the AB&W Bus Company, told the writer's father that the future of public transportation was on rubber tires, not steel tracks, and true enough, by 1932, the interurban trolley lines came to an end. (No one realized that the phenomenal population growth of the post-World War II era would bring back the necessity for the steel tracked Metro system.) In April 1865 a violent explosion rocked this intersection when a wagon full of fireworks exploded in the middle of the street. A near tragedy occurred here in 1881 when President Rutherford B. Hayes, who was watching a George Washington Birthday parade, was nearly crushed when the grandstand collapsed. Clearly seen are the Auto Accessories store on the right and Timberman's Drug Store on the left. Unfortunately of all the buildings shown in this view, only the Amos Alexander Building on the northeast corner (right side) is still standing.
Loeb Collection

Among several schisms which occurred within the old "Alexandria Station" of the Methodist Church (later Trinity), one of the earliest took place in 1828 with the formation of the Methodist Protestant Church under the national leadership of Nicholas Snethen, a former pastor in the Alexandria church. This division came about over the form of church government. A chapel was built on the west side of the 100 block of North Washington Street in 1830 and a subsequent enlargement in 1890 resulted in the Gothic-style edifice shown here. A left-hand tower was later lowered to the same height as that on the right. This was demolished in the 1950s when the congregation moved to West Braddock Road and the building was replaced by a neo-Colonial J. C. Penney store. The three-and-one-half story residence to the right, later serving as doctor's offices, was torn down at about the same time to make room for a new Christ Church parish hall.
Photograph by Virgil Davis, circa 1950

Christ Church (1773) with its belfry (1818) stands in this 1929 view in the middle of Cameron Street as it always has but its early date of construction and its location "in the woods" caused little concern for a later extension of that street. Looking west across North Washington, there appear two houses (semi-detached) in the Italianate style built in 1875 by brick layer-contractor Emmanuel Francis on land which he had purchased from the German Cooperative Building Association (established in 1868 and which continues to exist today under the title of First Commonwealth Savings Bank. Graves from the Christ Church cemetery were discovered during construction (Alexandria Gazette, May 31, 1875). These buildings located on the 700 block of Cameron Street, were demolished in the late 1950s, to provide a parking lot for an adjoining office building.
National Archives

This unique photograph is taken from Christ Church cemetery before 1885 looking east across the 100 block of North Washington Street. In the center of the picture is the formidable residence of Dr. M. M. Lewis who restyled the house in the Second Empire style in 1870. To the left is a row of historic homes on the 600 block of Cameron Street. The one with the recessed arch and horizontal strong string course was constructed by William Yeaton, circa 1800. Yeaton, designer of the tomb of George Washington at Mount Vernon, also constructed the original fabric of the Dr. Lewis House around 1805. The flat-roofed building to the far left (201 North Washington Street) belonged to the Powell family, and the Alexandria Gazette on August 20, 1885, reported that Dr. R. C. Powell was enlarging his house by having a third-story mansard roof added. Mary G. Powell, well-known Alexandria historian, resided here much of her adult life. Her son, Dr. Llewellyn Powell, was living here in the 1930s with his family and his daughter, Grace, a local violinist and music teacher who had her studio in the building. The elderly frame house just beyond the Powell House on Cameron Street was just another example of the type of structure which was fast disappearing from the Alexandria scene for it was removed shortly after the date of this picture.
Gift of William Triplett

This picturesque view of the 100 block of North Washington Street looking south shows the Dr. Lewis House (southeast corner of Cameron and Washington Streets) and a lovely bower of shade trees. Before the twentieth century, Washington Street was an elegant avenue of beautiful Victorian and Greek Revival structures.
Alexandria-Washington Lodge No. 22

The northwest corner of North Washington and Cameron streets had two Italianate-style houses which were erected about 1872 under the auspices of the German Building Cooperative Association by Messrs. Risheill and Hooge, members of that institution. These structures were part of a planned development of vacant land north of Christ Church in the early 1870s and were designed and built by Benjamin Franklin Price, one of Alexandria's most successful and prolific architects. At his death in 1894, it was stated "he loved the town of his birth and was deeply interested in its welfare and progress . . . and hundreds of the neat as well as the more costly residences, stores and other buildings, among them the Market House steeple are monuments of his intelligent handiwork." (Penny Morrill Who Built Alexandria?) The corner structure housed the Alexandria Chapter of the American Red Cross for a time during World War II and later served as a tourist and rooming house. To their right stands the town's first synagogue, home of the Beth El Hebrew Congregation. The small Jewish community had by 1859 formed a congregation which met in rented rooms. The period of the War Between the States saw a heavy influx of Jewish merchants and their families so that by 1871 the Beth El Congregation built and dedicated this

structure which remained in active use until about 1955 when it moved to new quarters on Seminary Road. These three structures were demolished to accommodate a new bank and office building at this location.
Gamble Collection

The Benjamin Hallowell and C. C. Carlin House was located at 215 North Washington Street (east side). After returning to Alexandria in the early 1850s, Benjamin Hallowell designed this lovely dwelling for his residence. He states in his autobiography that "in 1854-55, I built a house on a lot I owned opposite the boarding school (Brimstone Castle). As I expected to end my days in this new building, I furnished it with every known convenience, and supplied it with all modern improvements." Unfortunately, Hallowell was unable to continue the operation of his boarding school and departed Alexandria for good in the late 1850s. Like the Brimstone Castle, this elegant old home was seized by Union military authorities during the war and converted into a major military hospital. Joseph Broders, president of the first National Bank was the occupant in the late 1890s. During the twentieth century, Charles C. Carlin, Alexandria businessman and U.S. congressman resided here and entertained numerous notables including President Taft. In 1965 after an unsuccessful effort by the Historic Alexandria Foundation to save the dwelling, the Alexandria Board of Architectural Review granted permission to demolish it. Historic Alexandria Foundation, December 1959

173

Benjamin Hallowell, respected Quaker teacher purchased this real estate about 1832 and converted an old sugar house (right) and a tobacco warehouse (left) into a school which was called "Brimstone Castle" by his students. Hallowell, who had operated his school at this site from 1828, moved his family here after an unsuccessful effort to purchase Lloyd House in 1832. He wrote in his autobiography that he "immediately engaged George Swain to do the carpenter work and Robert Brockett to do the brick work." About this time he joined the buildings with an addition containing an observatory and bell tower. By 1842, Hallowell had transferred his school to his nephews, Caleb and James Hallowell, and returned to Sandy Spring, Maryland, to farm. During the War Between the States, the school building was converted into a military hospital for Federal troops. When hostilities ceased in 1865 the old structure became the home of Blackburn's Academy and was operated by John Blackburn and Charles Taylor. The building has been demolished.
Milton Grigg Collection

174

The Lloyd House at 220 North Washington Street was built in 1797 by John Wise, Alexandria's tavern King, and is a fine example of late Georgian architecture. Particularly interesting are the fluted keystone lintels above the windows and the beautiful doric pedimented doorway. Wise, who resided briefly at Lloyd House, leased the property in 1800 to Charles Lee, attorney general under the Washington and Adams Administrations; in 1801 to 1804 to James Marshall, brother of Supreme Court Justice John Marshall; in 1805 to 1806 to Nicholas Fitzhugh, circuit court judge. Jacob Hoffman, mayor of Alexandria in 1804 and 1818, was a wealthy entrepreneur who resided at Lloyd House and was proprietor of a successful sugar refinery on the southern half of the lot. Later, after its purchase by the widow of James H. Hooe in 1825, Benjamin Hallowell, prominent Quaker teacher and educator, rented it and moved his already established school here in the same year. It attracted the sons of lawmakers, judges, and ambassadors. John Lloyd, who had married Ann Harriotte Lee, Robert E. Lee's first cousin, purchased the real estate in 1832. His family occupied the home until 1918 when it was subsequently sold to William Albert Smoot, who while mayor of the city entertained President Herbert Hoover on the celebration of George Washington's birthday in 1928. During World War II, the fine old building was turned into barracks for WAVES who worked at the U.S. Naval Torpedo Plant on Union Street. Thereafter, it became a rooming house and geological offices, and finally was purchased by the city with donations from the Hoge and Historic Alexandria Foundations for use as a historical and genealogical library. Presently an adjunct to the Alexandria Library, Lloyd House houses an impressive collection of volumes and documents on Virginia, Alexandria, and the South. The photograph, taken before 1900 shows a rear building which served as the kitchen wing. It was demolished after 1924.
O'Brien/Hulfish Collection

This group of frame buildings on the northeast corner of Washington and Queen, 300 block, known locally as Brockett's Row, was built in 1808 by Robert Brockett "for private families or business." Remodeled and updated about 1852, this row remained in possession of Brockett's heirs until 1925. Interestingly enough, these units continue to serve both commercial and residential occupants to this day.
Photograph by Victor Amato, 1968, Historic Alexandria Foundation

Originally owned by Light Horse Harry Lee, the lot of 329 North Washington Street (southeast corner with Princess) was purchased by John C. Mandell in 1821 for four hundred dollars. In 1829 he advertised a two-story house for rent at this location. It was William Gregory, the proprietor of a dry goods store who sold carpets and other woolen goods from his family factory in Kilmarnock, Scotland, who acquired the dwelling in 1832 for four thousand dollars. The third floor was probably added during his ownership. His daughter, Mary Gregory Powell, a noted Alexandria historian, wrote an interesting account of the town entitled: The History of Old Alexandria, Va. In 1937 the Gregory heirs sold the charming edifice to Dr. Martin Delaney who resided here until his death in 1987. Amazingly, four of his sons also became medical doctors.

The smaller two-story house to the right (323 North Washington) was built between 1877 and 1885. During the 1930s it was occupied by the George Grim family.
National Archives, 1929

On the east side of the 300 block of North Washington Street was located the home of Robert H. Miller who, born in 1798, was an industrious Quaker entrepreneur who shaped the fabric of nineteenth-century Alexandria society. He was an original incorporator of the Mount Vernon Manufacturing Company, president of the Alexandria Water Company, first president of the First National Bank and trustee of the Female Orphan Society. Miller married Anna Janney of Loudoun County, Virginia, by whom he fathered eleven children. During his later life, he inhabited this elegant three-story Greek Revival house where he died in 1874. The 1877 Hopkins City Atlas shows that the Miller estate owned the entire middle half of the block including equal frontage on St. Asaph Street. The house has long since been torn down.
Gift of Landmarks Society of Alexandria

The second photograph pictures Mr. and Mrs. Miller with much of their family at the time of their golden wedding anniversary about 1870.
Alexandria Library

This photograph depicts the west side of the 300 block of North Washington Street during the 1950s. The large Second Empire house with its distinctive mansard roof was constructed for Herbert Bryant in 1881 and designed by B. F. Price. When it was finished the Alexandria Gazette remarked: "Of all the residences in the city, none are handsomer than the one recently erected by Captain Herbert Bryant. The building inside is supplied with all the modern improvements. The workmanship on this building reflects credit upon Alexandria mechanics." Capt. Herbert Bryant (1834-1914) served as adjutant of the Seventeenth Virginia Regiment throughout the War Between the States. Upon the termination of the conflict he returned to Alexandria and opened an agricultural store at 117 King Street and later established a large fertilizer plant at the foot of Duke. His martial spirit was not quenched by the war and in 1871 he became captain of the Alexandria Grays, a local militia unit. Captain Bryant also served in several other municipal positions including: membership in the Board of Aldermen, School Board member and city police commissioner. During the first third of the twentieth century, the Catholic Brothers operated the Xavier School, usually referred to as the "Brothers School," in the old Bryant House. Many parties and festivals were held on the school lawn during these years. At the time of this photograph, a large house between the two shown here had just been demolished and these two were soon to follow.
Photograph by Virgil Davis

View taken in 1924 of the west side of the 300 block of North Washington Street looking south. The house to the immediate right is the Brockett House, built after 1877 but whose rear extension, or ell, was much older. Directly beside it is 316 North Washington Street. This dwelling was owned by John Dixon in the late 1870s and 1880s. Dixon (1814-1895), a local businessman, was involved in numerous commercial enterprises. Along with his brother George O., he commenced a mercantile establishment on the west side of Union between Prince and Duke streets. During this epoch (1840s and 1850s) much of the town's trade was concentrated on that thoroughfare or the Strand. The Dixon's business flourished and the brothers moved to the corner of the Strand and King Street until there was a dissolution of the firm occasioned by the indisposition of George. Later John moved to the southeast corner of Prince and Pitt streets where he conducted a grocery business. With the outbreak of the war the firm was dissolved. Dixon devoted himself mainly to the pursuit of his real estate interests after the hostilities. "Mild mannered and meek, John Dixon enjoyed the respect of all who knew him." He had a wife and two children. A subsequent owner was the family of Judge Nichol, president of

Alexandria National Bank.
Photograph by W. P. Gray, Valentine Museum

This view of the rear of the Brockett House, 318 North Washington, taken about 1950, shows a considerably older building than the one to which it was attached. It was probably erected in the early nineteenth century and was likely not intended to become an append-age to a later structure. Scotsman Robert Brockett owned this lot before his death in 1829. His son Robert served as a lieu-tenant in the army during the War of 1812, was president of the City Council for a number of years, and represented the interests of Alexandria before the U.S. Congress. Of three grandchildren of the original Robert, one, Robert L., be-came a prominent teacher and constructed a large boarding school at 603 Queen Street; another, Walter, who died at this address in 1889, served as a captain in the Fourth Louisiana Volunteers and later was president of that state's Board of Assessors; and Edgar L. also served in the Confederate Army. Edgar's son, A. D. Brockett, founded a brokerage firm under that name in Alexandria. In December 1925, the Brockett estate was purchased by St. Mary's church to ex-pand the operation of the Brother's School, which already occupied the Bry-ant House at the south end of the block. Photograph by Virgil Davis

This fine postcard view of President Taft, Vice President Sherman, and Governor Swanson was taken at Princess and North Washington streets upon the president's attendance of a homecoming ceremony in May 1909. Later the official retinue was whisked away to Shuter's Hill where President Taft participated in the cornerstone laying of a proposed new monument to George Washington. ". . . The ceremonies in connection with the laying of the cornerstone were very impressive. When the President accepted the invitation to visit Alexandria . . . he was not expected to make a speech. He, however, partook of the enthusiasm of yesterday . . . and was introduced on the hill by the Governor. Mr. Taft was greeted with great applause. He said: 'It has been a great pleasure to be here this afternoon and to join with hospitable Alexandria and Virginia in celebrating the memory of George Washington . . . When your committee kindly invited me to be present . . . It was left to me to remain silent . . . so I will after expressing to you in behalf of the Vice-President, the Speaker of the House and the whole government that has moved down, here from Washington our appreciation of Virginia hospitality . . .

The crowds kept up an incessant cheer, and their shouts were taken up by the soldiers. With much shaking of hands and farewells the president . . . was whisked back to this city where they were en-

tertained at the residence of Mr. W. B. Smoot, president of the George Washington Park Association." (804 Prince Street)
(Alexandria Gazette, May 1, 1909)

Of the many antique structures which dot the streetscape of Alexandria, few have such a diverse heritage as the Lee-Fendall House at 429 North Washington Street (southeast corner with Oronoco). Its inhabitants have not only left their imprint on the town but also on the nation's history. Constructed in 1785 by Philip Richard Fendall, prominent Charles County, Maryland lawyer, the Lee-Fendall House is an interesting example of Maryland telescopic architecture. Its graceful dependencies are tied together to form a harmonious whole and its verdant gardens are a delight to all. From 1785 to 1903, more than thirty-five members of the Lee family lived in this residence. In 1852, Louis Cazenove who married Harriott Stuart, the great-granddaughter of Richard Henry Lee, completely remodeled the structure in the popular Greek Revival fashion. During the War Between the States, the house was converted into a ward of the Federal Grosvenor House military hospital. One can just imagine the shrieks and groans of the dying patients as their voices reverberated through the halls which once echoed the merriment of parties and receptions for Gen. George Washington. History, however, did not come to a grinding halt upon the departure of the last member of the Lee family in 1903. In 1937, John L. Lewis, president of the United Mine Workers, purchased the edifice. His figure loomed large on the national scene during the famous coal

strikes of World War II and afterwards as a giant in the labor movement. Until his death in 1969, Lewis entertained many prominent politicians here. In 1974 the Virginia Trust for Historic Preservation purchased the house from the Lewis heirs and since that time it has become a well-known Virginia landmark and house museum. It was placed on the National Register in 1979.

Laws were on the books in the early 1800s which prohibited animals from roaming at large, yet this early photo-

graph from the 1870s clearly shows a cow trodding down the 400 block of North Washington Street in front of the Lee-Fendall House. Frequently these bovine creatures would wreak havoc by munching on the well-manicured gardens of local inhabitants. To prevent such occurrences, it was the duty of constables to round up these animals and advertise their whereabouts in local newspapers. A group of court records called estray accounts list abandoned animals found throughout the town.

A fascinating view of the circular stairway in the Lee-Fendall House is shown prior to the erection of an elevator by John L. Lewis which occupies a large portion of the open area encircled by the balustrade. Fortunately, the stairway was not destroyed and could be restored fairly easily if the elevator should ever be removed.

Washington St. General Corse Residence, Alexandria, Va.

This early twentieth-century view of the west side of the 400 block of North Washington Street shows a group of handsome residences, most of which have been destroyed since 1960. Only the Edmund Jennings Lee home in the far background (428 North Washington Street) and the Buckingham dwelling (No. 420) third from the left, are still standing. The General Montgomery Corse House to the immediate left was razed in 1960 and the Queen Anne-style house (No. 418) with its distinctive tower fell victim to progress in 1982. No. 418 was constructed in 1886 and was the home of George A. Mushbach, a prominent Alexandria lawyer and member of the Virginia General Assembly from 1877 to 1880 and state senator from 1891 to 1898. Shortly after his purchase of the lot in March 1886, the Alexandria Gazette stated: "Captain G. A. Mushbach has awarded to Mr. W. F. Vincent the contract for building a handsome residence . . . The house is to be a two-story brick, with French roof, to be fitted with all the modern improvements and will be an ornament to that part of the city." The structure next to the Lee House was the home of the family of Justus Schneider, a member of the small but tightly-knit German community in Alexandria. He first operated a restaurant at the foot of King Street and later started a very successful insurance business. He was a founding member of the German Cooperative Building Association established in 1868. Courtesy of Mrs. Lewis Gordon Porter

This attractive colonnaded gallery along the side of the rear extension (or ell) of the Lee House at 428 North Washington Street is a sight becoming more and more rare in Alexandria. In earlier times the two galleries were quite common because the extension was usually flounder-shaped and one room deep. Having these porches eliminated the necessity of an inside hallway or the need to walk through one room in order to reach the next. Unfortunately the construction was normally of wood which, if not properly cared for, would rot and the extraordinary cost of repair or replacement resulted in the complete removal of the deteriorated structure. Thus many naked rear wings are to be seen throughout the city today. *O'Brien/Hulfish Collection, circa 1900*

This view of two houses facing Oronoco Street is included because the open side yard of the nearer structure (609 Oronoco) runs for several hundred feet along the east side of the 500 block of North Washington Street. Besides its strong Lee family connections, the house is sometimes referred to as the "Hallowell House" because it was here that the Quaker schoolmaster occupied and started his school in 1824. He moved to the Lloyd House the next year. The adjoining house is the Robert E. Lee boyhood home and the photograph shows both buildings in a sad state of disrepair, around 1900. Fortunately both were rescued and 609 Oronoco has been owned by the Arthur Herbert Bryant family for many years. *O'Brien/Hulfish Collection*

This building was originally the old Mount Vernon Cotton Factory. Constructed in 1847, it employed upwards of 150 hands, mostly industrious females who worked for twelve dollars to seventeen dollars a month. There were 3,840 spindles for 124 looms, weaving daily nearly five thousand yards of sheeting. During the War Between the States, the building became the largest prison in Alexandria and housed more than one thousand Confederate soldiers. Attempts to revitalize the business after the war failed and the structure was purchased by Robert Portner as a bottling works for his extensive brewery between 1902 and 1915. When Prohibitions closed the brewery, it was sold to the Express Spark Plug Company which operated a factory in it from 1918 to 1930. By 1935 the massive edifice had been gutted and converted into an apartment house. A plaster dummy which was left in the building after it was occupied by the Department of Agriculture in the early 1930s now inhabits the cupola. For years it was the talk of town and the mascot of thousands of motorists who drove by it each day. Renovated about 1982, the old Cotton Factory currently houses several businesses including the offices of patent attorneys.

Courtesy of the National Archives

EPILOGUE

t the end of the First World War, Alexandria, Virginia, suffered from an economic and political malaise. The old mayor-council form of government was not providing the leadership essential to the economic and fiscal well-being of the city. As the historic town struggled along under an antiquated, obsolete form of municipal government, it became impossible for members of city council to give detailed attention to the increasingly complex affairs of the city. Frequently council meetings were not well attended and lacked a quorum to do business. On August 20, 1918, only eight out of the sixteen members of the council appeared in chambers. Other city agencies also suffered staff and morale problems. For instance, it was hinted that only one-half of the members of the police force were performing their duty and that the employees at the City Gas Works had dwindled to less than a corporal's guard. Indeed, those who remained at their posts were sometimes compelled to labor thirty-six hours at a time. In addition, the street department was unable to secure laborers to work on the roads. (*Alexandria Gazette,* August 24, 1918)

The deficiencies of the old mayor-council form of government were multiple. Among the inherent problems were: (1) no responsible head of the administrative affairs of the city; (2) the responsibility of the city government was divided between the mayor, Common Council, Board of Aldermen, and a large number of committees. To remedy many of these ills, it was suggested that a city-manager plan of government be implemented. As early as 1919 such an initiative had been proposed and was de-

feated by five votes. (*Alexandria Gazette,* September 27, 1921, page 6)

Again in the fall of 1921 a plan for a new municipal government was suggested. Under this system the Council would be composed of five officials elected at large instead of the unwieldy sixteen members. In addition the council would have the power:

> to pass all city ordinances; to levy taxes, pass on all appropriations of city money, to provide what city officers are necessary to conduct the city affairs and to fix their salaries; to appoint a city manager. The council elected one of its members chairman of the Council, who is, by reason of the office, ex officio Mayor of the city . . . (*Alexandria Gazette,* September 27, 1921, page 6)

The important feature of the system was that there would be a city manager. As established in 1922, this individual had broad power to conduct the affairs of the city.

At a special election held in June 1922 the new form of government was approved and five at-large councilmen elected. They included: W. Albert Smoot, Robert J. Jones, Edmund F. Ticer, Thomas J. Fannon, and Arthur H. Bryant. (*Alexandria Gazette,* June 8, 1922) On September 1, 1922, the city manager system of government became operative and Wilder M. Rich of Sault Sainte Marie, Michigan, was appointed as the town's first city manager. To date, nineteen individuals have held this important Alexandria city post.

Unfortunately after World War I, much of Alexandria's historic housing stock, especially in the area now known as old town, had fallen into a state of disrepair. In 1927, members of Alexandria American Legion Post No. 22 actively began the restoration movement by volunteering to clean up the graveyard of the old Presbyterian Meeting House. Many town notables including John Carlyle, Dr. Craik, and personal lieutenants and acquaintances of George Washington are buried in the Meeting House cemetery. During the restoration the remains of an old Revolutionary War soldier were discovered and subsequently a marker was placed on his grave by the Children of the American Revolution. Dedicated in 1929, this site became known locally as the Tomb of the Unknown Revolutionary War soldier.

Fired with enthusiasm, the American Legion in 1928 also purchased the dilapidated old City Hotel (Gadsby's Tavern) and commenced raising money for its restoration. With the assistance of the American Legion Auxiliary, the Mount Vernon Chapter of the D.A.R., the Colonial Dames, and the Garden Club of Alexandria, the old tavern was restored and a non-profit corporation chartered by the state was appointed to keep the building open for tourists and special events.

An influx of new residents who were vitally interested in historic preservation began to arrive in 1929. Among the early "foreign legionnaires," an epithet assigned by the native population, were Col. and Mrs. Charles Beatty Moore and architect Ward Brown. The Moore's purchased and restored the William Hodgson House at 207 Prince Street and several additional properties. Ward Brown, who acquired 123 Prince Street, became enamoured with the houses in this row (Captain's Row) and developed a master plan to rehabilitate the entire block. Publicity for his project attracted the attention of federal officials in Washington, numbers of whom moved to Alexandria, hoping to make it into another Georgetown. One of the first to become enchanted with the history and ambience of old Alexandria was Supreme Court Justice Hugo Black who bought and restored the old Snowden homestead at 619 South Lee Street. Other prominent transplants included:

George Kennan, future ambassador to the Soviet Union; Senator and Mrs. Henry Keyes; and Blondelle Malone, a local artist. Not only private residences but commercial buildings on North and South Washington Street were renovated. The old Mount Vernon Cotton factory at 515 North Washington was converted into apartments while the Paff Shoe Manufactory was purchased by the Demaine Funeral Home. Unfortunately in 1929, Alexandria's largest mansion, Colross, located on the 1100 block of Oronoco Street, was carted off brick by brick to Princeton, New Jersey, after being ravaged by a tornado in 1927. Arch Hall, the former townhouse of Lawrence Lewis and Nelly Custic, on the north side of the 800 block of Franklin Street met a similar fate in 1950 when it was removed to Belmont Bay.

To protect its historic housing stock, Alexandria created an old and historic district in 1946 which extended south from Montgomery Street to Hunting Creek and east from Alfred Street to the Potomac River. "All structures therein dating from 1846 or earlier were protected from unwarranted demolition and/or extensive architectural treatment out of character with their history or surrounding." A Board of Architectural Review was established to enforce these provisions.

In 1949, the city celebrated its Two Hundredth Anniversary by sponsoring a pageant called "Alexandria, Thy Sons" at Windmill Hill (600 block South Lee Street) which presented historical highlights of the seaport's distinguished legacy.

Today, Alexandria is a vibrant community which boasts boutiques and shops, historical museums, art galleries, and delightful gourmet restaurants. In addition, a number of trade associations and businesses have recently moved into town. Each year thousands of tourists crowd Alexandria's cobblestone streets and alleys to drink deeply from the chalice of history. As it enters the twenty-first century, it is to be hoped that Alexandria will retain its unique charm and delightful character.

BIBLIOGRAPHY

Abdill, George B. *Civil War Railroads.* Seattle, Washington: Superior Publishing Co., 1961.

Alexandria, Virginia. Proceedings of the Board of Trustees of Alexandria, Virginia, 1749-1767. Alexandria Library, Lloyd House: photostatic copy.

Alexandria Gazette, 1784-1920. Library of Congress, Washington D.C.: microfilm.

Barnard, Major General John G. *A Report on the Defenses of Washington to the Chief of Engineers, U.S. Army.* Washington, D.C.: U.S. Government Printing Office, 1871.

Brockett, F. L. & Rock, George W. *A Concise History of the City of Alexandria, Va., from 1669 to 1883, with a Directory of Reliable Business Houses in the City.* Alexandria, Virginia: Printed at the Gazette Book and Job Office, 1883.

Caton, James R. *Legislative Chronicles of the City of Alexandria, Virginia.* Alexandria, Virginia: Newell-Cole, 1933.

Cox, Ethelyn. "Alexandria, Virginia, May 1774—December 1783." Alexandria Bicentennial Commission, May 1971.

_____ . *Historic Alexandria Virginia—Street by Street.* Alexandria, Virginia: Historic Alexandria Foundation, 1976.

The Fireside Sentinel. ed. T. Michael Miller. Alexandria, Virginia: Alexandria Library, Lloyd House.

Fitzgerald, Oscar. *The Green Family of Cabinetmakers—An Alexandria Institution—1817-1887.* Alexandria, Virginia: The Lyceum, 1986.

Glasgow, Col. William *Northern Virginia's Own—A History of the 17th Virginia Infantry Regiment, Confederate States Army.* Alexandria, Virginia: Gobill Press, 1989.

Hambleton, Elizabeth and VanLandingham, Marian, eds. *A Composite History of Alexandria.* Alexandria, Virginia: Alexandria Bicentennial Commission, 1975.

Hedman, Kathryn Pierpoint. *Washington Street United Methodist Church—Alexandria, Virginia Reflections 1849-1974.* Alexandria, Virginia: n.p., 1974.

Hurd, William B. *Alexandria, Virginia, 1861-65.* City of Alexandria, Virginia: Ft. Ward, 1970.

Kaye, Ruth Lincoln. *The History of St. Paul's Episcopal, Church, Alexandria, Virginia.* Springfield, Virginia: the Goetz Printing Co., 1984.

MaColl, John D., ed. *Alexandria: A Towne in Transition, 1800-1900.* Alexandria, Virginia: Alexandria Bicentennial Commission, Alexandria Historical Society, 1977.

Miller T. Michael. "A Brief History of the Alexandria Waterfront." unpublished research at the Lloyd House, Alexandria Library.

_____ . "Charles Lee, Collector of Customs: Portrait of an Early Alexandrian on the Waterfront." *The Alexandria Waterfront Forum: Birth and Rebirth 1730-1983.* Published by the Alexandria Archaeology Center, City of Alexandria, 1983.

_____ . *Murder & Mayhem—Criminal Conduct in Old Alexandria, Virginia, 1749-1900.* Bowie, Maryland: Heritage Press, Inc., 1989.

_____ . *Pen Portraits of Alexandria, Virginia, 1739-1900.* Bowie, Maryland: Heritage Press, 1987.

_____ . "Some Lee Homes in Alexandria, Virginia" *Northern Virginia Heritage.* June 1981, vol. 3, no. 2.

Moore, Gay Montague. *Seaport in Virginia: George Washington's* Richmond, Virginia: Garrett & Massie, Inc., 1949.

Morrill, Penny C. *Old Town Alexandria Architecture, 1750-1900.* Arlington, Virginia: Vol. 1, no. Inc., 1979.

_____ , ed. "Alexandria Academy." *The Plague.* Historic Alexandria Foundation, 1987.

_____ . *Who Built Alexandria/Architects in Alexandria 1750-1900.* Northern Virginia Regional Park Authority, 1979.

Munson, Dr. James. *Col. John Carlyle, Gent.—A True and Just Account of the Man and His Home.* Northern Virginia Regional Park Authority, 1986.

Our Town: 1749-1865. Alexandria Association, 1956.

Powell, Mary. *History of Old Alexandria, Virginia.* Richmond, Virginia: 1928.

Preisser, Thomas M. "Eighteenth-Century Alexandria, Virginia, before the Revolution, 1749-1776." Unpublished dissertation, College of William & Mary, Virginia, 1977: typescript.

Scribner's Monthly. "An Old Virginia Town." From midwinter number, February, 1881.

Schomette, Donald. "Maritime Alexandria—An evaluation of Submerged Cultural Resource Potentials." City of Alexandria, Virginia: Alexandria Archaeology Center, 1987.

Stoessel, John. "The Port of Alexandria, Va. in the 18th Century," page 61. Dissertation, Catholic University of America, 1969.

Tilp, Frederick. *This Was Potomac River.* Alexandria, Virginia privately published, 1978.

Wedderburn, A. J. *Souvenir Virginia Tercentennial of Historic Alexandria, Virginia 1607-1907.* Alexandria, Virginia: 1907.

INDEX

R.E. Lee Camp Hall 95
R.F. & P. R.R. Station 131
R.H. Miller & Sons 131
Race Tracks 41
Rainbow Tavern 37, 86, 109
Ralph's Gut 15
Ramsay House 19, 118, 128
Ramsay, Col. Dennis 24, 40, 43
Ramsay, G. Wm. 118
Ramsay, Wm. 14, 16, 19, 127
Reading, Pierson Barton 45
Reed Theatre 152
Reed, F.A. 166
Reeder's Tavern 37
Reliance Fire Co. 110
Relief Fire Co. 26
Relief Society 110
Retail Merchants Association 139
Rexall Drugstore 138
Rich, John 41
Rich Wilder M. 185
Ricketts, John 66
Ricketts, Mrs. John 29
Rickman, Dr. Wm. 16
Risheill & Hooge 172
Roberdeau, Daniel 31
Robert Portner Brewery 106, 113, 184
Robert's Chapel 77, 154
Roberts, Reuben 156
Robinson, Joseph 34
Rochambeau, Count 28
Rodgers, J.D. 142
Rogers, Capt. G.W. 94
Rosemont 106
Roundhouse-Railroad 90, 91, 152, 153
Royal St.-200 Block N. 111
Royal St.-300 Block S. 65
Royal, Ann 52
Rozier, Mary Helena 143
Rumney, Dr. Wm. 16
Ryan, Michael 35

S

S.H. Lynn 132
Saint-Memin 29
Sanderson, James 148
Sanford, Gen. Charles W. 83
Sanitary Grocery 146, 147
Sarapta Hall 25
Saunders & R.C. Acton Jewelry Store 138
Scarce, W.B. 42
Schneider, Justus 182
Schoepf, Johann 27
Schuylkill Barges 87
Scott, Margaret 46
Scottish Rite Club 107
Seaport Inn Restaurant 126
Second Presbyterian Church 66, 166
Serepta Hall 78
Service Drugstore 140
Seventeenth Va. Regiment 95
Shadow's (Hill House) 156
Sharpe, Horatio 20
Sharps & Flats 118
Shepherd's Landing 116
Shield's Plumbers 142
Ship's Tavern 37
Shirley, Wm. 20
Short, John 34
Shuter's Hill 36, 74, 77, 84, 92, 97, 99, 145, 150, 151, 152, 153, 180
Simms, Col. Charles 16
Simon Waterman's Clothing Store 132
Sisters of Charity 108
Slater, John 48
Slave Pen 64, 98
Slave Trade 54
Slaymaker, H.C. 131
Slocum, Gen.-Brigade Hospital 105
Slough, Gen. John P. 84, 89, 95
        Military Band 89
Smith & Perkins Locomotive Works 73, 77, 147
Smith Motor Supply Co. 139
Smith, Francis L. 89, 95
Smith, Hugh 128
Smith, Hugh Charles 52, 61, 107
Smoot, J.D.H. 166
Smoot, Wm. A. 55, 175, 185
Snethen, Nicholas 169
Snowden Family 131
Snowden Flounder House 164
Snowden, Edgar 87

Society of Friends 57
Soldier's Cemetery 86
Soldier's Rest 98
Southern Memorial Association 97
Southern R.R. Freight Station 131
Spanish American War 104, 121
Spring Field 14, 17, 63
St. Asaph & Cameron St.-N.E. Cor. 118
St. Asaph St.-100 Block S. 26
St. Asaph St.-109 S. 111
St. Asaph St.-211 S. 89
St. Asaph St.-300 Block S. 57
St. Asaph St.-301 S. 62
St. Asaph St.-322 S. 117
St. Asaph St-403 N. 63
St. Asaph St.-717 N. 131
St. John's Demosthenian Society 142
St. John's Military Academy 76
St. Mary's Academy 108
St. Mary's Roman Catholic Church 77, 99, 155, 167, 179
St. Paul's Church 60
Stabler, Dr. Richard H. 163
Stabler, Edward 131
Stabler-Leadbeater Apothecary Shop 33, 131, 162
Stagecoach Travel-18th Century 57
Steamboats 117
Steiner & Yoho 128
Stewart, Rev. Kenzie J. 60
Stone, Thomas 28
Strand 71, 78, 88, 178
Strangman, C.A. 113
Strawberry Vale 49
Streetcar Tracks 137
Sugar Refinery 107
Sully Plantation 47
Summers, Francis 12
Summers, John 12
Sun Engine House 17
Sun Fire Co. 110
Surratt, Mary 108
Swain, George 174
Swann Brother's Department Store 131
Swann Building 132
Swann, Thomas 165
Swanson, Governor 180
Swift, Jonathan 55

T

Tackett's, Mrs. 118
Taft, President 173, 180
Tatspaugh, John 73
Taverns 37
Taylor, Charles 174
Taylor, Charles H. 83
Taylor, George 49
Taylor, Robert J. 36
Tefft, Thomas 81
Telephone Service 104
Thompson, Jonah 105, 108
Thornton, Benjamin 55
Ticer, Edmund F. 185
Tilp, Capt. Fred 107
Timberlake, Mrs. 108
Timberman's Drugstore 168
Tobacco Traders 1
Tom's Garden 133
Toonerville Trolley 113
Torpedo Inn 129
Torpedo Plant 106, 126, 175
Town Crier 19
Townsend, George Alfred 86
Tressler, Peter 75
Trinity Methodist Church 77, 167
Triplett, Thomas 38
Trowbridge, John T. 101
True, Wm. 53
Turner, Lucy Lyons 45
Twinning, Thomas 30

U

U.S. Army Commissary Office 96
U.S. Court House 80
U.S. Military R.R. 82, 87, 90, 92, 93
U.S. National Cemetery 86, 97
U.S. Shipping Board Emergency Fleet Corp. 106, 115
Union Bank 129
Union St.-100 S. 71
Union Station 150, 153
Union Tavern 37

Unknown Revolutionary War Soldier 186
Urban Renewal Program 135, 136

V

Vepco (Virginia Public Service Bldg) 162
Vepco Building 168
Vermonnet, Jean 53
Vincent, Wm. 121, 182
Virginia Bowling & Athletic Supply Co. 142
Virginia Declaration of Rights 23
Virginia House Hotel 42, 142
Virginia Safe Deposit & Trust Co. 131
Virginia Ship Building Corp. 115
Virginia Shoe Repair Co. 144
Virginia Trust For Historic Preservation 180
Vowell, John 95
Vowell, Thomas Jr. 87

W

W.A. Smoot & Co.-Fire-1909 122
W.E. Hinken & Son 143
Wagar Apartments 123
War Between the States-Prisons 63, 184
War Between the States-Union Provost Office 136
War of 1812 52
Warfield's Drugstore 134
Warfield, Edgar 94
Warfield, Edgar Sr. 134
Washington & Old Dominion R.R. Station 131
Washington Free School 159
Washington Hall 25, 138, 139
Washington Monument Commission 42
Washington School 142, 159
Washington Southern R.R. Co. 113
Washington St. 155
Washington St. Methodist Church 77, 141, 167, 168
Washington St.-200 Block S. 81
Washington St.-220 N. 47
Washington St.-407 N. 44, 46
Washington St.-414 N. 64
Washington St.-428 N. 43, 44
Washington St.-617 S. 108
Washington St.-700 Block N. 94
Washington Steamboat Co. 117
Washington Tavern 41
Washington, Alexandria, Mt. Vernon Electric R.R. 131
Washington, George 13, 14, 15, 16, 17, 21, 24, 25, 27, 28, 32, 34, 36, 40, 41, 60, 65, 107, 128, 158, 170, 180
Washington, Judge Bushrod 110
Washington, Lawrence 14, 17, 24, 25
Washington, Martha 33, 71
Water Co. 68, 74, 77, 145
Wattles, Richard H. 109
Waves 175
Webster, Police Chief 112
Weil Brothers 138
Wells 68
West End 42
West, George 20
West, John 12, 14, 24
West, Thomas Wade 55
West, Wm. E. 45
Wheat, Benoni 119
Wheat, J.J. 73
Whelan's Drugstore 141
White, Thomas 156
White, Thomas W. 156
Whittlesey Family 160
Whittlesey, Sarah J.C. 160
Wildt, Henry R. 100
Wilkins, Francis 79
Williams, Harriet 26
Williams, Jon 54
Wilmer, Rev. Wm. H. 60, 63, 139
Windmill Hill 186
Wise's Tavern 31, 35, 40
Wise, John 37, 47, 175
Withers, John 140
Wm. H. May & Co. 128
Wm. McKnight's Tavern 35

Y

Young, Genl. Robert 54, 64

Z

Zimmerman's Oyster House 41

ABOUT THE AUTHORS

illiam Francis Smith was born in Alexandria, the son of deeply rooted Tidewater Virginians and whose mother was descended from several early Alexandria families. He was graduated from George Washington High School, attended the Episcopal High School and received a B.A. degree in history from the University of Virginia. In between times he served as an Ensign in the Navy, taught in the public school for one year, and finally ended up as a banker, a career he has continued to pursue to the present time. Nancy Leith of Michigan became his bride many years ago and they are parents of three good children, all married. His interest in history, especially of the local variety, never abated during the years of family raising, bank-working, and taking an active part in a number of organizations, particularly the Alexandria Library, the Historic Alexandria Foundation, and church activities. The collecting of old photographs of Alexandria began about forty years ago and this interest is as strong as ever but the availability of new sources becomes increasingly rare. It is unlikely that anything short of mental disability will ever lessen his hope of finding that long lost view, so spectacular that it will always remain as the crown jewel of his photographic collection.

ichael Miller has long had a fascination with Alexandria, Virginia, and its brick-lined streets, museums, manicured gardens, and distinctive eighteenth and nineteenth century architecture. After receiving degrees in history, political science, and international relations, he was employed by the federal government before settling in Alexandria during the mid-1970s. The charm of the old seaport community soon cast its spell over him and from 1978 to 1980 he served as Curator of the Lee-Fendall House Museum. In July 1980, he accepted employment with the Alexandria Library, Lloyd House, and is currently research historian with that organization. Mr. Miller has penned numerous articles and monographs on Alexandria including two recent books entitled: *Murder & Mayhem*—criminal conduct in Old Alexandria, Virginia and *Pen Portraits of Alexandria—1739-1900*, a compilation of travelers' accounts. He is currently editor of the *Fireside Sentinel*—a historical journal published by the Library and he lectures extensively on the town's history.